ON ISLAND TIME

A TRAVELER'S ATLAS

Illustrated Adventures ON & AROUND THE ISLANDS OF

WASHINGTON & BRITISH COLUMBIA

~CHANDLER O'LEARY~

SASQUATCH BOOKS

SEATTLE

Printed in China

SASQUATCH BOOKS with colophon is a registered trademark of Penguin Random House LLC

27 26 25 24 23   9 8 7 6 5 4 3 2

Editor: Hannah Elnan | Production editor: Rachelle Longé McGhee
Cover design: Anna Goldstein | Interior design: Alison Keefe & Anna Goldstein

Library of Congress Cataloging-in-Publication Data
Names: O'Leary, Chandler, author.
Title: On island time : a traveler's atlas : illustrated adventures on and
  around the islands of Washington and British Columbia / Chandler O'Leary.
Description: Seattle : Sasquatch Books, [2023] | Includes index.
Identifiers: LCCN 2022031595 | ISBN 9781632173386 (trade paperback)
Subjects: LCSH: San Juan Islands (Wash.)--Guidebooks. | Puget Sound
  (Wash.)--Guidebooks. | Gulf Islands (B.C.)--Guidebooks. |
  Islands--Salish Sea (B.C. and Wash.)--Description and travel. |
  Islands--Salish Sea (B.C. and Wash.)--Maps. | Salish Sea Region (B.C.
  and Wash.)--Guidebooks
Classification: LCC F897.A19 O54 2023 | DDC 979.7/74--dc23/eng/20220810
LC record available at https://lccn.loc.gov/2022031595

ISBN: 978-1-63217-338-6

Sasquatch Books
1325 Fourth Avenue, Suite 1025
Seattle, WA 98101

SasquatchBooks.com

FSC®
MIX
Paper | Supporting
responsible forestry
www.fsc.org
FSC® C008047

For Gale, a force of nature

CONTENTS

Dear Reader vi • *On This Land viii*

Island Basics

INTRODUCTION 2

HOW TO USE THIS BOOK 4

AN ISLAND PRIMER 6

GET STARTED 12

SAFE AND SOUND 18

1 Puget Sound

AREA MAP 24

BAINBRIDGE 26

VASHON-MAURY 34

WHIDBEY 42

THE SOUTH SOUND 54

OTHER ISLANDS 62

2 San Juan Islands

AREA MAP 76

FIDALGO 78

SAN JUAN 86

ORCAS 100

LOPEZ 112

OTHER ISLANDS 120

3 British Columbia

AREA MAP 138

VANCOUVER ISLAND 140

THE GULF ISLANDS 158

THE SUNSHINE COAST 176

Field Notes

CARVING A NICHE X

A FERRY TO CATCH 10

PACK YOUR BAGS 16

TIME AND TIDE 20

AT THE MARINA 32

GREEN CANOPY 40

CATCH OF THE DAY 52

EITHER/OAR 60

LOOK SKYWARD 72

THE WORKING WATERFRONT 84

THAR SHE BLOWS 98

FRESH AND FORAGED 110

FLIPPER AND FIN 118

BARN BEAUTY 134

GONE FISHING 156

WILD BOUQUET 174

BEACONS IN THE NIGHT 184

Afterword 186 • *Pronunciation Guide 188*
Index of Places 192 • *Thank You 194*

EAR READER

I have lived and worked in the Pacific Northwest since 2008, after many years of wandering around the United States and elsewhere. Though I have, at last, found my permanent home, I can't seem to stop behaving like a perpetual tourist. I go exploring as often as possible. I work daily to expand my "mental map." I document what I see, hear, and taste in my sketchbooks. I try not to take my surroundings for granted. Applying the principles of my former nomadic life has expanded and deepened my love for the Salish Sea.

   Though it's hard to play favorites in this beautiful corner of the world, my heart belongs to the islands. My small home studio in Tacoma, Washington, overlooks Commencement Bay and Maury Island, and on summer nights a pair of lighthouses flashes through my open windows, casting a faint glow onto my bedroom walls. For me, the islands represent a constant dance of home and away. I visit often enough to feel a sense of stewardship, yet my mainlander status keeps the islands just unfamiliar enough to never lose their getaway feeling. Instead of the coffee shop, the ferry is often my "third place," where I go to clear my head or work out new ideas—there's always a saltwater view and plenty of fresh air. I have the good fortune to spend time on San Juan Island every year, filling sketchbooks, creating my own writing retreats, or simply relaxing with my family. When my son was born in 2019, the islands seemed like the perfect place to introduce him to his home region and the joys of travel.

▼ A view from my neighborhood in Tacoma. In the Salish Sea region, more than a million people live on an island, and millions more live within a few miles of salt water.

He rode his first ferry at two months old, and some of his earliest outings included visiting Vashon and Fox Islands to look for banana slugs or comb the beaches.

My son has not been the only audience for my island enthusiasm. This book has been brewing in my mind for many years. Every time I played tour guide to a visitor, or jotted down a note in my sketchbook, or recounted a story to a friend, I was unconsciously planning these pages. Once I began the formal research and drafting process for the book, it didn't take long to realize that what I was really crafting was a love letter. Learning to see the islands with fresh eyes, revisiting old favorites, and discovering new ones gave me the chance to attempt translating the experience for someone else—you.

My wish is that in some small way, this book may have succeeded on that front. If you are reading this somewhere far from the Salish Sea, I hope these pages entice you to come here and discover this place for yourself. If you are a local like me, perhaps you'll still find something new to explore, or a perspective that hadn't occurred to you before. This book is only a dim reflection of reality, but if it can serve as a gateway to the real thing, I'll be prouder than I can express. I hope it will inspire you to fall in love with the islands as I have.

Chandler O'Leary

▲ One of my favorite places to work is on the ferry. Most crossings are just long enough to complete a sketchbook drawing or two.

 # ON THIS LAND

▼ Tribal Canoe Journeys, oceangoing canoe gatherings, bring Salish Sea Indigenous communities together. The tradition was revived in 1989, a century after US and Canadian governments forcibly repressed Indigenous cultural practices (page 154), including banning and burning dugout canoes.

This book acknowledges that the Salish Sea region is situated on the unceded traditional homelands of many Indigenous peoples and cultures. The territories in the southern and eastern portions of the region are home to the Coast Salish peoples—members of the larger Salishan ethnic group. This group encompasses many tribes—like the Tulalip, Malahat, Skagit, Lummi, and Squamish peoples—and several language groups, such as Lushootseed, Nooksack, and Klallam. Most of the Pacific shore of what is now Vancouver Island is the traditional territory of the Nuu-chah-nulth peoples (previously called the Nootka by white colonizers—this name is now considered offensive by some), who encompass fifteen tribes and are closely related to the Makah and Quileute peoples of northwestern Washington State. The Kwakwaka'wakw peoples (whom non-native people historically lumped together as the Kwakiutl, the name of a single tribe) traditionally inhabit northern Vancouver Island and the northern shore of mainland British Columbia. The Kwakwaka'wakw encompass several Kwak'wala-speaking nations, and share some cultural customs with their northern neighbors such as the Haida and Tlingit peoples.

Coast Salish, Nuu-chah-nulth, and Kwakwaka'wakw craftspeople all carry on a long tradition of wood carving and a graphic aesthetic known as the formline style (page xi). Though totem poles are historically associated with northern Pacific Coast cultures (Seattle's poles were originally stolen from Alaska by white people), many contemporary Northwest Indigenous artists have incorporated totem carving and other cross-cultural techniques and motifs into their visual storytelling and studio practices. (Author's note: Where necessary, I have depicted a handful of Indigenous carvings throughout

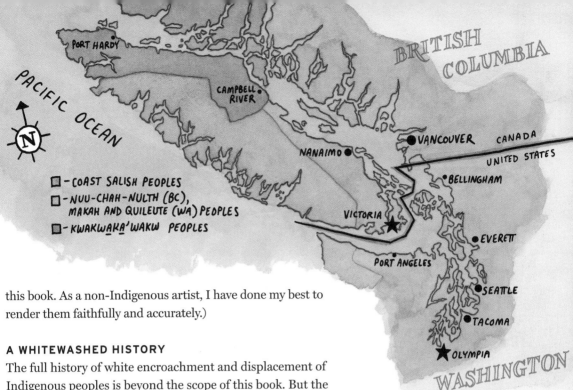

this book. As a non-Indigenous artist, I have done my best to render them faithfully and accurately.)

A WHITEWASHED HISTORY

The full history of white encroachment and displacement of Indigenous peoples is beyond the scope of this book. But the result is that today's islands are overwhelmingly inhabited by white people, with Indigenous communities largely pushed to mainland reservations. Some tribes, like the Duwamish (whose ancestral territory includes what is now Seattle), have still not had the terms of their treaty honored with federal recognition or the promised reservation allotment.

CONTINUING TRADITIONS

Despite marginalization by mainstream Northwest customs, Indigenous culture is very much alive and active in the Salish Sea region. Traditional celebrations and processes continue with each generation: new tribally owned museums and cultural centers open each year, and many groups are revitalizing spoken Indigenous language instruction (both for tribal members and the general public).

KNOW BEFORE YOU GO

Throughout this book, you'll find tribal reservations and landmarks marked on maps, and where possible in the text, Indigenous names included alongside English ones. You'll also find a number of Indigenous names and terms in the Pronunciation Guide (page 188). For each island you visit, learn the names of the cultures who call it home, and remember their place there. Make time to visit Indigenous cultural museums, parks, or events where the general public is welcome—and adhere to all tribal laws and rules (as well as basic courtesy and respect) when you are invited to participate. Research tribal berry gathering and fishing rights, and know when and where Indigenous people have the legal right of way for harvesting. Treat your visit with respect for past and future generations, just as the Indigenous people of the Salish Sea region do.

▼ The Suquamish Tribe's House of Awakened Culture emulates a traditional longhouse. It is located near the site of Old-Man-House, the winter home of Si'ahl (Chief Seattle). It was destroyed by the federal government in 1870, when they forced the Suquamish to abandon traditional communal living for individual family allotments.

Carving A Niche

The famous cedar carvings created by Indigenous artists and craftspeople are some of the Northwest's most iconic and powerful symbols. You can find many historic and contemporary examples on your island adventure, including:

◀ **TOTEM POLES.** Usually carved from a single tree, totem poles employ symbolic images of animals and human figures to tell a story.

TLO:KWA:NA (WOLF RITUAL) MASK, c. 1900
ARTIST UNKNOWN (NUU-CHAH-NULTH)
PRIVATE AUCTION GALLERY, BURNABY, BC

◀ **MASKS.** Many Northwest Indigenous artisans create ceremonial masks and other wearable pieces. These frequently incorporate iconic animals—like the raven, eagle, thunderbird, or, in this case, wolf—to tell or act out traditional stories.

▲ **RETURN THE REGALIA.** Until recently, ceremonial objects were frequently stolen by collectors and confiscated by government officials (page 154). Indigenous communities are still working to recover and repatriate their historic artifacts and regalia.

HOUSE POST, 1954
BY MUNGO MARTIN (KWAKWA̱KA̱'WAKW)
NEAR Q'EMÁSƏŊ (ROYAL BC MUSEUM, VICTORIA, BC)

TOTEM POLE, DATE UNKNOWN
ARTIST UNKNOWN (KWAKWA̱KA̱'WAKW)
TSAX̱IS (FORT RUPERT, BC)

◀ **THEN AND NOW.** Historically, totem poles were mainly associated with Kwakwa̱ka'wakw and Alaska Native peoples. Today, contemporary Northwest Indigenous artists from many different cultures carve totem and other poles.

▶ **HOUSE POSTS.** Often created in pairs or groups for structural support of a building, house posts are generally shorter and fatter than totem poles. These are usually associated with more northern cultures, but some Coast Salish carvers create them as well.

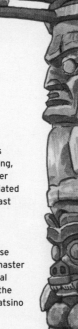

▶ **LAID TO REST.** This Victoria, BC, house pole, created in 1954 by Kwakwa̱ka'wakw master carver Mungo Martin, had begun the natural process of returning to the earth. In 2019 the Royal BC Museum repatriated it to the Quatsino First Nation for burial.

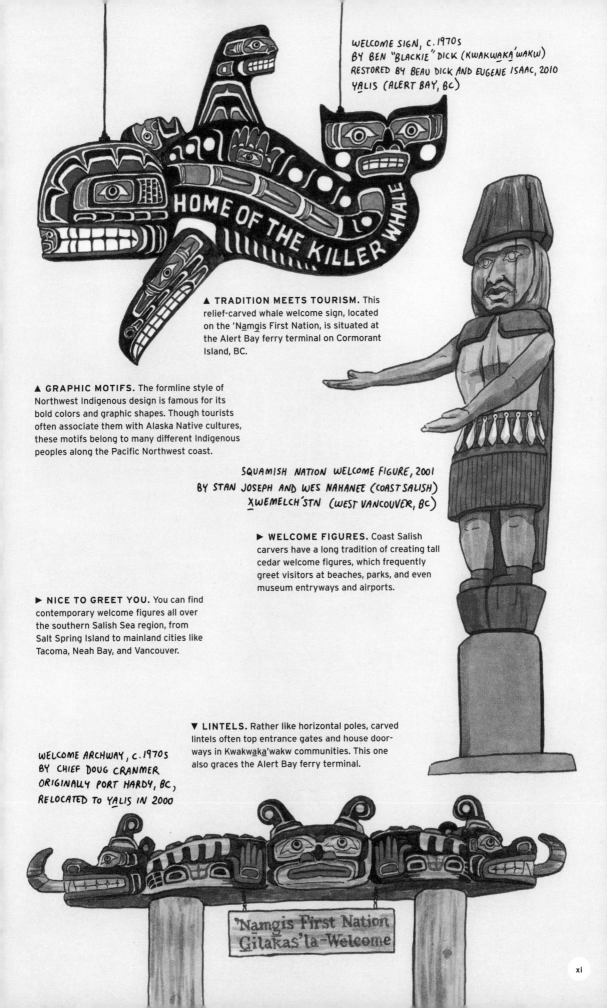

WELCOME SIGN, C. 1970S
BY BEN "BLACKIE" DICK (KWAKWAKA'WAKW)
RESTORED BY BEAU DICK AND EUGENE ISAAC, 2010
YALIS (ALERT BAY, BC)

HOME OF THE KILLER WHALE

▲ **TRADITION MEETS TOURISM.** This relief-carved whale welcome sign, located on the 'Namgis First Nation, is situated at the Alert Bay ferry terminal on Cormorant Island, BC.

▲ **GRAPHIC MOTIFS.** The formline style of Northwest Indigenous design is famous for its bold colors and graphic shapes. Though tourists often associate them with Alaska Native cultures, these motifs belong to many different Indigenous peoples along the Pacific Northwest coast.

SQUAMISH NATION WELCOME FIGURE, 2001
BY STAN JOSEPH AND WES NAHANEE (COAST SALISH)
XWEMELCH'STN (WEST VANCOUVER, BC)

▶ **WELCOME FIGURES.** Coast Salish carvers have a long tradition of creating tall cedar welcome figures, which frequently greet visitors at beaches, parks, and even museum entryways and airports.

▶ **NICE TO GREET YOU.** You can find contemporary welcome figures all over the southern Salish Sea region, from Salt Spring Island to mainland cities like Tacoma, Neah Bay, and Vancouver.

▼ **LINTELS.** Rather like horizontal poles, carved lintels often top entrance gates and house doorways in Kwakwaka'wakw communities. This one also graces the Alert Bay ferry terminal.

WELCOME ARCHWAY, C. 1970S
BY CHIEF DOUG CRANMER
ORIGINALLY PORT HARDY, BC,
RELOCATED TO YALIS IN 2000

'Namgis First Nation
Gilakas'la-Welcome

ISLAND

Before you embark on your Salish Sea adventure, make sure you're well prepared. This section will give you a taste of what to expect, local quirks, travel rules and etiquette, essential packing lists, and a host of other resources to get you started.

 # INTRODUCTION

The Salish Sea is a 270-mile-long marginal sea—a saltwater body partially enclosed by land—that straddles northwestern Washington State and southwestern British Columbia. The area is part of the region called the North American Pacific Fjordland, which stretches from Oregon to Alaska. The name Salish Sea refers to the Coast Salish people, and both the United States and Canada made it the official term for these waters in 2009. Locals still refer to more specific bodies of water instead: Puget Sound, the Strait of Georgia, etc.

The Salish Sea encompasses hundreds of islands and "named rocks" (bare, uninhabited islets). Within these are many topographic or climatic differences, but there are some commonalities. The landforms and mountains were created by volcanic eruptions and the movement of tectonic plates on the earth's crust. The deep waterways were then carved out by ice-age glaciers. Today's islands are characterized by vast evergreen forests, occasional mountains, rolling valleys dotted with small farms, treeless prairies, and a mild, rainy (technically Mediterranean) climate.

Small towns or unincorporated communities are common, and for outsiders, the island pace of life can sometimes feel a bit more relaxed or less "modern." This leads visitors and mainlanders to use the phrase "on island time" when they cross over—meaning that time seems to behave differently here. Depending on whom you ask, this might seem like a compliment or an insult—but visitors tend to use the phrase lovingly, referring to a joyful, vacation-like feeling.

DON'T LIKE THE WEATHER? WAIT FIVE MINUTES

There are four seasons here (including a few hot summer days and, rarely, snow in winter), but it's more useful to think in terms of the wet and dry seasons. The rainy season (October through June) features gentle, near-daily rain and a seemingly endless cover of low clouds. The mountains disappear for days or even weeks at a time, and some days bring

▼ The rainy season is dominated by grays and indigo blues, as the short winter days limit the daylight hours.

ever-changing conditions and "sun breaks" (brief sunny spells). Winters are fairly mild—only occasionally does it dip below freezing—but punctuated by storms. These can be severe and last for days: wind speeds of forty knots (forty-six miles per hour), torrential rain, downed trees, and power outages are all common.

The arrival of the dry season, around the Fourth of July, feels like the flip of a switch. Suddenly, the sky clears, temperatures are warm but not hot, and the long northern days seem jewel bright and endless. Climate change has made summers hotter and drier, and sadly, days on end of thick smoke from distant wildfires have become a regular occurrence in recent years. Furthermore, you'll encounter microclimates here: patches of rain forest, sunny slopes, rain shadows (page 44), even subalpine extremes. That's why it's best to pack for every type of weather (page 16).

ISLANDERS AND OFF-ISLANDERS

On any given day, you'll find a mix of islanders, visiting mainlanders, tourists from afar, and folks who own summer or second homes here. Island summer cabins (or "camps" as some families called them) became popular among middle- and working-class families in the 1920s. Other main-landers send their kids to island summer camps, another long-standing tradition. Many "year-rounders" run errands on the mainland (though most larger islands have at least a general store), and time their trips for off-hours ferries to avoid the crowds.

Sometimes tourists can feel unwelcome, given the num-ber of "no trespassing" signs you'll find on any island. And islanders (including Indigenous people with ancestral roots here) can easily resent the real estate prices that rise along-side the region's popularity. But the relationship between islanders, off-islanders, and tourists has to be a symbiotic one to find a balance. With many historic local industries diminished or vanished, the islands rely on tourism and the tax base of summer homes. If you're a visitor, try adopting the stewardship of year-rounders and Indigenous communities to help preserve the environment and way of life here—without it, the islands risk being loved to death.

▲ There are still many historic shoreline summer cabins up and down the region—some of these are available as vacation rentals.

▼ The dry season is the best time to see the mountain ranges that surround the Salish Sea region—including the Olympic Mountains and the volcanoes of the Cascade Range.

# HOW TO USE THIS BOOK

This is not your typical guidebook, nor is it an exhaustive list of features and attractions. Instead, think of it as an illustrated starter kit for your own island adventure—part travel guide, part visual dictionary.

GET YOUR BEARINGS

This book breaks the Salish Sea region down into three distinct subregions. Part One (page 22) focuses on Puget Sound, radiating outward from Seattle, Washington, and beginning with the larger or more populous islands. Part Two (page 74) moves north to the San Juan Islands, an archipelago midway between Puget Sound and Vancouver Island (page 140).

Part Three (page 136) extends into British Columbia, Canada. *BC* is used wherever the province is mentioned. As the map on page v shows, the Salish Sea really only extends as far north as Campbell River, BC (page 152), and west to the mouth of the Strait of Juan de Fuca. However, some authorities include a wider range of areas in their reckoning, so this book includes all of Vancouver Island and a few smaller islands off of its northern shore.

While this book uses the term *Pacific Northwest* throughout, that's not the term Canadians use to refer to the BC coast. Instead they simply call it the West Coast— keep this in mind, as you'll see that term crop up if you visit any Canadian islands. Also, many Americans get one important distinction mixed up: Vancouver is not the same as Vancouver Island! Vancouver Island is the largest island in the Salish Sea (and on the West Coast of the Americas,

▼ Located just beyond Victoria, BC's, Inner Harbour (page 142) is the small enclave of house boats and floating homes at Fisherman's Wharf.

for that matter), and home to the provincial capital, Victoria (page 142). The *city* of Vancouver, BC, which is more familiar to Americans, is located on the mainland, near the international border. And while Vancouver and Seattle are mentioned tangentially throughout, Victoria is the only major metropolitan area covered by this book.

X MARKS THE SPOT

The maps in this book are as close to scale as possible, though they are for reference, not precise navigation. Each map includes points of interest for both land-based and marine travelers. Wherever possible, lighthouses and camp-grounds are indicated on each map, as well as marinas with public moorage (see the map key to the right). Note that some campgrounds are reserved for visitors arriving in their own kayaks or other human-powered watercraft—these are marked with a blue triangle.

VISUAL CHECKLISTS

Also sprinkled throughout the text are a number of Field Notes. These pages collect and define different categories of island icons—birds, marine mammals, boat types, etc.—to help you make sense of your surroundings and identify what you see. While you'll find these placed in one chapter or another, remember that most of these lists can apply to the Salish Sea region as a whole.

A WHOLE LOT OF WAYFINDING

Throughout your journey you'll come across a number of important signals, wayfinding symbols, trail markers, and more. Train yourself to pay attention to these—sudden road construction is common, viewpoints are often tucked away, and ferry directions can be convoluted. Also, signage depends heavily on regional differences. Canadian signs are often bilingual—usually English and French, but sometimes the local Indigenous language instead of French. Canadian speeds are measured in kilometers per hour, and miles per hour in the United States. Distances in the United States are Imperial (miles and feet), and metric (kilometers and meters) in Canada.

Boaters must also understand nautical markers, signals, and buoys. Wind and craft speeds are measured in knots (one mile per hour equals 0.869 knots), and distances in nautical miles (one mile equals 1.1508 nautical miles). Most jurisdictions require boaters to take a boating safety course (list on page 14), which will cover this information.

MAP KEY

■ = POINT OF INTEREST
○ = LIGHTHOUSE
▼ = PUBLIC MARINA
◄ = PUBLIC FISHING PIER
▲ = CAMPING AVAILABLE
△ = CAMPING FOR PADDLERS ONLY
▣ = ACCESSIBLE FACILITIES
= TRIBAL RESERVATION
= PARK OR OTHER NATURAL AREA
= OTHER SPECIAL AREA
—— = MAIN ROUTE
—— = ALTERNATE ROUTE
—— = OTHER ROAD
----- = FERRY ROUTE
······· = TRAIL
▬▬▬ = INTERNATIONAL BORDER

AN ISLAND PRIMER

▼ The sprawling Marine Supply & Hardware store in Anacortes, Washington (page 82), sells everything from nautical charts and souvenirs to vintage stock of marine tools, fishing lures, and spare parts.

Every island and community is different, but here are a few island travel basics to help you get started. While you travel, remember also to tread lightly on the land. Conserve water (drinking water is a precious commodity on the islands), keep wildlife wild, take only pictures, prevent wildfires, pack out all trash when hiking, and leave no trace.

FROM BEHIND THE WHEEL

If you're planning on covering a lot of ground or visiting remote areas, bringing your own car with you will give you the most flexibility. Almost all of the major ferry routes can accommodate cars. (Some locals leave one car on the island and another on the mainland to save on the ferry commute.) Island roads tend to be well maintained, though often curvy and narrow. Inclement weather can cause landslides and road washouts, so drive with care. Obey the speed limit, watch for wildlife (especially deer at dawn and dusk!) and loose pets, and respect the rights of pedestrians and cyclists.

FOOT AND PEDAL POWER

Ferries are pedestrian and bike friendly, and many island communities are walkable. Smaller and flatter islands are especially great for pedestrians and cyclists. Bike rentals are available on the more touristy islands—and on a few islands you can rent a moped or scooter. Or, if you have a larger budget, you might consider a multiday cycling or hiking tour; these can be booked through many local tour companies. Some of the more populous islands offer public bus transit, and a few places have tourist trollies, taxi services, and even ridesharing. Service is not available to all areas, however, and schedules are limited—especially in the off-season or on Sundays or holidays. Research schedules and options ahead of time to avoid being stranded.

UP, UP, AND AWAY

If you'd rather take to the air for your island trip, Kenmore Air serves the San Juans from SeaTac International Airport and from the shore of Lake Union in Seattle. Harbour Air serves a number of British Columbia destinations, as do smaller companies like Gulf Island Seaplanes and Sunshine

Coast Air. Or you might try a day trip via floatplane—you'll find these available at Friday Harbor (page 88), Rosario Resort & Spa (page 107), Victoria, and more. Residents on rural, "non-ferry" islands often rely on charter flight services (which can be surprisingly inexpensive) for transporting both themselves and goods to and from the mainland. Charter flights are available to many destinations, departing from hubs like Bellingham, Victoria, and Nanaimo. If you happen to have a pilot's license and want to arrive on your own wings, there are many small municipal and private airports and airstrips throughout the region (several, though not all, are marked on the maps in this book).

MESSING ABOUT IN BOATS

If you have your own boat, you have access to many islands and attractions that aren't reachable by ferry. This book is primarily geared toward landlubbers, but in these pages you'll still find plenty of information, destinations, and activities for boaters—including owners and users of human-powered vessels, sailboats, and power craft. For those hoping to get their feet wet in the boating world, many islands have boat- or kayak-rental businesses, as well as charter boat services. And some sea-kayak trip outfits operate out of larger cites, offering everything from day outings to full-service, multiday paddling trips.

ISLAND ACCESSIBILITY

Unfortunately, travelers with disabilities may find accessibility on the islands to be a mixed bag. Municipal ferries are wheelchair accessible, but drivers have to ask for accommodation. Island communities can be hilly with few paved sidewalks, though larger towns are better about accessible infrastructure. In many places, public shorelines are accessed by wooded trails, boardwalks, or stairs. Few of these are paved or wheelchair accessible, and many are steep, slippery, or muddy. Regional tourism and chamber-of-commerce websites are getting better about listing accessible lodging, businesses, and attractions, so it pays to do your research ahead of time.

FERRIES AND MORE FERRIES

Ferries might be a special treat for tourists, but they're a part of everyday life (as well as the public transit system) on the Salish Sea. Even some highways around the region include a ferry as part of the official route.

▼ The tiny floatplanes that zip in and out of Friday Harbor and other ports provide an unforgettable vantage point for sightseeing.

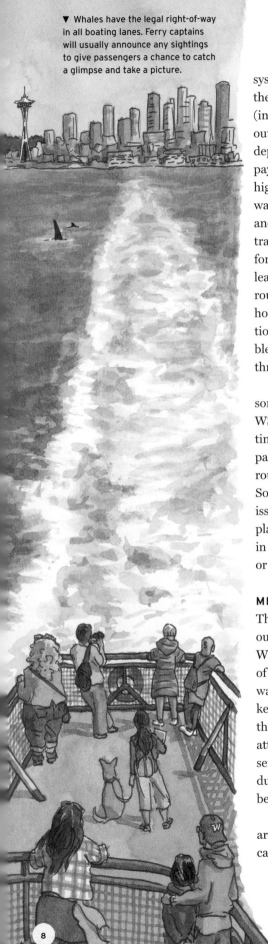

Washington State Ferries (WSF), the most-used ferry system in the world, serve many of the state's islands and are the vessels most often referenced in this book. Pedestrian (including bicyclist) fares are collected one-way only, usually outbound from the more urban terminal. Vehicle fares depend on size—so motorcycles cost less than RVs. Drivers pay going both directions for many routes, but not all. A few high-demand crossings accept reservations for cars (not for walk-on passengers), but many routes do not. Both stairs and elevators connect the car deck to the passenger cabin; travelers needing elevator access can alert the ticket agent for priority parking. Drivers must be in line for the boat at least twenty minutes ahead of departure (and more for some routes); during the peak season, wait times can stretch on for hours. Especially in the summer, if you *can* make a reservation on your selected route, it's best to do so. Wherever possible, routes with special rules or requirements are highlighted throughout this book.

The sailing schedule changes with the seasons (and sometimes extreme tides) as well, so it helps to consult the WSF website ahead of your trip for the correct departure times. And every boat and terminal offers free pocket-size paper schedules containing that season's schedule for every route in the system (pro tip: keep one of these in your car!). Sometimes crossings can be delayed en route by maintenance issues, fog, or other weather conditions; make alternate plans, and have plenty of snacks handy to help keep tempers in check (especially since on-board snack bars may be closed or nonexistent).

MIND YOUR MANNERS

The rules of ferry travel may seem self-evident, but it's worth outlining a few etiquette basics. The following is based on WSF protocol, but other ferry lines have similar rules. Most of these pertain to car travelers: never idle your engine while waiting or on board, stick to the lane you're directed to use, keep your headlights off when boarding at night, and engage the emergency brake when parked on the boat (a ferry attendant will guide you into the right place). If you have a sensitive car alarm, disable it or it will most certainly go off during the crossing—and then you'll have the ignominy of being singled out over the loudspeaker.

WSF crossings allow leashed pets in exterior passenger areas; other pets must be in carriers to enter the passenger cabin or else confined to a vehicle on the car deck. For a full list of what else can and cannot be brought on board, check the WSF (or other carrier) website.

One of the lesser-known services WSF provides is the chance for passengers to get married or buried at sea. Passengers who wish to scatter cremated remains must make arrangements in advance, but the captain will stop the vessel en route to allow for the ceremony (the boat will not stop for a wedding). If you happen to be on one of these rare, special crossings, be patient during the short delay, and keep your distance from the event, out of respect.

Last of all, get out and explore the vessel! Most of the ship is open to passengers, and most of the vessel models (page 10) have multiple decks, as well as indoor and outdoor areas. Commuters and other locals tend to skip the scenery and stay in their cars for the whole crossing (author's note: I will never understand this). Yet all but the foulest weather crossings offer beautiful scenery at least, and sometimes surprises like a sea otter cameo or a pod of orcas along the way. If you're at all able, take the time to get out of your car and enjoy the view.

▲ Read the signs and follow ferry protocol closely—knowing the rules gives you the best chance of blending in with local island commuters.

INTERNATIONAL CROSSINGS

If you're including Canada (page 136) in your adventures, you'll need to plan ahead for crossing the international border. Since 2007 a valid passport has been required for visitors over age sixteen to cross in and out of Canada. Alternately, US citizens can present an enhanced driver's license to cross by land or sea (though not by air). Travelers with minors under sixteen must present the child's birth and/or adoption certificate for entry into Canada.

▼ Older WSF models include outdoor covered seating areas on the top deck. The deck on the now-retired MV *Elwha* also sported a mini captain's wheel for kids.

Vancouver Island is accessible via the Black Ball Line from Port Angeles, Washington; the passenger-only Victoria Clipper from Seattle; a WSF sailing from Anacortes or Friday Harbor; or BC Ferries from Vancouver and other Canadian ports. The Gulf Islands (page 158) and the Sunshine Coast (page 176) are served by BC Ferries.

A Ferry TO Catch

For more than a century, public and private ferries have connected the communities of the Salish Sea region. Each vessel has its own history and unique design—as well as hidden stories or fun features to share.

▶ **WASHINGTON STATE FERRIES.** An extensive municipal network of RoPax (roll-on/roll-off car) ferries, WSF vessels of varying sizes are swapped around the region as capacity needs change. The largest boats hold 200 cars and are more than 450 feet long.

WSF ISSAQUAH CLASS

WSF JUMBO MARK II CLASS

▶ **PUZZLE AHOY.** Regular passengers donate puzzles for communal use aboard many WSF vessels. Put in a piece or two on a short crossing, or solve the whole thing to kill time during an en route weather delay.

◀ **CHOCKABLOCK.** If you're an end car on the ferry, or parked on the ramp to an upper deck (which happens on crowded sailings), a ferry attendant will chock your wheels during the crossing.

▼ **WED ON THE WATER.** Many couples choose to get married on WSF crossings. Though boat captains are often sought to officiate weddings, WSF captains are not allowed to perform these ceremonies.

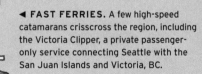

WEST SEATTLE WATER TAXI

◀ **FAST FERRIES.** A few high-speed catamarans crisscross the region, including the Victoria Clipper, a private passenger-only service connecting Seattle with the San Juan Islands and Victoria, BC.

VICTORIA CLIPPER

▼ **THE MOSQUITO FLEET.** Until the 1930s, this former network of private ferries once carried all of Puget Sound's ferry traffic. The last still-operating vessel is the *Carlisle II*, built in 1917 and now running as a foot ferry between Bremerton and Port Orchard.

◀ **FOOT FERRIES.** This local term refers to passenger-only ferries. Iconic examples include BC's tiny "pickle boat" taxis that cruise Victoria's Inner Harbour and Vancouver's False Creek.

PICKLE BOAT

MV CARLISLE II

HARBOUR FERRY TAXI'S WATER BALLET

◀ **PICKLE PIROUETTES.** Victoria's water taxis put on a "water ballet" performance for tourists each summer.

BC FERRIES ISLAND CLASS

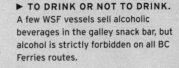

▶ TO DRINK OR NOT TO DRINK. A few WSF vessels sell alcoholic beverages in the galley snack bar, but alcohol is strictly forbidden on all BC Ferries routes.

PIERCE COUNTY FERRY

◀ OTHER MUNICIPAL FERRIES. BC Ferries also runs a large network of vessels around the upper Salish Sea, while county ferries make the Washington runs to Anderson, Lummi, and Guemes Islands.

▶ PRIVATE FERRIES. The *Coho*, a former BC ferry, now makes the Port Angeles to Victoria (page 9) run as the Black Ball Line, an homage to a historic Puget Sound private ferry network (and Bing Crosby song!).

MV COHO

▶ TELLTALE SIGNS. WSF vessels carry their wooden name plaque on the wheelhouse, and some islands welcome visitors with an artistic sign at the ferry terminal.

▼ RETIRED VESSELS AND GHOSTS. A number of historic ferries, now either decommissioned or even destroyed, have become local legends.

MV RHODODENDRON

◀ "THE RHODY." Built in the 1950s, the *Rhododendron* served on many WSF runs before ending her career in 2012 on the Vashon to Point Defiance route (page 35). As of this writing, she is moored off of Fanny Bay, BC (page 152).

MV CHILKAT

◀ THE "BLUE CANOE." The first ferry on the Alaska Marine Highway (page 124) was built in 1957, decommissioned in 1988, and sold to a shellfish outfit in Anacortes, Washington, in 2012. A January 2021 storm severed her mooring, and she sank just off of Guemes Island.

MV KALAKALA

◀ THE "SILVER SLUG." The *Kalakala*, a glamorous art deco ferry that plied Puget Sound's waters from 1935 to 1967, met a sad end in 2015, when her rusted hull forced her to be scrapped—despite local efforts to save her.

# GET STARTED

Before you set sail for the islands, make sure you're prepared by looking into ferries, passes, maps, and rules ahead of time. This is not an exhaustive list of resources and services, but it should help you get your travel research off to a strong start. Note that island bookstores stock a wealth of hyper-local books and maps, so it helps to build a browsing trip into each island you visit.

Travel Information

FERRY INFORMATION

Washington State Ferries: wsdot.wa.gov
/travel/washington-state-ferries
BC Ferries: bcferries.com
Lasqueti Ferry: lasqueti.ca/island-info
/lasqueti_ferry
Lummi Island Ferry: lummi-island.com/ferry
Anderson Island Ferry: piercecountywa.gov
/1793/ferry
Guemes Island Ferry: guemesislandferry.com
Kitsap Transit Fast Ferry: kitsaptransit.com
/service/fast-ferry
Victoria/San Juan Island Clipper:
clippervacations.com
Black Ball Ferry Line: cohoferry.com
Argosy Cruises: argosycruises.com
Alaska Marine Highway System: dot.alaska.gov
/amhs

OTHER INFORMATION

Washington State Department of Transportation:
wsdot.wa.gov
DriveBC: drivebc.ca
Kenmore Air: kenmoreair.com
Harbour Air: harbourair.com
Backroads bicycle tours: backroads.com
Canadian travel and border information:
cbsa-asfc.gc.ca/travel-voyage/menu-eng.html
US travel and border information:
dhs.gov/how-do-i/cross-us-borders

Park Information

WASHINGTON STATE

Washington State Parks: parks.wa.gov
Washington State Department of Natural
Resources: dnr.wa.gov
National Park Service: nps.gov
US Forest Service: fs.usda.gov
San Juan County Parks: sanjuanco.com
/430/parks-recreation-fair
Island County Parks: islandcountywa.gov
/publicworks/parks/pages/home.aspx
King County Parks: kingcounty.gov/services
/parks-recreation/parks.aspx
Bainbridge Island Parks: biparks.org
Vashon Park District: vashonparks.org

BRITISH COLUMBIA

BC Parks: bcparks.ca
BC Provincial Coastal Marine Parks:
bcparks.ca/recreation/marine_parks
Gulf Islands National Park Reserve:
pc.gc.ca/en/pn-np/bc/gulf
Parks Canada: pc.gc.ca
Capital Regional District parks:
crd.bc.ca/parks-recreation-culture/parks-trails
/crd-regional-parks/park-maps
Victoria parks: victoria.ca/en/main/residents
/parks/our_parks.html
Saysutshun (Newcastle Island) Marine
Provincial Park: newcastleisland.ca

Passes and Permits

National Park Service passes:
nps.gov/planyourvisit/passes.htm
Parks Canada passes:
pc.gc.ca/en/voyage-travel/admission
Discover Pass (Washington's annual state park pass):
discoverpass.wa.gov
BC Parks day-use passes and permits:
bcparks.ca/reserve/day-use
BC Parks backcountry permits:
bcparks.ca/registration
Washington State Boater Education Card:
boat.wa.gov/boating-information-portal
/boaters-card
**Canada boaters' proof of competency for
recreational boaters:** tc.canada.ca/en
/marine-transportation/marine-safety
/proof-competency-recreational-boaters
**Washington Department of Fish and Wildlife (WDFW)
aquatic invasive species prevention permits:**
wdfw.wa.gov/species-habitats/invasive/permits

FISH AND SHELLFISH PERMITS
WDFW fishing and shellfish permits:
wdfw.wa.gov/fishing/shellfish
British Columbia shellfish harvesting information:
pac.dfo-mpo.gc.ca/fm-gp/rec/shellfish-coquillages
-eng.html
**British Columbia tidal waters fishing license
information:** pac.dfo-mpo.gc.ca/fm-gp/rec
/licence-permis/application-eng.html
British Columbia fishing regulations:
pac.dfo-mpo.gc.ca/fm-gp/rec/index-eng.html
WDFW fishing regulations:
wdfw.wa.gov/fishing/regulations
British Columbia shellfish biotoxin information:
pac.dfo-mpo.gc.ca/fm-gp/contamination
/index-eng.html
Washington State shellfish biotoxin map:
fortress.wa.gov/doh/biotoxin/biotoxin.html

▼ The west coast of Vancouver Island boasts many sea
stacks—towers of rock that long ago eroded away from
the coastal cliff, and now stand alone just offshore.

Navigational Aids

AAA (maps are free for members): aaa.com
Better World Club: betterworldclub.net
Great Pacific Maps: greatpacificmaps.com
DeLorme Atlas & Gazetteer: bit.ly/36QTs2W
Waggoner Guide Books: waggonerguidebooks.com
Rand McNally *Road Atlas*: randmcnally.com
/product/road-atlas
Google Maps: google.com/maps

Emergency Contacts

Washington emergency boat information:
nwboatinfo.com/emergency-information.html
**Emergencies in Washington and most places
in British Columbia:** dial 911
**US and Canadian Coast Guard emergency
channel for ship radios:** channel 16
**US and Canadian citizens band distress
channel for ship radios:** channel 9
Royal Canadian Marine Search and Rescue:
ccga-pacific.org

Conservation

Report invasive species (WA): invasivespecies
.wa.gov/report-a-sighting
Report invasive species (BC): bcinvasives.ca/report
Orca Network: OrcaNetwork.org
Guide to Green Boating: georgiastrait.org/work
/cleanmarinebc/greenboatingguide
Bainbridge Island Land Trust: bi-landtrust.org
Islands Trust (BC): islandstrust.bc.ca
San Juan County Conservation Land Bank:
sjclandbank.org
Vashon-Maury Island Land Trust:
vashonlandtrust.org
Whidbey Camano Land Trust:
wclt.org

Boating Resources

GENERAL INFORMATION

Cascadia Marine Trail:
wwta.org/water-trails/cascadia-marine-trail

BC Marine Trails: bcmarinetrails.org

Kayak locations and launch maps: paddling.com

National Oceanic and Atmospheric Administration:
noaa.gov

Online tide tables: tide-forecast.com

Tidelog (tide almanac): tidelog.com

Boating navigation rules: boatus.org/navigation-rules

Waggoner boating information: waggonerguide.com

Washington boating information: nwboatinfo.com

Real-time marine traffic: vesselfinder.com

BOATING SCHOOLS AND COURSES

Northwest Maritime Center: nwmaritime.org

Northwest School of Wooden Boatbuilding:
nwswb.edu

The Center for Wooden Boats: cwb.org

Community Boating Center: boatingcenter.org

San Juan Sailing: sanjuansailing.com

US Coast Guard's Boating Safety Division:
uscgboating.org

Washington State boater education requirements:
parks.state.wa.us/442/mandatory-boater-education

BC boating certification: boatingbc.ca/cpages
/get-certified

Nanaimo Yacht Charters & Sailing School:
nanaimoyachtcharters.com

MARINAS AND MOORAGE

Washington State Parks moorage:
parks.state.wa.us/648/moorage

BC marinas and harbors:
ahoybc.com/chart-your-course/marinas-harbours

Gulf Islands marina directory:
nwboatinfo.com/marinas-gulf-islands.html

Puget Sound marina directory:
nwboatinfo.com/marinas.html

San Juan Islands marina directory:
nwboatinfo.com/marinas-san-juans.html

BOAT CHARTERS AND TOURS

**Fishing Booker (travel agency for charter fishing
trips):** fishingbooker.com

Silver Blue Charters: silverbluecharters.com

Get West Adventure Cruises: getwest.ca

Sea Wolf Adventures: seawolfadventures.ca

k'awat'si Tours: kawatsitours.ca

T'ashii Paddle School: tashiipaddle.com

Island Express Charters: islandexpresscharters.com

Outer Island Excursions: outerislandx.com

Paraclete Charters: paracletecharters.com

San Juan Excursions: watchwhales.com

Sunshine Coast Tours: sunshinecoasttours.ca

Discovery Sea Kayak Tours: discoveryseakayak.com

Anacortes Kayak Tours: anacorteskayaktours.com

Whidbey Island Kayaking: whidbeyislandkayaking.com

Gulf Island Kayaking: seakayak.ca

CHANDLERIES AND MARINE SUPPLIES

The Chandlery at Winslow Wharf:
chandlerymarine.net

Marine Supply & Hardware:
marinesupplyandhardware.com

Wooden Boat Chandlery:
shop.woodenboatchandlery.org

Harbour Chandler: harbourchandler.ca

Trotac Marine: trotac.ca

Kings Marine: kings-market.com/marine.html

Oak Bay Marina: oakbaymarina.com

Roche Harbor Marine Services:
rocheharbormarine.com

Ocean Pacific Marine Store:
oceanpacificmarine.com/marine-store

▼ Nearly every major island in the Salish Sea has a
local farmers' market in the tourist season. Others have
indoor public markets—a Northwest specialty—or even
seasonal night markets.

Camping Resources

GENERAL INFORMATION
All Trails: alltrails.com
Washington Trails Association: wta.org
BC camping permit information: bcparks.ca/fees
**Washington State Parks camping and cabin
  reservations:** parks.state.wa.us/223/reservations
Parks Canada West Coast Trail:
  pc.gc.ca/en/pn-np/bc/pacificrim/activ/sco-wct
ADA recreation in Washington State Parks:
  parks.state.wa.us/156/ada-recreation
Recreational Equipment, Inc. (REI): rei.com

WEATHER AND FIRE INFORMATION
Government of Canada weather: weather.gc.ca
National Weather Service: weather.gov
Washington State burn bans: dnr.wa.gov
  /burn-restrictions
BC burn bans: gov.bc.ca/gov/content/safety
  /wildfire-status/fire-bans-and-restrictions
Washington State wildfire information:
  dnr.wa.gov/wildfires
BC wildfire information: gov.bc.ca/gov/content
  /safety/wildfire-status/wildfire-situation

Markets

Anacortes Farmers Market: anacortesfarmersmarket.org
Bainbridge Island Farmers Market:
  bainbridgeislandfarmersmarket.com
Snow Goose Produce: snowgooseproducemarket.com
Heyday Market: heydayfarm.com
Bayview Farmers Market: bayviewfarmersmarket.com
Coupeville Market: coupevillemarket.com
3 Sisters Market: 3sistersmarket.com
The Star Store: starstorewhidbey.com
Camano Commons Marketplace: camanocommons.com
San Juan Island Farmers Market: sjifarmersmarket.com
Lopez Island Farmers Market: lopezfarmersmarket.com
Orcas Island Farmers Market: orcasislandfarmersmarket.org
Pike Place Market: pikeplacemarket.org
Victoria Public Market: victoriapublicmarket.com
Oak Bay Village Night Market: visitoakbayvillage.ca
  /index.php?area_id=1003&article_id=3
Sidney Outdoor Markets: sidneystreetmarket.com
Market on Ship Point: gvha.ca/events/ship-point-market
Old Country Market: oldcountrymarket.com
Salt Spring Saturday Market: saltspringmarket.com
Gibsons Public Market: gibsonspublicmarket.com
Gabriola Growers and Makers Market:
  gabriolaagriculturalcoop.ca/growers-and-makers-market
Cortes Island Farmer's Markets: ourcortes.com/activities
  /farmers-markets

Learn More

INDIGENOUS RESOURCES
Cowichan Tribes: cowichantribes.com
Hibulb Cultural Center:
  hibulbculturalcenter.org
Indigenous Tourism BC: indigenousbc.com
Nuu-chah-nulth Tribal Council:
  nuuchahnulth.org
Nuyumbalees Cultural Centre:
  museumatcapemudge.com
Puyallup Tribal Language Program:
  puyalluptriballanguage.org
Samish Indian Nation Timeline:
  samishtribe.nsn.us/who-we-are/timeline
Saysutshun cultural experiences:
  newcastleisland.ca/culture-and-history
**Squaxin Island Museum Library and Research
  Center:** squaxinislandmuseum.org
**Signs of Lekwungen markers,
  Victoria, BC:** songheesnation.ca/community
  /l-k-ng-n-traditional-territory
Suquamish Tribe: suquamish.nsn.us
Talaysay Tours: talaysay.com
tems swiya Museum:
  shishalh.com/culture-language/shishalh
  -nation-tems-swiya-museum
U'mista Cultural Centre: umista.ca

WEBSITES AND FILMS
atlasobscura.com
drawntheroadagain.com
lighthousefriends.com
roadarch.com
roadsideamerica.com
Blackfish by Gabriela Cowberthwaite
  (documentary)

BOOKS
Afoot & Afloat series by Marge and Ted Mueller
Birds of the Puget Sound Region by Bob Morse,
  Tom Aversa, and Hal Opperman
By the Shore by Nancy Blakey
Farewell to Manzanar by Jeanne Wakatsuki
  Houston and James D. Houston
*Go Do Some Great Thing: The Black Pioneers
  of British Columbia* by Crawford Kilian
Gulf Islands: A Boater's Guidebook by Shawn
  Breeding and Heather Bansmer
Island Year by Hazel Heckman
Looking for Betty MacDonald by Paula Becker
*Native Seattle: Histories from the Crossing-
  Over Place* by Coll Thrush
Onions in the Stew by Betty MacDonald
Turn Around Time by David Guterson
We Hereby Refuse by Frank Abe and Tamiko
  Nimura

Pack *Your* Bags

Whether you prefer to pack heavy or travel light, you'll need a variety of essentials to get the most out of your island adventure. Here's a packing list to get you started and help keep you warm, dry, comfortable, and prepared:

▼ **PERSONAL ITEMS.** Weather in the region can vary widely, even on the same day. Dress in layers, prepare for both wet and sun, and consider investing in good waterproof footwear.

GALOSHES

HIKING BOOTS OR WATERPROOF TRAIL RUNNERS

DAY PACK

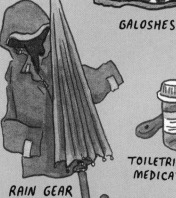

RAIN GEAR

TOILETRIES AND MEDICATIONS

WARM LAYERED CLOTHING

HEADWEAR AND SUN PROTECTION

INSECT REPELLENT

TICKETS AND PRINTED RESERVATIONS

PARK PASSES

PASSPORT (OR EDL)

DRIVER'S LICENSE

TIDE AND FERRY TIMETABLES

◄ **IMPORTANT PAPERS.** You'll need a valid driver's license for a road trip, proper ID for hotel check-in, and current legal documents for crossing an international border. Also make sure to keep all your tickets, passes, and schedules together in a safe place!

PAPER MAPS

GUIDEBOOKS

◄ NAVIGATION AND SAFETY. Stock up on paper maps and guides, especially for when you lose internet or cell access. Use common sense when it comes to car and safety gear, but a few basic tools will never go amiss. And don't skip the toilet paper—it might make you laugh now, but it won't when you need it!

PHONE

FLASHLIGHT AND BATTERIES

CAR REPAIR AND EMERGENCY KIT

EXTRA BATTERY CHARGERS

FIRST AID KIT

TP

BLANKETS

ELECTRIC KETTLE

TRAVEL MUGS

TRAVEL COOLER

◄ FOOD AND DRINK. Not every island has a grocery store or restaurant (and many island businesses close early, despite late ferries), so it's good to keep picnic supplies on hand at all times. Bringing a jug of water is a good idea, too, as potable water isn't available everywhere. The kettle can be a lifesaver if you want hot tea in your hotel room or cabin.

INSTANT HOT BEVERAGES

SNACKS AND PICNIC FOODS

POSTCARD STAMPS

BINOCULARS

► JUST FOR FUN. Bring extra camera batteries and memory cards (or film, if you're old-school). Journals or sketchbooks are handy for jotting down the day's observations. And people *love* receiving travel postcards, so keep some stamps on hand!

CAMERA

WRITING OR DRAWING SUPPLIES

SAFE AND SOUND

Here are a few tips to help you stay safe and get the most out of your Salish Sea adventure:

In General

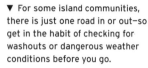

▼ For some island communities, there is just one road in or out–so get in the habit of checking for washouts or dangerous weather conditions before you go.

PACE YOURSELF. Travel around the islands can involve long distances. Give yourself enough time to get to your destinations safely. Plan extra time in each day's itinerary as a buffer, in case of ferry delays or other mishaps.

PAPER MAPS ARE YOUR FRIENDS. GPS isn't accurate (or even functional) everywhere. Carry paper maps and learn to read them properly. Regional and local atlases are wonderfully detailed and especially great for back roads.

ON SHAKY GROUND. The entire region is located within the Cascadia Subduction Zone—which means earthquakes are a possibility. Carry basic emergency supplies with you, and familiarize yourself with earthquake survival procedures.

In the Car

BE A SAFE DRIVER. Obey all posted speed limits, traffic laws, and warnings, and respect construction zones. Always carry your license and proof of insurance.

PULL OVER ON NARROW ROADS. Use traffic pullouts to allow faster cars behind you to pass. This allows you to travel safely, without stressing out or feeling pressured to speed up.

KEEP YOUR GAS TANK FULL. Gas and service stations can be both scarce and expensive on an island. Get in the habit of topping off your tank on the mainland, and get your car serviced at home before you embark on an island road trip.

DON'T SLIDE AWAY. The wet Northwest climate makes landslides and road washouts a common occurrence during the rainy season. Keep an eye on road conditions throughout your trip, and be ready to make alternate plans if necessary.

CALLING FOR HELP? If you need roadside assistance, note the nearest mile marker or landmark and memorize your license plate number so help can find you as quickly as possible.

In the Wild

RESPECT THE WILD. If you venture into remote or wilderness areas, take your surroundings seriously, pack accordingly, and let others know of your travel plans.

KNOWLEDGE BEFORE FORAGE. Safely foraging for mushrooms, berries, and other wild edible plant life requires a good deal of knowledge and experience. If you're not absolutely sure of what you're doing, stick to the farmers' market!

BE BEAR AWARE. Black bears (and also raccoons) that get used to people can become a public nuisance—as well as a danger to themselves and humans. Never litter or feed wild animals, and use bear-proof food containers when camping.

BUY ANNUAL PARK PASSES. State and national park entry fees can add up quickly (see the long list of parks in this book on page 193), so buy an annual pass if you can. Your investment will pay for itself after just a handful of parks.

▲ Some campgrounds require visitors to use bear-proof food canisters—but to deter ever-savvier raccoons, not black bears!

On the Water

BE BEACH SAVVY. Not every beach is open to the public, and property owners are protective. Be certain and careful of public-private beach boundaries to avoid trespassing.

LICENSE TO KRILL. Fishing and shellfish harvesting require a license or permit. Do your research so you know when, where, and how you may participate (as well as whether your lodging allows you to keep your catch on the premises). Also check local toxicity updates and heed all warnings.

NEVER TURN YOUR BACK ON THE OCEAN. On the beach, note posted warnings about tsunamis and sneaker waves. Stay off jetties and breakwaters; evacuate if you hear a siren. Carry tide tables to help plan your activities.

BE SAFE AT SEA. Whether you'll be boating for an hour or a week, always wear a correctly fitting life jacket and take a recreational boating safety course before your trip.

THIS AIN'T SUNNY SOCAL. The Salish Sea is cold, even at the height of summer. Hypothermia is a real concern, especially for kayakers—always have a companion on the water, dress in layers, and wear a neoprene wetsuit under your life jacket.

KEEP AN EYE ON THE WEATHER. Conditions can change rapidly on the water. Look for "small craft advisory" language on weather reports before setting out, and review inclement-weather procedures from your boating safety course.

▼ Life jackets even come in dog sizes! Canine sailors are a common sight at marinas and liveaboard communities.

Time AND Tide

The Salish Sea is dotted with tide pools—and positively teeming with diverse intertidal life. Many locations are easily accessible from the shore, and a well-timed visit can yield huge rewards. Just don't forget your wading boots!

▼ **THANK A PLANT.** Seaweed provides critical habitat for countless species. Whiplike bull kelp forms entire underwater forests (and commonly washes ashore after storms), and rockweed is one of the first organisms to appear as the tide ebbs.

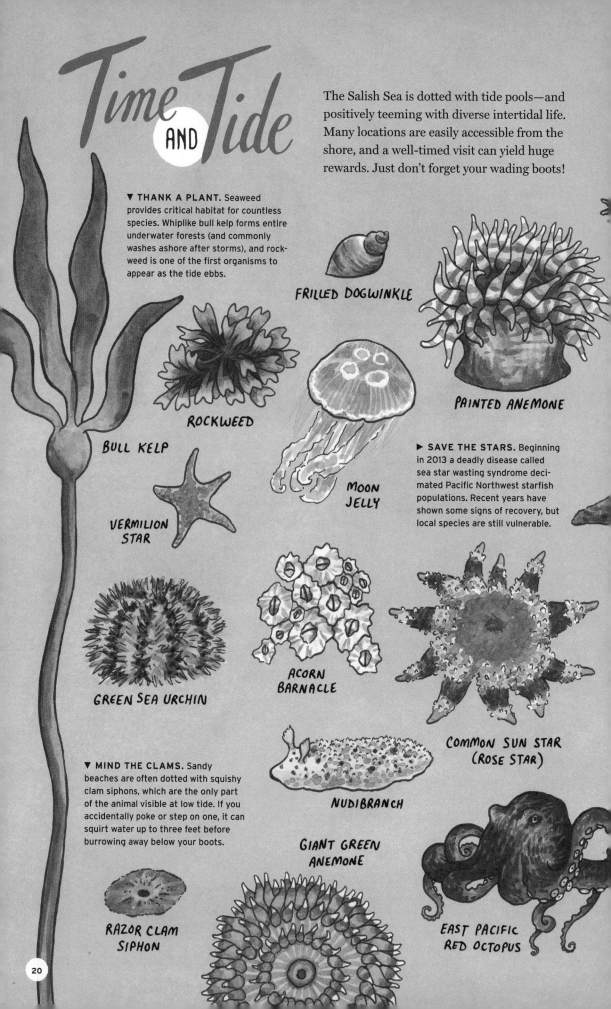

FRILLED DOGWINKLE

ROCKWEED

BULL KELP

PAINTED ANEMONE

MOON JELLY

VERMILION STAR

▶ **SAVE THE STARS.** Beginning in 2013 a deadly disease called sea star wasting syndrome decimated Pacific Northwest starfish populations. Recent years have shown some signs of recovery, but local species are still vulnerable.

GREEN SEA URCHIN

ACORN BARNACLE

COMMON SUN STAR (ROSE STAR)

NUDIBRANCH

▼ **MIND THE CLAMS.** Sandy beaches are often dotted with squishy clam siphons, which are the only part of the animal visible at low tide. If you accidentally poke or step on one, it can squirt water up to three feet before burrowing away below your boots.

GIANT GREEN ANEMONE

RAZOR CLAM SIPHON

EAST PACIFIC RED OCTOPUS

PLUMOSE
ANEMONE

KEYHOLE LIMPET

GIANT RED
SEA CUCUMBER

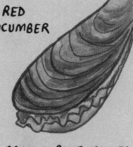

PACIFIC BLUE MUSSEL

▲ **"IF YOU PRY, IT WILL DIE."**
Remember this rhyme and take it
to heart. It's best to avoid touching tidal creatures altogether, but
attempting to detach or remove
them can easily kill them.

PURPLE SEA STAR

SLIME
STAR

MOON SNAIL
WITH EGG CASE

▼ **CHOOSE YOUR CHART.** Most tide
tables are just dense numerical charts.
But illustrative tide charts also exist—
these list the tides as visual graphs that
are much easier (and more fun) to read.

TIDE TABLE

FEATHER
DUSTER WORM

GREENMARK
HERMIT CRAB

▼ **KNOW YOUR TIDES.**
This chart explains the
different tides you might
encounter. Minus tides offer
the best chance to explore
tide pools. The highest
(spring) tides happen at the
full moon; super moons (when
the full moon is closest to
Earth) cause king tides.

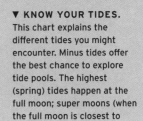

STORM LINE

KING TIDE (HIGH)

SPRING TIDE (HIGH)

MEAN HIGH TIDE

NEAP TIDE (HIGH)

NEAP TIDE (LOW)

MEAN LOW WATER
(ZERO TIDE)

SPRING TIDE (LOW)

KING TIDE (LOW)

← FLOOD

EBB →

← INTERTIDAL ZONE →

← MINUS TIDES →

PART

1

PUGET

SOUND

A hundred-mile-long estuary home to dozens of islands, peninsulas, and waterways, Puget Sound is the southernmost portion of the Salish Sea. Its islands lie within easy reach of Seattle—some just a few miles as the gull flies—yet they seem to belong to a different world. Whether your itinerary allows for a day or many weeks, the Puget Sound region offers an endless array of natural beauty, local flavor, and cultural attractions.

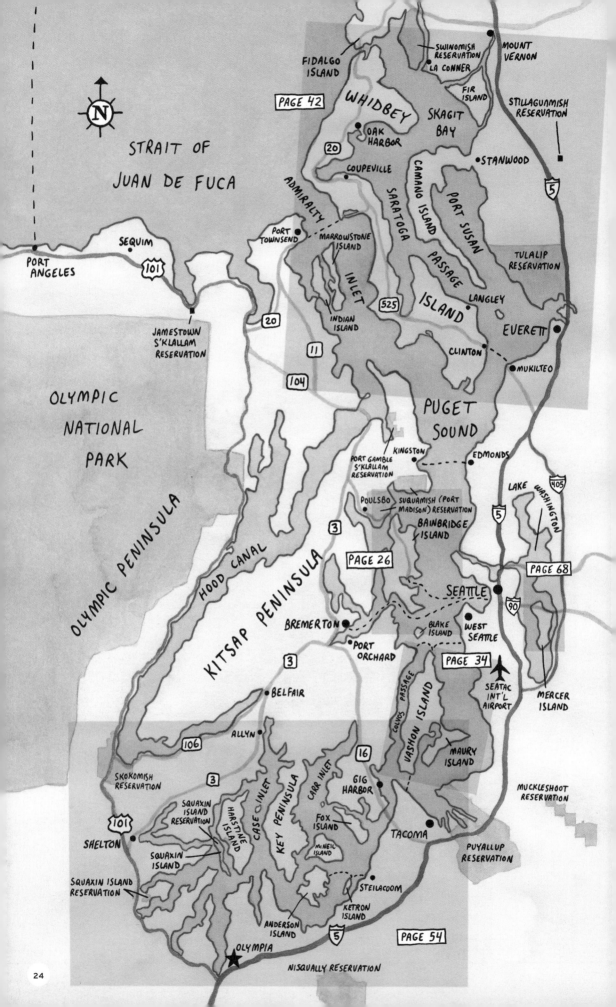

mpossibly labyrinthine, Puget Sound crams many twists, turns, nooks, and crannies into one small section of the Washington State map. Yet the region's network of highways and ferries brings much of the Sound within reach for landlubbers.

As a rule, Puget Sound is largely urban along the eastern shore and more rural on the west side. The greater Seattle area dominates the central region, with several ferries crossing the main channel of the Sound to communities on the other side. Thanks to the glacial history of the region, the landscapes of the Sound's lowlands are surprisingly uniform: nearly everywhere you'll find thick evergreen forests and cleared areas occupied by farmland. Most of the islands are characterized by rocky or pebbly shores (sandy beaches are rare here), sharp slopes rising up from the waterline, and rolling hills in the interior of each island. Yet every island offers its own unique flavor and breathtaking vistas in every direction. Note that public beach access in many places—especially state or county parks—requires a steep walk downhill, sometimes via a woodland trail.

SO CLOSE, AND YET SO FAR

The Sound is long and narrow, just ten miles across at its widest point. Yet embarking on an island adventure takes planning—and time. Ferry crossings take about thirty to sixty minutes on average, though wait times for the next vessel can be long during the summer. If a ferry is out of service or a bridge is under construction, driving an alternate route around a waterway can take hours. Be sure to have a backup plan, and expect heavy traffic along the Interstate-5 corridor.

CHOOSE YOUR OWN ADVENTURE

This section highlights Puget Sound's largest and most popular ferry-served islands first, starting closest to Seattle and radiating outward. Next come a number of smaller and lesser-known islands that even locals tend to overlook. The more you explore, the more you'll find yourself steeped in Pacific Northwest life.

▲ Almost everywhere you turn in Puget Sound, there's a spectacular view—the Olympic Mountains dominate westward-facing prospects on clear days.

▼ Like many other Puget Sound harbors, the Bainbridge Island Marina is home to many liveaboards who make their boat their primary residence.

BAINBRIDGE

▼ Pedestrian-only Madrone Lane functions like a piazza, offering visitors a shady spot to sit and relax after a stroll down adjacent Winslow Way.

Located across the Sound from Seattle, Bainbridge Island is roughly the size of Manhattan. With ferries leaving Seattle about every forty-five minutes, adding a Bainbridge jaunt to even a short Seattle vacation is easy. And thanks to the bridge at the northern end of the island, so is connecting your sojourn to places like Olympic National Park or Vancouver Island (page 140).

The island is the ancestral home of the Suquamish people, whose name means "people of the clear salt water" in Lushootseed. Bainbridge, like many islands, was given arbitrary English names by naval commanders who surveyed the area starting in the late-eighteenth century. The Suquamish were forced onto a mainland reservation by the 1855 Treaty of Point Elliott (and the tribe still struggles against treaty violations by white encroachers). White settlers then used the island for logging and shipbuilding, as its old-growth conifers were prized for masts.

As logging depleted Bainbridge's old-growth forests around 1900, Japanese American laborers turned the scars into arable land. These Issei (first-generation immigrants) pulled the stumps of huge cedars and firs with dynamite and horsepower, then removed the many rocks strewn by ice-age glaciers. As redlining and other racist systems prevented many Issei from buying the farmland they cleared, most of them leased it instead, saving up until the second and third generations (the Nisei and Sansei) could buy it outright. Along with their land, many of these farmers also passed along to their children the vendor leases for the highstalls, the permanent produce stands at Seattle's Pike Place Market.

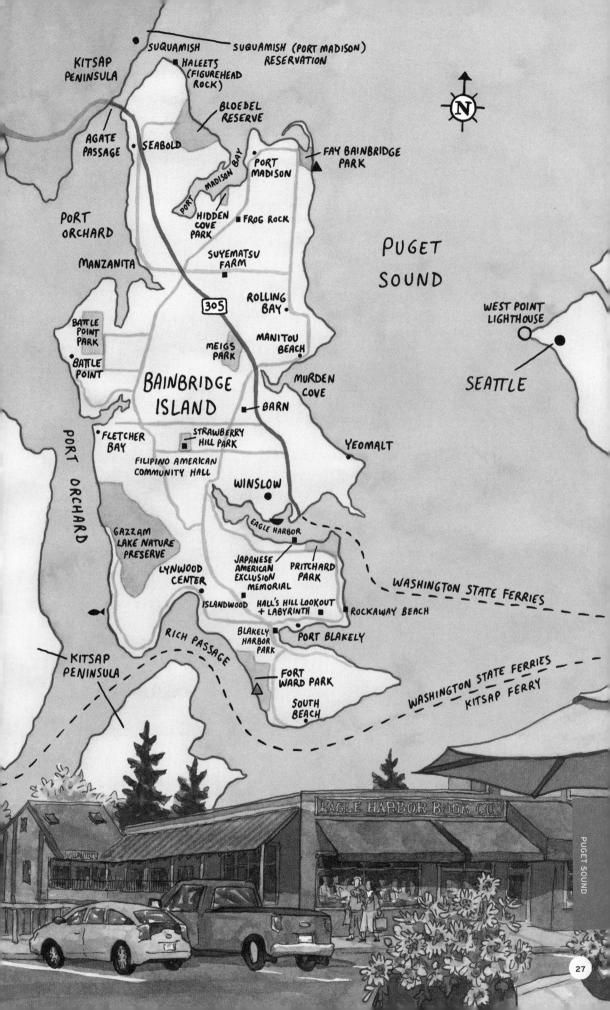

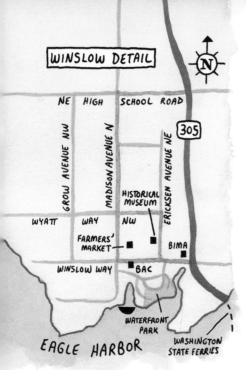

WINSLOW DETAIL

N

NE HIGH SCHOOL ROAD

305

GROW AVENUE NW

MADISON AVENUE N

ERICKSEN AVENUE NE

HISTORICAL
MUSEUM

WYATT WAY NW

FARMERS'
MARKET

BIMA

WINSLOW WAY BAC

WATERFRONT
PARK

EAGLE HARBOR

WASHINGTON
STATE FERRIES

STRAWBERRY FIELDS FORGOTTEN

Issei farmers discovered the perfect crop for the island's misty, cool climate: strawberries. One particular variety, the delicate Marshall, became Bainbridge's most famous crop. These large berries were both sweeter and juicier than today's grocery-store variety. Popularity peaked in the 1930s—even King George VI ordered eight hundred crates of them for his 1939 royal visit to Vancouver. Yet with a short harvest period and a thin skin that made them highly perishable and vulnerable to disease, the Marshall just wasn't viable for nationwide commercial production. The berry disappeared from island farms by the 1960s, and exists today only as a rare heirloom variety.

A DARK HISTORY

The removal of Indigenous people was not the only shameful moment in Bainbridge's past. After the 1941 World War II attack on Pearl Harbor, President Roosevelt issued Executive Order 9066, sending nearly 120,000 West Coast Issei and their American-born descendants to remote inland internment camps, where they were incarcerated until 1946, well after the war ended. The forced relocation began on Bainbridge Island, when 227 islanders, including children, were herded onto the Seattle ferry on March 30, 1942.

Many interned families came home to the West Coast in 1946 to find their property looted or sold out from under them. On Bainbridge, at least, some neighbors offered help. Filipino and Indigenous farmworkers kept strawberry farms running, and the *Bainbridge Island Review* was a rare outspoken opponent of internment—even hiring internees as correspondents and publishing their reports.

There is little evidence of this history here today, unless you know where to look. Suyematsu Farm is the last historic Japanese American farm still in operation—it's open by appointment for tours. The Bainbridge Island Historical Museum features an award-winning exhibit on local Japanese immigrant history. The Strawberry Festival at Filipino American Community Hall is still held each June. And across Eagle Harbor from the ferry terminal is the beautiful and poignant Japanese American Exclusion Memorial, completed in 2011 and operated by the National Park Service.

▼ The Japanese American Exclusion Memorial's cedar "story wall" is festooned with gifts and mementos left by visitors: pebbles, notes, and origami cranes.

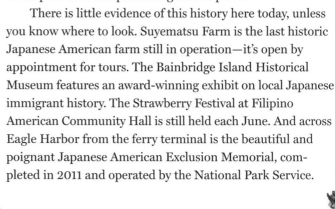

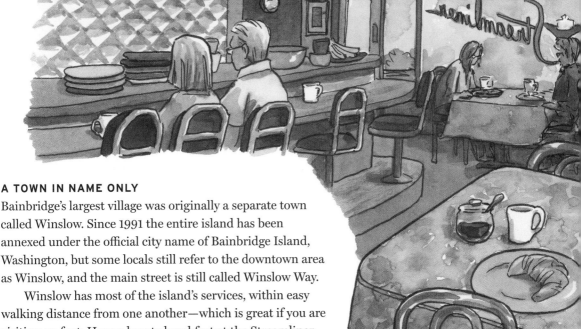

A TOWN IN NAME ONLY

Bainbridge's largest village was originally a separate town called Winslow. Since 1991 the entire island has been annexed under the official city name of Bainbridge Island, Washington, but some locals still refer to the downtown area as Winslow, and the main street is still called Winslow Way.

Winslow has most of the island's services, within easy walking distance from one another—which is great if you are visiting on foot. Have a hearty breakfast at the Streamliner Diner, then get a historical overview at the Bainbridge Island Historical Museum, a 1908 one-room schoolhouse that was relocated downtown in 2004. Recharge with a snack at the Blackbird Bakery, or if you're there on a Saturday between April and October, browse the farmers' market for local produce or fresh (and cheap!) oysters. Then do a bit of shopping: crafty types will love Esther's Fabrics or Churchmouse Yarns & Teas (online-only since 2020, but local pickups are available); the outdoorsy can stock up on gear at Wildernest; and bookish folks can explore the Eagle Harbor Book Co. Sit down for an island-to-table dinner at Hitchcock, then finish the day with a scoop at MORA Iced Creamery.

▲ Streamliner Diner, serving breakfast and lunch since 1980, is ever popular, especially on weekends. Arrive for an early meal, or prepare for a wait for the next open table.

▼ The Bainbridge Island Historical Society keeps a few Marshall strawberry beds alive behind the Historical Museum building in Winslow.

ARTISTIC ACRONYMS

Like many Salish Sea islands, Bainbridge is a hub for artists and art patrons. A number of island organizations provide creative opportunities to art enthusiasts of all stripes—the trouble is getting their names straight. The Bainbridge Island Museum of Art (BIMA on the map, page 28) features rotating exhibits, live performances, and an impressive permanent collection of handmade artist books. To shop for original artwork and artisan gifts, visit Bainbridge Arts and Crafts gallery (BAC). And to try your hand at different media and materials, take a class at the BARN (Bainbridge Artisan Resource Network), located just north of Winslow.

IT TAKES A VILLAGE

Other small burgs dot the Bainbridge map as well—though you'll likely need a car to reach them. Many occupy the same historic locations as the nine ancestral Suquamish winter

villages that once populated the island (see Suquamish Museum, page 31, to learn more).

Southwest of Winslow is Lynwood Center, home to a historic movie theater and newer condos. Food options include the Treehouse Café, Hammy's Burgers, and the Heyday Market, an outpost of Heyday Farm, a working farm south of Lynwood that hosts private events.

At the south end of the island is Fort Ward, a historic military base that is now part public park, part planned community of private homes. At the other end of the island are Rolling Bay (home of the excellent historic general store Bay Hay & Feed), Battle Point Park (where you'll find the John Rudolph Planetarium), and the residential enclaves of Seabold and Port Madison. Near the latter is Frog Rock, a giant boulder that a farmer tried (and failed) to dynamite away in the 1950s. Teenagers later painted the remaining split rock green, and it's been a local fixture ever since.

A WALK IN THE WOODS

If sylvan silence is more your cup of tea, Bainbridge has many forested parks, trails, and meditation spots to offer. Blakely Harbor Park, once the site of a nineteenth-century sawmill, is now a great picnic or wildlife-watching spot. Gazzam Lake Nature Preserve sets aside more than three hundred acres of wood and wetland areas, and maintains an extensive network of hiking trails. Or if you'd rather combine the forest with human creature comforts, attend a retreat or class at IslandWood, a beautiful nonprofit event space dedicated to education and environmental stewardship.

Hall's Hill Lookout, located along a quiet forest roadside, is extra special. Artist Jeffrey Bale created the park as a meditative space in 2014. Walk the circuits of the stone mosaic labyrinth, then head over to the bronze prayer wheel and spin it nine times to make its interior bell ring.

▲ The labyrinth at Hall's Hill Lookout, created using symbolic materials and measurements, is built in the same medieval style as the floor labyrinth at Chartres Cathedral in France.

▼ The Bloedel Reserve Mid-Pond was the first garden feature added to the property by landscape architect Thomas Church.

Best of all is the Bloedel Reserve, the formal garden that was once the private estate of a logging baron. The 150-acre grounds feature a midcentury Japanese-style tea house and Zen garden; several reflecting pools and ponds; a forest boardwalk with carnivorous pitcher plants; and many native and cultivated flowers and shrubs. The Reserve also hosts cultural events throughout the year.

OF SEASHELLS AND SKYSCRAPERS

Many of the island's beaches and waterfront drives offer spectacular views of the Seattle skyline, including Pritchard Park, Manitou Beach, Eagle Harbor, and the ferry landing (not to mention the ferry ride itself). Rockaway Beach, tucked among swanky waterfront homes, features tide pools as well as a killer view. Fay Bainbridge Park, at the northeastern tip of the island, offers a campground as well. Be mindful of public-private beach boundaries—and motorists, pedestrians, and cyclists alike should take road sharing and safety seriously.

BEYOND THE BRIDGE

Just off-island are a few Kitsap Peninsula attractions worth noting as well. In Suquamish, just across the bridge, you can visit the grave of Chief Si'ahl (Seattle's namesake) and the Suquamish Museum, where you can learn more about the millennia-old ancestral images carved on Haleets (or Xalilc, pictured right). Then sample the Norwegian flavor of the historic town of Poulsbo. Or you can go all the way to the lovely waterfront of Port Orchard, then catch a different ferry back to Seattle from Bremerton (map on page 24).

▲ Haleets (Figurehead Rock), a monolith covered with ancient petroglyphs, is visible from the water at low tide near Agate Point. The beach is private, so permission from the property owner is required to approach.

▼ The Bloedel Reserve Residence was built in 1931 in the style of an eighteenth-century French country manor.

PUGET SOUND

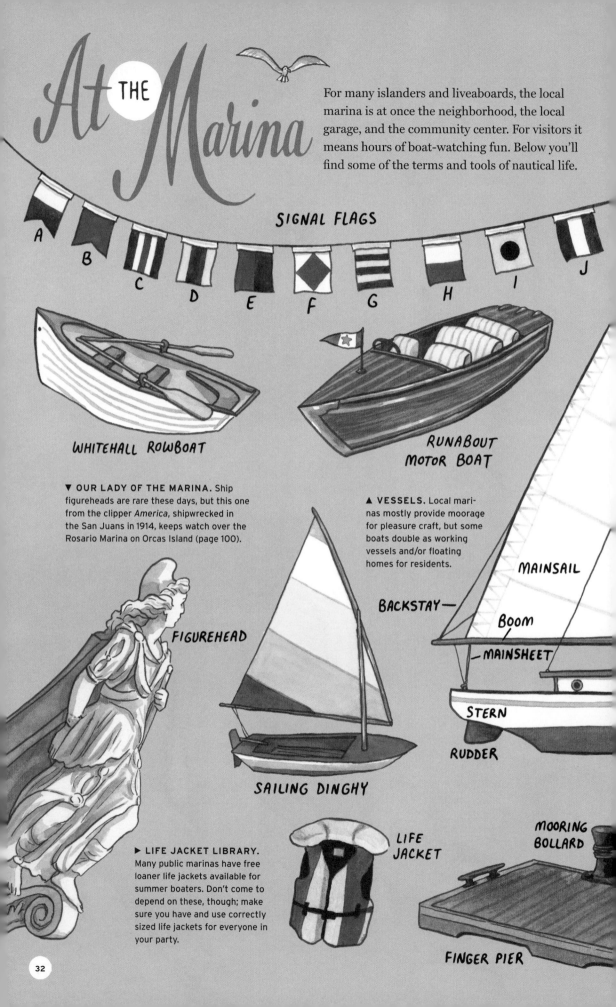

At _{THE} Marina

For many islanders and liveaboards, the local marina is at once the neighborhood, the local garage, and the community center. For visitors it means hours of boat-watching fun. Below you'll find some of the terms and tools of nautical life.

SIGNAL FLAGS

A B C D E F G H I J

WHITEHALL ROWBOAT

RUNABOUT MOTOR BOAT

▼ **OUR LADY OF THE MARINA.** Ship figureheads are rare these days, but this one from the clipper *America*, shipwrecked in the San Juans in 1914, keeps watch over the Rosario Marina on Orcas Island (page 100).

▲ **VESSELS.** Local marinas mostly provide moorage for pleasure craft, but some boats double as working vessels and/or floating homes for residents.

FIGUREHEAD

SAILING DINGHY

MAINSAIL

BACKSTAY—

Boom

MAINSHEET

STERN

RUDDER

▶ **LIFE JACKET LIBRARY.** Many public marinas have free loaner life jackets available for summer boaters. Don't come to depend on these, though; make sure you have and use correctly sized life jackets for everyone in your party.

LIFE JACKET

MOORING BOLLARD

FINGER PIER

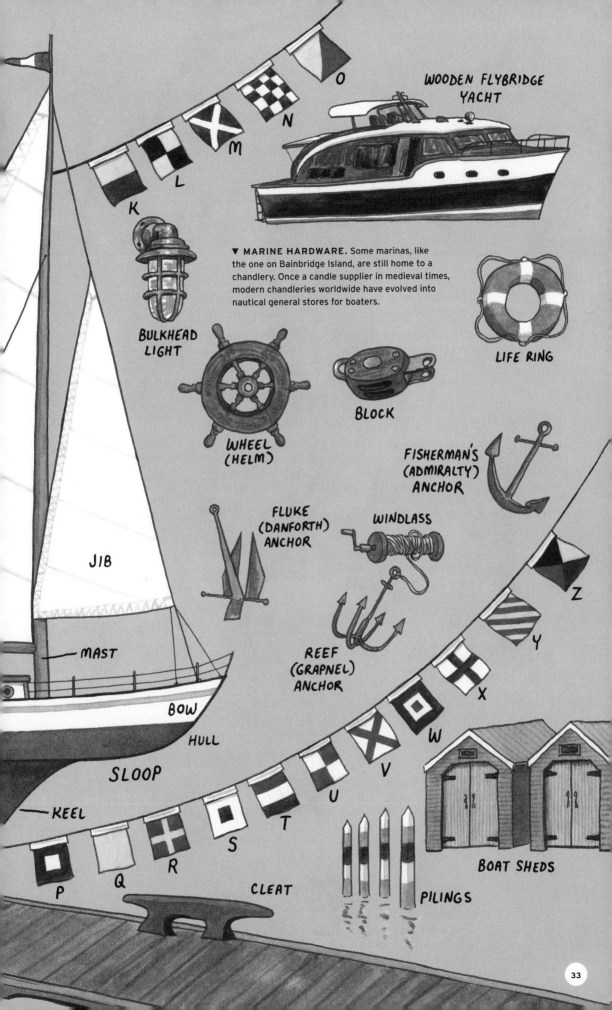

O

N

M

L

K

WOODEN FLYBRIDGE YACHT

BULKHEAD LIGHT

▼ MARINE HARDWARE. Some marinas, like the one on Bainbridge Island, are still home to a chandlery. Once a candle supplier in medieval times, modern chandleries worldwide have evolved into nautical general stores for boaters.

LIFE RING

WHEEL (HELM)

BLOCK

FISHERMAN'S (ADMIRALTY) ANCHOR

FLUKE (DANFORTH) ANCHOR

WINDLASS

JIB

Z

Y

REEF (GRAPNEL) ANCHOR

X

MAST

W

BOW

HULL

V

SLOOP

U

KEEL

T

S

BOAT SHEDS

R

Q

P

CLEAT

PILINGS

VASHON-MAURY

▼ The tiny community of Burton straddles the isthmus between inner and outer Quartermaster Harbor, providing picturesque views of quiet coves and Victorian-era structures.

The largest Puget Sound island south of Whidbey (page 42), Vashon-Maury sits in the main channel of the Sound, roughly midway between Tacoma and Seattle. This is the ideal location for its commuter residents, who are numerous enough to support a ferry at either end of Vashon-Maury.

An important historic fishing ground for the Puyallup people, Vashon and Maury Islands were originally connected only at low tide. White homeowners permanently tied the islands together with a man-made isthmus in 1913. Today some locals still refer to them as distinct islands, but for most, Vashon-Maury or simply "Vashon" apply to the pair as a whole.

Vashon shares a similar agricultural and immigrant history with Bainbridge (page 26), with one major distinction: unlike Bainbridge, no bridge has ever been built on Vashon. Early growth proponents saw an opportunity to create another Mercer Island (page 68), and many bridge proposals were floated (no pun intended) beginning in the 1930s. In 1953 the state legislature passed the Cross Sound Bridge Bill to link the northern tip of Vashon with Port Orchard and West Seattle, and add a four-lane freeway to the island. Despite local support of the bill, it died in committee, and to this day there is no bridge across the main channel of the Sound. As a result, Vashon has largely preserved its rural character—which has become its main attraction.

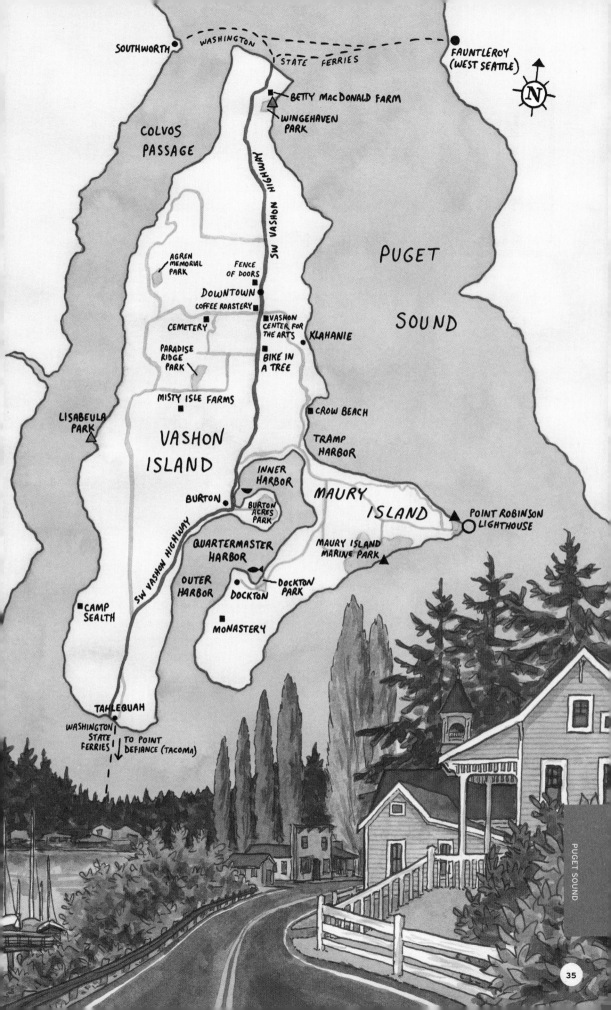

SOUTHWORTH

WASHINGTON STATE FERRIES

FAUNTLEROY (WEST SEATTLE)

N

COLVOS PASSAGE

Betty MacDonald Farm

Wingehaven Park

SW VASHON HIGHWAY

PUGET

SOUND

Agren Memorial Park

Fence of Doors

DOWNTOWN

Coffee Roastery

Cemetery

Vashon Center for the Arts

Klahanie

Paradise Ridge Park

Bike in a Tree

Misty Isle Farms

Crow Beach

Lisabeula Park

VASHON ISLAND

Tramp Harbor

Inner Harbor

MAURY ISLAND

Burton

Burton Acres Park

Point Robinson Lighthouse

Quartermaster Harbor

Maury Island Marine Park

Outer Harbor

Dockton

Dockton Park

Camp Sealth

SW VASHON HIGHWAY

Monastery

Tahlequah

Washington State Ferries

To Point Defiance (Tacoma)

BEAUCOUP BUCOLIC

Soon after white settlement, Vashon transitioned from a fishing economy to logging to agriculture. Like Bainbridge, Vashon enjoyed an ideal berry-growing climate, and strawberries quickly became the dominant crop. Somewhat less well-known is the island's poultry history. In 1923 (the same year then-101-year-old Melissa Jaynes was crowned the first Vashon Strawberry Queen), Vashon had 150,000 laying hens and produced 35,000 cases of eggs for shipping. With the exception of a few local egg stands, today the only reminder of these historic hens is a barn that stands at the corner of Cemetery Road and 87th Avenue SW. In 2008 artist Annie Brulé painted a mural-size replica of a 1920s Vashon chicken-farming cooperative advertisement on the building.

In recent decades vanishing farmland has been a concern on Vashon-Maury. The big commercial agricultural producers are gone now, and as suburban commuters have flocked to Vashon, wealthy bedroom enclaves have encroached upon the coastal real estate. To combat this Vashon-Maury has been designated an official King County rural area, and acreage minimums apply to land parcels in the interior to favor growers.

Vashon's contemporary rural life tells a tale of slow food and small scale, organic family farms, open-air markets, craft brewers, and heritage properties. Strawberry and egg farms have given way to wineries and perry (apple cider's fermented-pear sibling) producers. Large commercial producers have been replaced by the farm-to-table movement. A small-town atmosphere prevails, and locals still celebrate the cycle of the agricultural year. The Strawberry Festival still happens every July, and off-islanders flock to the annual Sheepdog Classic, where herding dogs compete in athletic trials straight out of a movie like *Babe*. Spend just a little time immersed in this culture, and it's easy to see why Vashon residents still feel no need for a bridge to the mainland—or to let in the city hustle.

▲ Nashi Orchards produces perry from heirloom Asian pears and is open for tours and tastings year-round on weekends or by appointment on weekdays.

▼ The Vashon Sheepdog Classic is inspired by the working dog competitions that began in New Zealand in the nineteenth century.

AN ARTIST'S RETREAT

For many Vashon denizens, the bucolic rural setting is a source of inspiration. The area has developed a reputation as a vibrant artist colony, with many painters, sculptors, jewelers, glassblowers, photographers, and others practicing here. Each May and December since the 1970s, Vashon's artists (now organized as VIVA, or Vashon Island Visual Artists) have hosted a multiweekend studio tour circuit. A newer event is the Wandering Reel Traveling Film Festival, which brings international short films to the Vashon Theatre each November. The Church of Great Rain is a local variety show that performs at the Open Space arts center. Voice of Vashon, a homegrown radio station, operates out of a downtown studio. And in 2016 the Vashon Center for the Arts transformed the 1912 Blue Heron Art Center into a gleaming five-acre campus, including a sculpture garden, restored wetlands, a gallery space, and a three-hundred-seat performance hall.

Vashon-Maury is home to a collection of somewhat less-highbrow art, too, in the form of quirky landmarks, roadside attractions, and conversation pieces. All around the island are seemingly random roadside sculptures, improvised statues, and offbeat decor—like the fence made of brightly painted doors tucked away in an alley off of Vashon Highway SW. Most famous is the Vashon Island Bike in the Tree, where a 1950s-era child's bicycle is suspended halfway up a living cedar, where the wood grew around it and "ate" the frame.

If you prefer your inspiration in the form of meditation, several local yoga studios offer classes and organized day, weekend, and seasonal retreats. The Hestia Retreat hosts small-group gatherings for women, and Camp Burton and Camp Fire offer religious retreats and other events. There is even a Russian Orthodox monastery on the island: an onion-domed chapel sits on land donated by the actor John Ratzenberger (one of the island's famous part-time residents). The monastery is open to the public for reflection or pilgrimages (visitors must call ahead), though overnight accommodations are available to male visitors only.

EAT, DRINK, AND BE MERRY

With so many local growers providing ingredients, Vashon is a great place to dine on farm-to-table treats. Bramble House offers a rotating menu of locally grown seasonal dishes, and The Hardware Store downtown—which really did sell hardware from 1890 until it became a restaurant in 2005—

▲ In 2014 vandals stripped the Bike in the Tree so that only a rusted frame remains. That has not, however, stopped people from making pilgrimages to see it.

▼ All-Merciful Saviour Monastery was established in 1988, and now includes a campus of several buildings on eleven acres of protected land.

◀ The Vashon Island Coffee Roasterie is the origin of the Seattle's Best brand. It still roasts and sells shade-grown heirloom beans, a local specialty of the famous Seattle-area coffee culture.

has a more classic menu peppered with local ingredients. Wine lovers will want to visit Vashon, Maury Island, or Palouse Wineries. Beer enthusiasts can try Vashon Brewing and Camp Colvos Brewing, while Dragon's Head Cider and Nashi Orchards keep the cider and perry fans happy. All these places have tasting rooms, or you can sample local libations at the Vashon Blues and Brews Festival in June, or the annual Oktoberfest. And for an old-fashioned Northwest cuppa, don't miss the historic coffee roastery at the corner of Vashon Highway SW and SW Cemetery Road.

ISLE OF BOOKS

Writers have long sought refuge on Vashon Island and found its rural setting to be the perfect writers' retreat. Most famous among these is Betty MacDonald, author of the 1945 memoir *The Egg and I*, which became a popular series of mid-twentieth-century films. That book is set on the Olympic Peninsula (not far from Marrowstone Island, page 70), but her third memoir, *Onions in the Stew* (1954), chronicles her time on Vashon. During that period she also wrote her well-known Mrs. Piggle-Wiggle series for children. MacDonald's waterfront cabin is still a private home, but the main property, including the red barn that belonged to her second husband, Don, is now part of a bed-and-breakfast called the Betty MacDonald Farm.

Michael Chabon also called Vashon home for a time; his 2002 novel *Summerland* is set on fictional Clam Island, which is modeled after Vashon. Berkeley Breathed, creator of the Bloom County comic strip, wrote the children's story *Red Ranger Came Calling*, which is based on the Vashon Bike in the Tree. And Jean Davies Okimoto, author of many award-winning books for children and young adults, still calls the island home. You can find books written and illustrated by more than a hundred island authors at the Vashon Bookshop—or you can continue the tradition by writing your own. The Living Room Workshops, out of Seattle, offers

▼ A private residence in Dockton overlooks the former site of Codfish Dock, where the Bering Sea Packing Co. once processed and salted Pacific cod caught in Alaska.

▶ Vashon is home to a number of "walk-in communities," where shoreline homes are connected by wooded boardwalks, and residents haul in goods with communal wheelbarrows stationed at the pier.

occasional writing retreats on Vashon, and Vashon Center for the Arts hosts the Vashon Lit Con in the spring. Or you can rent the Cedar Loft at the Betty MacDonald Farm, and craft your own writers' retreat.

NAUTICAL NOTES

Like all the islands in the Sound, Vashon is steeped in maritime culture—and here, there are opportunities to become a part of it. The Quartermaster Yacht Club offers sailing lessons to both children and adults, and the Vashon Island Rowing Club hosts a junior racing crew, as well as adult rowing classes. In the summer kids can participate in many nautical activities at historic Camp Sealth, offering both day and overnight camps at its location on the western shore.

Even if you are navigating by car or bike, you can still take your own nautical tour. Start at Point Robinson Park, where a 1914 lighthouse sits adjacent to two older keepers' quarters buildings, both of which are available for vacation rentals. The annual Low Tide Celebration, a festival of tidal critters, is held here every July. Elsewhere on Maury Island, the small town of Dockton was home to the largest dry dock north of San Francisco in the late-nineteenth century; you can see remnants of it in Dockton Park and learn about Dockton's history through a series of interpretive signs around town. Watch shorebirds foraging at Crow Beach, or see the boats come in and out of Quartermaster Marina. In Colvos Passage off the west side of Vashon, you might glimpse humpback whales or orcas by day, or glowing bioluminescent organisms by night. And for the complete Vashon experience, plan your trip so that you take both ferries: the Tahlequah ferry heads to Tacoma, while the boat at the northern end of the island will take you either to Fauntleroy in West Seattle or to Southworth on the Kitsap Peninsula. (All fares to Vashon are one-way, collected on the mainland for inbound crossings. There are no ticket booths on Vashon, and outbound trips are free for walk-ons and drivers.)

▲ Island residents fund the annual Fourth of July fireworks, which are lit from a barge anchored in Quartermaster Harbor.

Green Canopy

The Northwest's dense evergreens and rain-forest microclimates give its woodlands a year-round emerald glow. Here are some common native trees and flowering shrubs you might encounter.

◀ **EVERGREENS.** Tall conifers lend Washington its "Evergreen State" moniker. But you'll also find a number of evergreen broadleaf species here, like madronas and rhododendrons, the state flower.

PACIFIC MADRONE (MADRONA, ARBUTUS)

▼ **IRONWOOD.** There are few hardwood species in the region but ocean spray, a flowering shrub, was once used to make nails, before metal hardware came to the islands.

VINE MAPLE

OCEAN SPRAY (IRONWOOD)

BIG-LEAF MAPLE

OREGON GRAPE

▶ **MAPLES.** No sugar maples grow west of the Rockies, but in recent years Northwest producers have begun tapping endemic big-leaf maples for syrup.

▼ **NEEDLES.** Learning to tell all those conifer species apart? Take a close look at their needles for clues.

WESTERN RED CEDAR

DOUGLAS FIR

LODGEPOLE PINE

WESTERN HEMLOCK

PACIFIC YEW

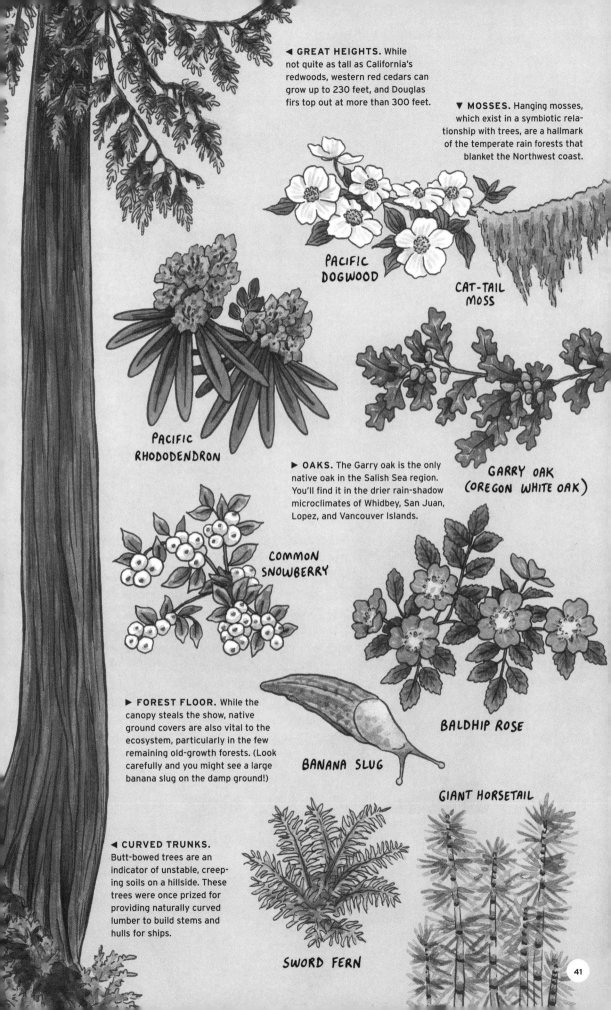

◄ **GREAT HEIGHTS.** While not quite as tall as California's redwoods, western red cedars can grow up to 230 feet, and Douglas firs top out at more than 300 feet.

▼ **MOSSES.** Hanging mosses, which exist in a symbiotic relationship with trees, are a hallmark of the temperate rain forests that blanket the Northwest coast.

PACIFIC DOGWOOD

CAT-TAIL MOSS

PACIFIC RHODODENDRON

GARRY OAK (OREGON WHITE OAK)

► **OAKS.** The Garry oak is the only native oak in the Salish Sea region. You'll find it in the drier rain-shadow microclimates of Whidbey, San Juan, Lopez, and Vancouver Islands.

COMMON SNOWBERRY

BALDHIP ROSE

► **FOREST FLOOR.** While the canopy steals the show, native ground covers are also vital to the ecosystem, particularly in the few remaining old-growth forests. (Look carefully and you might see a large banana slug on the damp ground!)

BANANA SLUG

GIANT HORSETAIL

◄ **CURVED TRUNKS.** Butt-bowed trees are an indicator of unstable, creeping soils on a hillside. These trees were once prized for providing naturally curved lumber to build stems and hulls for ships.

SWORD FERN

WHIDBEY

▼ The Whidbey Island Kite Festival, held every September at Camp Casey, highlights both family kite activities and the local Sport Kite Championships.

Welcome to the northern gatekeeper of Puget Sound. At about fifty-five miles long by road, Whidbey Island is Washington's largest, and the fourth largest and longest island in the lower forty-eight states. Like Bainbridge, Whidbey is connected by bridge (Deception Pass) at the northern end and by ferry at the southern end.

During the last ice age (about seventeen thousand years ago), Seattle was buried under the three-thousand-foot-deep Cordilleran Ice Sheet—the glacier that helped carve Puget Sound. As the ice retreated, Whidbey was one of the landforms that appeared, and Columbian mammoths roamed the region. Numerous mastodon and mammoth fossils have been found on the island over the years, including a large tooth dug up and relished by a resident's happy dog in 2018.

The island is the ancestral home of the Skagit, Swinomish, Suquamish, and Snohomish peoples—archeological evidence of their presence dates back more than ten thousand years. White settlers arrived in the mid-nineteenth century, and both clashed and intermarried with Indigenous groups (whose tribal seats were forced off-island, where they remain today). Northern Whidbey became a base for various military operations, from the 1890s to the present.

Today's Whidbey is a mix of work and pleasure. Summer homes, working farms, military life, and outdoor recreation all intermingle, and its parks attract tourists from around the country and beyond. Because of its proximity to Seattle, Whidbey is also a major destination for day trips and weekend getaways. The ferry runs every half hour, but, as it is the state's most popular, brace yourself for long waits to get your car aboard, especially on summer weekends.

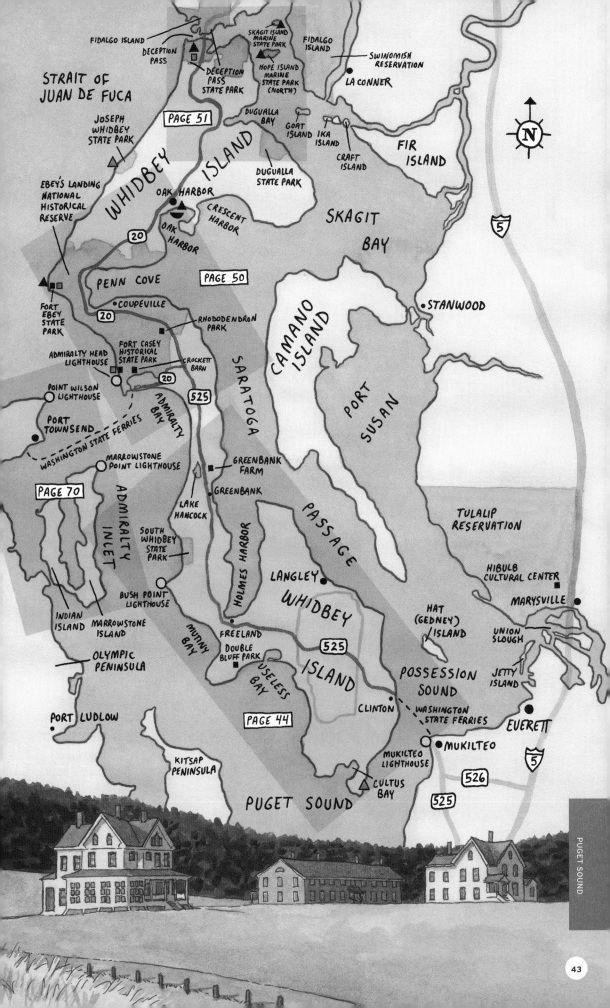

STRAIT OF JUAN DE FUCA

FIDALGO ISLAND

DECEPTION PASS

DECEPTION PASS STATE PARK

SKAGIT ISLAND MARINE STATE PARK

FIDALGO ISLAND

HOPE ISLAND MARINE STATE PARK (NORTH)

SWINOMISH RESERVATION

LA CONNER

JOSEPH WHIDBEY STATE PARK

PAGE 51

DUGUALLA BAY

GOAT ISLAND

IKA ISLAND

CRAFT ISLAND

FIR ISLAND

WHIDBEY ISLAND

DUGUALLA STATE PARK

EBEY'S LANDING NATIONAL HISTORICAL RESERVE

OAK HARBOR

OAK HARBOR

CRESCENT HARBOR

SKAGIT BAY

20

PENN COVE

PAGE 50

CAMANO ISLAND

STANWOOD

FORT EBEY STATE PARK

COUPEVILLE

RHODODENDRON PARK

20

ADMIRALTY HEAD LIGHTHOUSE

FORT CASEY HISTORICAL STATE PARK

CROCKETT BARN

20

525

PORT SUSAN

SARATOGA

POINT WILSON LIGHTHOUSE

PORT TOWNSEND

WASHINGTON STATE FERRIES

ADMIRALTY BAY

MARROWSTONE POINT LIGHTHOUSE

GREENBANK FARM

PAGE 70

GREENBANK

ADMIRALTY INLET

LAKE HANCOCK

SOUTH WHIDBEY STATE PARK

HOLMES HARBOR

PASSAGE

TULALIP RESERVATION

HIBULB CULTURAL CENTER

LANGLEY

WHIDBEY

MARYSVILLE

INDIAN ISLAND

MARROWSTONE ISLAND

BUSH POINT LIGHTHOUSE

HAT (GEDNEY) ISLAND

UNION SLOUGH

OLYMPIC PENINSULA

MUTNY BAY

FREELAND

DOUBLE BLUFF PARK

ISLAND

525

POSSESSION SOUND

JETTY ISLAND

PORT LUDLOW

USELESS BAY

PAGE 44

CLINTON

WASHINGTON STATE FERRIES

EVERETT

KITSAP PENINSULA

MUKILTEO LIGHTHOUSE

MUKILTEO

PUGET SOUND

CULTUS BAY

526

525

N

5

5

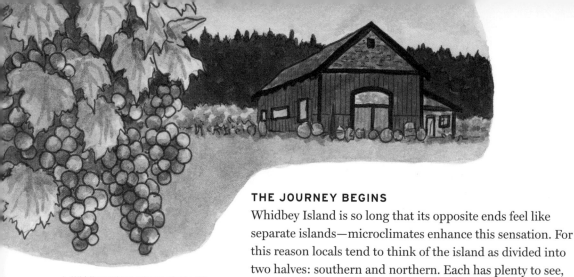

▲ Whidbey Island Winery planted its first vines in 1986, and now produces about 3,500 cases of wine a year.

THE JOURNEY BEGINS

Whidbey Island is so long that its opposite ends feel like separate islands—microclimates enhance this sensation. For this reason locals tend to think of the island as divided into two halves: southern and northern. Each has plenty to see, so many tourists focus on just one area. This chapter covers the whole island, moving south to north.

The town of Clinton, home of the island's main car ferry terminal since 1910, is the first stop for travelers arriving on Whidbey from Mukilteo. The small community is home to a few food markets and specialty shops, and Clinton Beach Park offers great views of the ferry landing. Whidbey Wonders specializes in goods and food made by island artisans and growers. Or try the blackberry liqueur at Whidbey Island Distillery.

Beyond Clinton, it's worth exploring some of the wooded back roads that meander around the southernmost portion of the island. To avoid trespassing you'll need to stay on the public roadside, but the picturesque houses and peekaboo views provide an idyllic glimpse of island life. Possession Beach Waterfront Park has views of the mainland, and Possession Point State Park offers campsites for boaters as part of the Cascadia Marine Trail (page 58).

WHIDBEY WINES

Part of the island lies in the rain shadow cast by the Olympic Mountains across the Sound. The mountains block much of the rain that falls elsewhere, making for a drier microclimate within the region's Mediterranean clime (dry, sunny summers and mild, wet winters). This is ideal for a number of surprising Mediterranean crops, including lavender and even wine grapes. Southern Whidbey has a handful of wineries (most of Washington's vintners are east of the Cascade Mountains), including Blooms Winery, Whidbey Island Winery, and Spoiled Dog Winery. Those that grow their own grapes specialize in rare northern European white varietals like Madeleine Angevine and Siegerrebe. Most of Whidbey's wineries have a public tasting room—if you can't decide which to visit, you can book a chauffeured sampling with Whidbey Wine Tasting Tours in Clinton.

PICK A BAY, ANY BAY

Southern Whidbey is carved up into several bays and inlets (many of which are lined with scenic drives and residential roads). The largest is Useless Bay—so named because at low tide it's too shallow for boating. There are two small public parks at either end: Dave Mackie County Park at the Maxwelton end, and Double Bluff County Park, near Freeland. Both offer sandy beaches and lots of beachcombing. Farther up the western shore is South Whidbey State Park, home to an old-growth forest grove (day use only; camping here is closed indefinitely due to falling trees). And at the island's narrowest point, Freeland sits at the end of Holmes Harbor. After a waterfront stroll at Freeland Park, stop for a fancy seafood meal with a view at Gordon's on Blueberry Hill.

SEASONAL SIGHTSEEING

Many of southern Whidbey's highlights revolve around seasonal events. In the growing season (April through October), the Bayview Farmers Market hosts farmers, artisans, and food vendors. Clinton has an annual Easter egg hunt for kids, and adults can enjoy the spring rhododendron blooms at Meerkerk Gardens (or visit in August for the annual bluegrass concert). You can combine nature and spirituality with a visit to Earth Sanctuary. The Whidbey Island Garden Tour features local private gardens each June, and Maxwelton hosts a small-town Fourth of July parade. Kids can partake of Whidbey summer camps, including the day camp at Full Moon Rising Farm. Knitters and weavers will love Fiber Quest, a November circuit of yarn shops and alpaca farms. And in Langley local businesses decorate their doors each December to celebrate the holidays.

THE VILLAGE BY THE SEA

The quaint town of Langley, perched on a bluff overlooking the Saratoga Passage and Camano Island (page 64), is southern Whidbey's focal point. With just over a thousand inhabitants, Langley is small enough to be walkable and

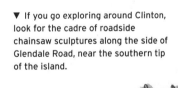

▲ Most of the beaches along Useless Bay are privately owned and lined with shoreline homes and vacation-rental cottages.

▼ If you go exploring around Clinton, look for the cadre of roadside chainsaw sculptures along the side of Glendale Road, near the southern tip of the island.

large enough to offer plenty of cuisine and shopping. Browse the shelves at Moonraker Books for local subjects and authors, or try the Star Store, an impressive combination of coffee shop, specialty grocer, kitchen store, and gift shop. For weekend brunch try the stuffed French toast at the Braeburn. Satisfy your sweet tooth with the house-made candy at Sweet Mona's. For Salish seafood grab a meal at Saltwater Fish House & Oyster Bar. And in mid-September don't miss the 2nd Street Community Feast, an open-air public dinner.

The Inn at Langley, a high-end hotel, spa, and restaurant, has become a tourism centerpiece. The multistory complex is unassuming from the street side, but its balconies cascade down the bluff to the beach. The hotel, founded by former Seattle mayor Paul Schell in 1989, blends a mix of Craftsman-era, Pacific Northwest, and Asian influences into its aesthetic, aiming for a quiet, zen-like ambiance for its guests. The Inn's restaurant, Chef's Kitchen, is open to the public for prix fixe dinners featuring seasonal, local fare—including herbs from the hotel's front garden.

If you're looking for offbeat, retro fun, visit the Machine Shop to play a vintage pinball or arcade game. For an interactive art experience visit Callahan's Firehouse to watch glass artisans at work in the hot shop—or even try your hand at glassblowing yourself. For a bit of quiet time, stop at the South Whidbey Commons—part library, part bookstore. Or in the summer try an after-dark kayak tour with Whidbey Island Kayaking for a chance to see bioluminescent organisms light up the Saratoga Passage.

WHALE-SOME TRADITIONS

Langley's central location on whale migration routes (also called the Whale Trail) makes it an ideal spot for cetacean lovers. Gray whales pass through the Saratoga Passage in the spring, and the Southern Resident orcas (page 98) can sometimes be seen around Whidbey Island in the fall. Transient orcas, humpbacks, and other cetacean species are occasional

▲ Visit Seawall Park, which overlooks the Saratoga Passage, and keep a sharp eye on the water. Then ring the Whale Bell if you spot a cetacean!

▼ The formal front garden at the Inn at Langley, designed by landscape architect Tom Berger, is open to the public and accessible from the street.

year-round visitors. Visit the Langley Whale Center for scientific exhibits and an up-to-date whale-sighting map; you can also call in your own sightings and help update the map. And celebrate at the Welcome the Whales Festival in mid-April—don't miss the whale-themed parade!

(DON'T) FALL DOWN THE RABBIT HOLE

Just south of Langley are the Whidbey Island Fairgrounds (formerly the Island County Fairgrounds), a cluster of historic fair buildings and barns that host the fair every July. A quintessential county fair, the event is a 4-H lover's dream, with crop displays, needlework exhibits, baking contests, and livestock competitions.

The fairgrounds are also the epicenter of the world's cutest pest control problem. Decades ago the fair held "barnyard scrambles," where chicks and bunnies were released for children to catch and keep as pets. A few escapees each year led to a firmly entrenched wild population today—and an erosion problem from ever-expanding warrens.

The feral European rabbits are easy to spot—they're much larger and more colorful than the native cottontail. They are remarkably nonchalant about humans, but don't approach them, touch them, or feed them—they are still wild animals, and they can transmit diseases to humans and pets. Beware of walking your dog around Langley—or of turning an ankle in one of the many rabbit holes!

THE CENTER OF THE COMPASS

As you head up-island, you'll thread a narrow midsection dotted with fields and farmhouses. In July you'll find Lavender Wind farm in full bloom. Visit for a farm tour and to buy plant starts or lavender products, or stop by their year-round shop in Coupeville. Nearby is Greenbank Farm, a former loganberry farm that is now a cluster of shops offering wine,

▲ The Pole Building, the centerpiece of the fairgrounds, was built from peeled logs in 1937 with Depression-era Works Progress Administration stimulus funding.

▼ The Langley bunnies have a gang of feathered allies: beware of rogue roosters and grumpy hens roaming the fairgrounds as well.

PUGET SOUND

47

▲ Greenbank Farm is where Whidbey Pies bakes its signature confections for sale at stores around the island. Loganberry (a blackberry-raspberry hybrid) pie is a local favorite.

▲ Many Whidbey Island restaurants prepare Penn Cove mussels in the traditional French method, steamed in white wine, garlic, and cream.

▼ The Coupeville Wharf building was built in 1905 to store island grain exported by boat. Today it houses a souvenir shop, a cafe, and a marine educational center.

cheese, local artwork, furniture, and homemade pies. In Greenbank itself is the Greenbank Pantry & Deli (no affiliation with the farm), which serves sandwiches on house-made bread, as well as artisanal groceries.

Whidbey is nearly bisected by Penn Cove, a shallow inlet famous for its shellfish beds—and made infamous in 1970 for the violent roundup that captured live orcas for distant aquariums. The surrounding rural area encompasses natural prairies (unique treeless areas found only on a few islands in the region), plus several farms, settlements, and military installations that date back to the mid-nineteenth century.

This entire section of the island is part of Ebey's Landing National Historical Reserve, a cultural and natural district devoted to preserving Whidbey's history. The effort is co-managed by several state and county parks, a number of private landowners and trusts, and the National Park Service. Historical buildings include the Crockett Barn (1895) and the Ferry House (circa 1858). Fort Casey Historical State Park houses the Admiralty Head Lighthouse (1903), arguably the most beautiful on Puget Sound. The park is also home to Camp Casey, a summer camp for kids with special needs. Fort Ebey State Park offers camping and seaweed- and shellfish-gathering opportunities. Several hiking and bike trails crisscross the Reserve; as some of these traverse private property, remember to respect the privacy of residents and crops within farm fields.

Just outside Fort Casey is the terminus for the Coupeville–Port Townsend ferry, your link to Marrowstone Island (page 70). Runs are infrequent, so reservations are crucial, especially

in the winter. Note that during extreme tides or very choppy seas, this ferry is sometimes canceled—reservation holders get first dibs on rescheduled sailings.

A REAL-LIFE MOVIE SET

Don't miss historic Coupeville, the small town that sits right on Penn Cove. This Victorian community is one of the oldest towns in the state and part of Ebey's Landing National Historical Reserve. The National Park Service website offers maps for a self-guided walking tour of downtown— which served as a principal film location for the 1998 movie *Practical Magic*. There are a surprising number of things to do here, and the picturesque setting might convince you to stay for days. Visit the Island County Historical Museum to learn about the town's Indigenous and settler history. Stop into the Kingfisher Bookstore, then look for real kingfishers around the Coupeville Wharf (you won't have to wait long to see one). Grab a snack at Little Red Hen Bakery, or a rustic Italian meal at Ciao. Or you can shop for organic meats and local gifts and food products at 3 Sisters Market. For historic lodging try one of Coupeville's Victorian bed-and-breakfasts or the Captain Whidbey Inn, a lodge and restaurant built in 1907 and still operating today as a hipster-friendly resort.

▲ Admiralty Head Lighthouse was built as a companion to Point Wilson Lighthouse, situated directly across the Admiralty Inlet in Port Townsend, four miles away.

▼ The 1866 Sedge Building is one of the oldest structures in Coupeville. It was featured in *Practical Magic*, and has been home to several businesses since then.

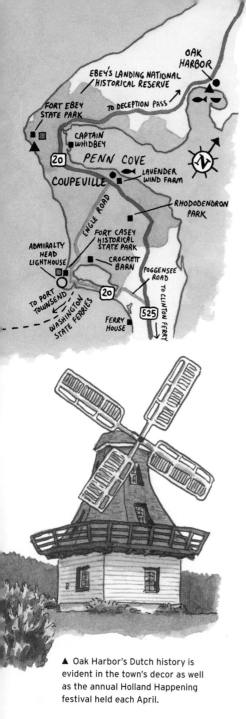

WISHING YOU FAIR WINDS AND CALM SEAS

Whidbey's largest town is a utilitarian hub thanks to nearby Naval Air Station Whidbey Island. Oak Harbor has a historic downtown, several shops and cafes, and any big-box suppliers you might need for provisions or camping gear. A handful of city parks line the harbor, and Dugualla State Park, just north of town, provides quiet hiking trails and beach access. The PBY Naval Air Museum shares the history of the "flying boat" aircraft based here during World War II. And you're likely to see (and hear!) naval jets flying overhead, as pilots practice for landing on aircraft carriers at sea. The experience lends extra meaning to the "fair winds and calm seas" phrase on the back of the welcome sign at either end of town—but it also brings up a word of caution. The flyover noise here (and at Deception Pass State Park) can be a deal-breaker for lodging guests looking for a quiet retreat. Make sure you read plenty of online reviews before you book anything.

THE GRAND FINALE

If your adventure follows this chapter from south to north, you've saved the best part for last. Deception Pass State Park—which straddles both sides of the namesake water passage between Whidbey and Fidalgo Islands (page 78)—is Whidbey's most famous attraction and Washington's most popular state park. The park receives more than two million visitors each year, outstripping even Mount Rainier National Park. Because of this popularity, you can expect to battle crowds here, particularly if you visit on a summer weekend. Aim for an off-season visit or an early weekday morning in the summer if you'd like more breathing room.

Deception Pass got its name in 1792, when Captain George Vancouver of the British navy made his survey of Puget Sound. He originally thought Whidbey was a peninsula, and named the passage when he learned, to his surprise, that it wasn't. Until the Deception Pass Bridge was completed in 1935, residents, travelers, and commercial businesspeople commuted by Mosquito Fleet ferry between Whidbey, Fidalgo, and the mainland.

▲ Oak Harbor's Dutch history is evident in the town's decor as well as the annual Holland Happening festival held each April.

▼ Deception Pass State Park offers many vantage points to watch boats navigating the tricky channel and swift currents swirling through the pass.

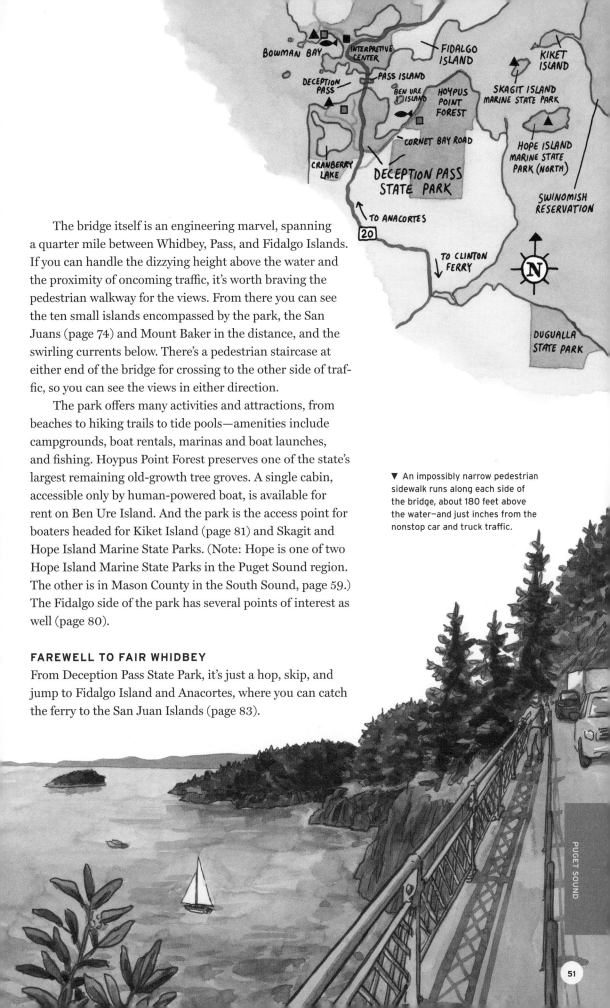

The bridge itself is an engineering marvel, spanning a quarter mile between Whidbey, Pass, and Fidalgo Islands. If you can handle the dizzying height above the water and the proximity of oncoming traffic, it's worth braving the pedestrian walkway for the views. From there you can see the ten small islands encompassed by the park, the San Juans (page 74) and Mount Baker in the distance, and the swirling currents below. There's a pedestrian staircase at either end of the bridge for crossing to the other side of traffic, so you can see the views in either direction.

The park offers many activities and attractions, from beaches to hiking trails to tide pools—amenities include campgrounds, boat rentals, marinas and boat launches, and fishing. Hoypus Point Forest preserves one of the state's largest remaining old-growth tree groves. A single cabin, accessible only by human-powered boat, is available for rent on Ben Ure Island. And the park is the access point for boaters headed for Kiket Island (page 81) and Skagit and Hope Island Marine State Parks. (Note: Hope is one of two Hope Island Marine State Parks in the Puget Sound region. The other is in Mason County in the South Sound, page 59.) The Fidalgo side of the park has several points of interest as well (page 80).

FAREWELL TO FAIR WHIDBEY
From Deception Pass State Park, it's just a hop, skip, and jump to Fidalgo Island and Anacortes, where you can catch the ferry to the San Juan Islands (page 83).

▼ An impossibly narrow pedestrian sidewalk runs along each side of the bridge, about 180 feet above the water—and just inches from the nonstop car and truck traffic.

PUGET SOUND

Catch of the Day

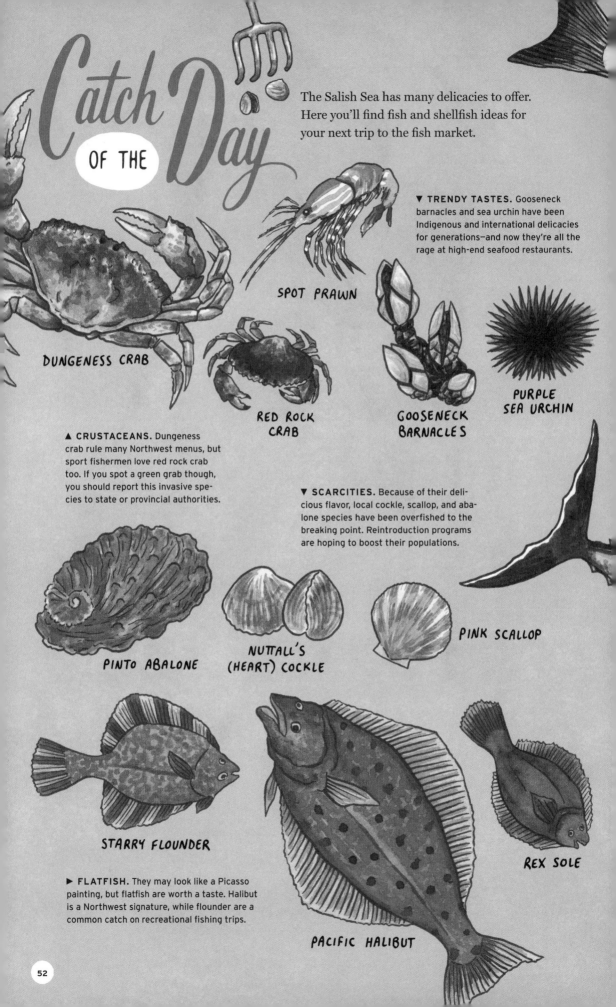

The Salish Sea has many delicacies to offer. Here you'll find fish and shellfish ideas for your next trip to the fish market.

▼ TRENDY TASTES. Gooseneck barnacles and sea urchin have been Indigenous and international delicacies for generations—and now they're all the rage at high-end seafood restaurants.

SPOT PRAWN

DUNGENESS CRAB

RED ROCK CRAB

GOOSENECK BARNACLES

PURPLE SEA URCHIN

▲ CRUSTACEANS. Dungeness crab rule many Northwest menus, but sport fishermen love red rock crab too. If you spot a green grab though, you should report this invasive species to state or provincial authorities.

▼ SCARCITIES. Because of their delicious flavor, local cockle, scallop, and abalone species have been overfished to the breaking point. Reintroduction programs are hoping to boost their populations.

PINTO ABALONE

NUTTALL'S (HEART) COCKLE

PINK SCALLOP

STARRY FLOUNDER

REX SOLE

► FLATFISH. They may look like a Picasso painting, but flatfish are worth a taste. Halibut is a Northwest signature, while flounder are a common catch on recreational fishing trips.

PACIFIC HALIBUT

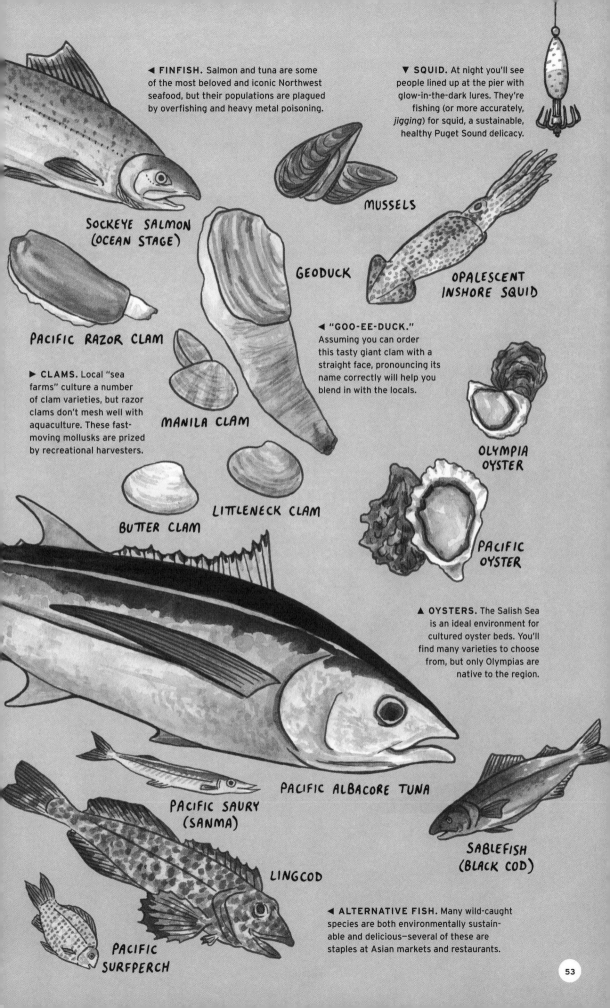

◀ FINFISH. Salmon and tuna are some of the most beloved and iconic Northwest seafood, but their populations are plagued by overfishing and heavy metal poisoning.

▼ SQUID. At night you'll see people lined up at the pier with glow-in-the-dark lures. They're fishing (or more accurately, *jigging*) for squid, a sustainable, healthy Puget Sound delicacy.

SOCKEYE SALMON
(OCEAN STAGE)

MUSSELS

GEODUCK

OPALESCENT
INSHORE SQUID

PACIFIC RAZOR CLAM

▶ CLAMS. Local "sea farms" culture a number of clam varieties, but razor clams don't mesh well with aquaculture. These fast-moving mollusks are prized by recreational harvesters.

MANILA CLAM

◀ "GOO-EE-DUCK." Assuming you can order this tasty giant clam with a straight face, pronouncing its name correctly will help you blend in with the locals.

OLYMPIA
OYSTER

LITTLENECK CLAM

BUTTER CLAM

PACIFIC
OYSTER

▲ OYSTERS. The Salish Sea is an ideal environment for cultured oyster beds. You'll find many varieties to choose from, but only Olympias are native to the region.

PACIFIC SAURY
(SANMA)

PACIFIC ALBACORE TUNA

SABLEFISH
(BLACK COD)

LINGCOD

◀ ALTERNATIVE FISH. Many wild-caught species are both environmentally sustainable and delicious—several of these are staples at Asian markets and restaurants.

PACIFIC
SURFPERCH

THE SOUTH SOUND

▼ Jarrell Cove State Park on Harstine Island boasts an excellent campground with easy access for both paddlers and boaters using the adjacent marina.

A complex region of fjords, inlets, and narrow passages, the South Sound is a large swath that includes everything south and west of Tacoma. Hardly any two destinations in this region are contiguous, so what is adjacent as the crow flies can become vast distances by road. Only a handful of islands are accessible by car or ferry; several others can be reached only by private or human-powered boat; and the rest are privately or tribally owned.

It's just under thirty miles from Tacoma to Olympia via Interstate 5, but reaching the islands will necessitate a lot of side trips down narrow, winding secondary roads. Watch for logging trucks and local traffic on weekdays, and RVs and other recreational traffic on weekends. Also, many roads hug the shoreline, which can be both beautiful and treacherous—beware of black ice in the winter, landslides after heavy rains, and patches of thick fog year-round. Finally, note that the Tacoma Narrows Bridge charges a one-way toll to eastbound drivers.

First up are the islands adjacent to Tacoma and Gig Harbor. These are largely bedroom communities for the cities, but there are still some public attractions worth visiting. At the outer reaches of the Sound, near the state capital of Olympia, are a handful of remote islands. Hopping between South Sound destinations requires time and patience, so take it slow—remember, you're on island time!

HOOD CANAL

ALLYN •

302

KITSAP PENINSULA

COLVOS PASSAGE

VASHON ISLAND

MAURY ISLAND

VAUGHN •

PAGE 58

N

CASE

CARR

GIG HARBOR

WASHINGTON STATE FERRIES

3

GRAPEVIEW •

STRETCH ISLAND

INLET

INLET

KEY PENINSULA

HERRON ISLAND

McMICKEN ISLAND

PAGE 57

FOX ISLAND

TACOMA NARROWS

TACOMA

OAKLAND BAY

SHELTON

HAMMERSLEY INLET

HARSTINE

ISLAND

LONGBRANCH •

McNEIL ISLAND

PUGET SOUND

16

5

LAKEWOOD

SQUAXIN ISLAND RESERVATION

SQUAXIN ISLAND

DRAYTON PASSAGE

PIERCE COUNTY FERRY

STEILACOOM

STEAMBOAT ISLAND

TOTTEN INLET

ANDERSON

ISLAND

KETRON ISLAND

NISQUALLY REACH

BUDD INLET

HOPE ISLAND MARINE STATE PARK (SOUTH)

ELD INLET

5

OLYMPIA ★

LACEY •

101

▲ Wide-Awake Hollow on Anderson Island, completed in 1883, is the oldest one-room schoolhouse in Pierce County. Now owned by the park district, it also has a protected bat breeding colony in the attic.

▲ The nubbly appendages often visible on concretions gave rise to the "claybaby" nickname. It is illegal to remove claybabies from Tacoma DeMolay Sandspit Nature Preserve.

▼ The late-1800s Johnson Farm is now home to the Anderson Island Historical Society. The farmhouse museum is open on weekends from spring through fall.

Near Tacoma

THE SOUTHERN NEIGHBOR

Anderson Island is the southernmost island in Puget Sound, just across the way from Steilacoom, a historic waterfront town between Tacoma and an active military installation. A frequent car ferry runs from Steilacoom; note that it is run by Pierce County rather than Washington State Ferries, so you won't find it in your folded paper WSF schedule. The boat also makes occasional stops at Ketron Island, a residential island home to fewer than twenty inhabitants. Ketron passengers need to call ahead to request a return ferry.

At just under eight square miles in size, Anderson Island is home to farms, parks, vacation rentals, and a whole lot of retirees (and also deer—the bane of island gardeners). For provisions, stop at the general store, Anderson's only storefront. For a sense of island history, visit the Historical Society museum at Johnson Farm or the beautifully restored one-room schoolhouse at Wide-Awake Hollow. The late Anderson writer Hazel Heckman chronicles the island's natural history in her lyrical book *Island Year*, modeled after Aldo Leopold's *A Sand County Almanac*.

For waterfront recreation visit Andy's Marine Park or Jacob's Point Park. Both offer extensive wooded hiking trails, beachside picnic spots, and water access for kayakers and other human-powered boaters (page 60). Jacob's Point Park also includes a hundred-foot-long walkway over a wetland, where you can watch birds and listen to frogs. Or you can paddle your way to Eagle Island Marine State Park, a 5-acre island located in Balch Passage, just 750 feet off Anderson's north shore. The park is maintained by Jarrell Cove State Park (page 58) and is available for day use only. Eagle Island is a popular haul-out for female harbor seals and their pups—the mothers leave the pups on the beach at low tide while they go hunting for food. Federal law prohibits disturbing marine mammals; wildlife watchers must stay at least one hundred yards away from seals and their pups.

FORBIDDEN ISLE

Just north of Anderson is McNeil Island, which has been government owned for most of its post-white-settlement history. From 1875 to 1981, the entire island was a federal penetentiary similar to Alcatraz in San Francisco, but with the addition of a dairy farm, beekeeping outfit, and other self-sufficient agricultural operations run by and for the inmates. It was the last US federal island prison accessible only by air or sea. Today the prison is state owned and houses the controversial Special Commitment Center, holding violent sexual predators under indefinite civil commitment. Recreational boaters are prohibited from visiting McNeil, though a passenger-only ferry brings facility employees and visitors in from Steilacoom and back.

A PLACE TO REST

Fox Island is connected by bridge to the Kitsap Peninsula. Adjacent to the bridge is Tanglewood Island, an islet sacred to the Nisqually people, who once interred their dead there in "tree burials" high above the ground. In the 1850s white settlers displaced and exiled many Puyallup and Nisqually families to Fox Island, until the 1854 Treaty of Medicine Creek removed them again to larger reservations on the mainland.

Contemporary Fox Island is largely a wealthy bedroom community, though its twentieth-century history as a vacation spot (*The Far Side* cartoonist Gary Larson spent childhood summers here) continues with a number of vacation rental properties. The main attraction on the island is the Tacoma DeMolay Sandspit Nature Preserve, a municipal park run by a seasonal caretaker. A quiet picnic post for day-trippers or boaters, the beach encompasses a large clay deposit, where tidal waters carve out and burnish unique shapes of sediment that pop off and wash up onto the beach. These formations, called concretions (or "claybabies" by locals), are a rare sight for beachcombers.

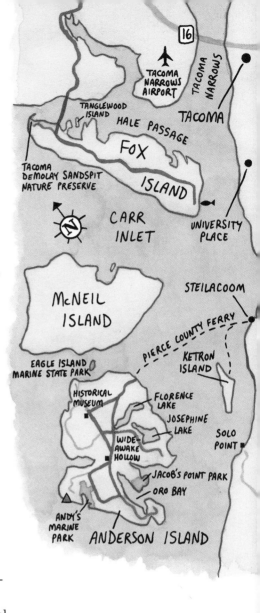

▼ The Fox Island bridge is one of the best spots in the South Sound to view Mount Rainier on a clear day.

Map labels

REACH ISLAND

TO ALLYN

STRETCH POINT STATE PARK

STRETCH ISLAND

3 GRAPEVIEW

N

TO SHELTON

CASE INLET

HERRON ISLAND

JARRELL COVE STATE PARK

PICKERING PASSAGE

COMMUNITY HALL

HARSTINE ISLAND STATE PARK

McMICKEN ISLAND MARINE STATE PARK

HARSTINE ISLAND

PEALE PASSAGE

SQUAXIN ISLAND

SQUAXIN ISLAND RESERVATION

TOTTEN INLET

STEAMBOAT ISLAND ROAD NW

ELD INLET

HOPE ISLAND MARINE STATE PARK (SOUTH)

STEAMBOAT ISLAND

DANA PASSAGE

BUDD INLET

▼ Beachcombers will find many treasures on the hike to McMicken Island, but make sure to hurry back before the tide rolls in!

Near Olympia

HIDDEN RETREAT

Rural Harstine Island (also sometimes spelled "Harstene") connects to the Olympic Peninsula by bridge and can be reached either through Shelton or via scenic back roads (recommended!) through the Kitsap Peninsula. On your way in stop at the Olympic Bakery for cinnamon rolls. There are no services on the island, but if you like the quiet, Harstine might be just what the doctor ordered. The island's interior is sadly scarred by clear-cut logging, but there are several shoreline vacation rentals (including some in the gated community at the northeastern tip of the island), as well as one of the most beautiful sites in the state park system.

Jarrell Cove State Park is the star of the show here. The park is accessible by car, but it's really designed for boaters—within are a marina (including gas station), moorage, and camping designed especially for sea travelers. This is part of a constellation of haul-outs, put-ins, and campgrounds throughout Puget Sound that comprise the Cascadia Marine Trail (CMT). You can find the full list of sites on the CMT website (page 14).

Just south of Jarrell Cove is Harstine Island State Park. This is an almost completely undeveloped park and a favorite of mushroom and huckleberry gatherers (no commercial foraging allowed). There's also a short wooded trail that picks its way down the hill to the beach. From there, at low tide only, it's possible to walk to nearby McMicken Island Marine State Park, as a narrow isthmus of sand will appear. The hike is approximately three miles round-trip from the trailhead, most of which must be completed before the tide comes in, unless you wish to hang out for hours at McMicken Island to wait for the tide to ebb again. McMicken is for day use only, so if you attempt the hike, be sure to plan carefully and avoid dawdling.

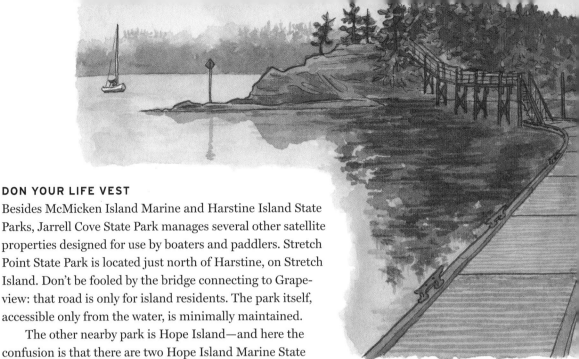

DON YOUR LIFE VEST

Besides McMicken Island Marine and Harstine Island State Parks, Jarrell Cove State Park manages several other satellite properties designed for use by boaters and paddlers. Stretch Point State Park is located just north of Harstine, on Stretch Island. Don't be fooled by the bridge connecting to Grapeview: that road is only for island residents. The park itself, accessible only from the water, is minimally maintained.

The other nearby park is Hope Island—and here the confusion is that there are two Hope Island Marine State Parks in Puget Sound, and both are reachable only by boat. (The other one is in Skagit County offshore from Whidbey Island, page 51). This Hope Island includes picnic tables for day use, plus eight campsites. There is no potable water, and all garbage must be packed out when you leave.

NOT-SO-PUBLIC ISLANDS

On your way to Harstine, you might see reference to a few other residential islands. Steamboat—technically part of Olympia, but easily a thirty-minute drive from downtown— has a bridge, and Herron is connected to the Key Peninsula by a private car ferry (a guest pass from the homeowners' corporation is required to board). You might find a vacation rental here, but otherwise these islands are not for tourists.

The Squaxin Island Tribe owns Squaxin Island, and only tribal members and their guests may visit. However, the tribe maintains a museum (including a sacred belongings collection) south of Shelton, and Kamilche Adventures offers guided canoe and kayak trips around the area.

▲ Jarrell Cove State Park is one of the South Sound's most placid, calming spots. Most of the park is accessible only by boat or via a wooden footbridge.

Either/Oar

Seeing the islands by boat is a worthy item to add to your travel to-do list. If you prefer to do your own paddling, there's a whole host of human-powered watercraft to choose from. And don't forget your life jacket!

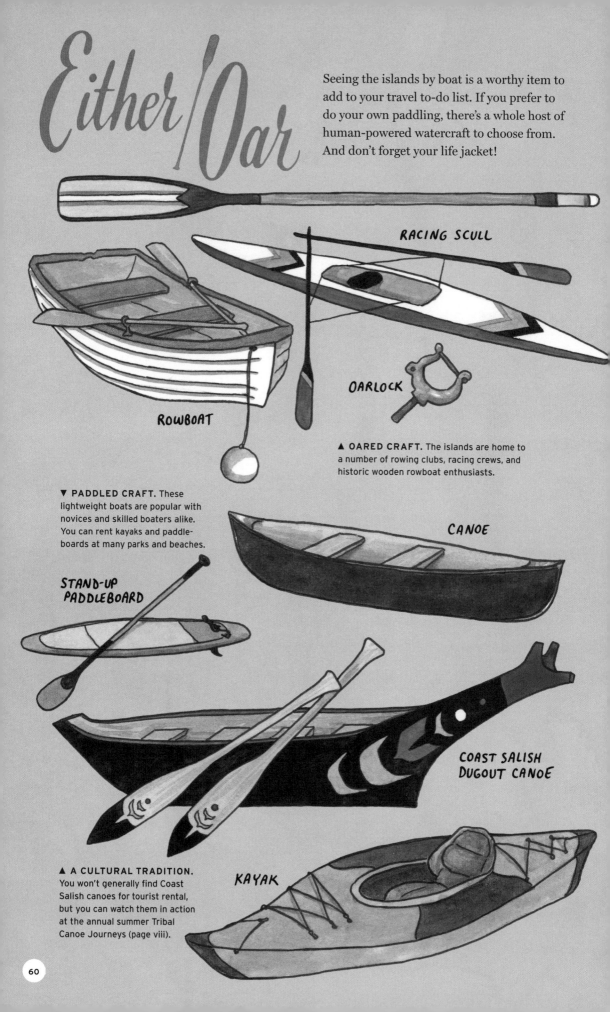

RACING SCULL

ROWBOAT

OARLOCK

▲ **OARED CRAFT.** The islands are home to a number of rowing clubs, racing crews, and historic wooden rowboat enthusiasts.

▼ **PADDLED CRAFT.** These lightweight boats are popular with novices and skilled boaters alike. You can rent kayaks and paddleboards at many parks and beaches.

CANOE

STAND-UP PADDLEBOARD

COAST SALISH DUGOUT CANOE

▲ **A CULTURAL TRADITION.** You won't generally find Coast Salish canoes for tourist rental, but you can watch them in action at the annual summer Tribal Canoe Journeys (page viii).

KAYAK

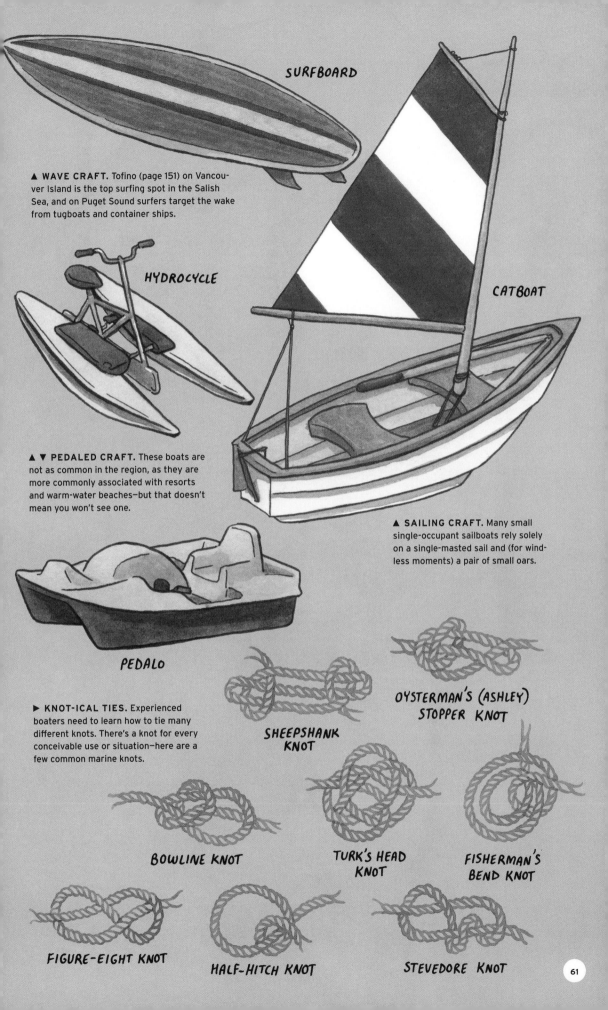

SURFBOARD

▲ **WAVE CRAFT.** Tofino (page 151) on Vancouver Island is the top surfing spot in the Salish Sea, and on Puget Sound surfers target the wake from tugboats and container ships.

HYDROCYCLE

CATBOAT

▲ ▼ **PEDALED CRAFT.** These boats are not as common in the region, as they are more commonly associated with resorts and warm-water beaches—but that doesn't mean you won't see one.

▲ **SAILING CRAFT.** Many small single-occupant sailboats rely solely on a single-masted sail and (for windless moments) a pair of small oars.

PEDALO

▶ **KNOT-ICAL TIES.** Experienced boaters need to learn how to tie many different knots. There's a knot for every conceivable use or situation—here are a few common marine knots.

OYSTERMAN'S (ASHLEY) STOPPER KNOT

SHEEPSHANK KNOT

BOWLINE KNOT

TURK'S HEAD KNOT

FISHERMAN'S BEND KNOT

FIGURE-EIGHT KNOT

HALF-HITCH KNOT

STEVEDORE KNOT

OTHER ISLANDS

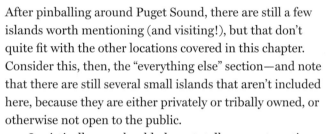

▼ Cama Beach Historical State Park is home to twenty-four restored waterfront cedar cabins, once part of a fishing resort built in the 1930s.

After pinballing around Puget Sound, there are still a few islands worth mentioning (and visiting!), but that don't quite fit with the other locations covered in this chapter. Consider this, then, the "everything else" section—and note that there are still several small islands that aren't included here, because they are either privately or tribally owned, or otherwise not open to the public.

Logistically, you should plan a totally separate outing or day trip for visiting each of the islands in this section. For one thing, most are not near one another. For another, while some are within easy distance of the major Puget Sound islands, getting there is not always straightforward. Camano and Fir Islands, for instance, are very close to Whidbey Island, but cannot be reached directly from Whidbey, unless you have your own boat. They are, however, very close to one another and easy to tour together. Mercer Island is centrally located on Interstate 90 between Seattle and Bellevue, but the near-constant gridlock of traffic makes it hard to do a quick jaunt there. Marrowstone Island requires either a long overland detour or doubling up on ferries to get there; the islands off the coast of Everett have their own tricky ferry logistics; and Blake requires either your own boat or a scheduled private cruise to visit.

Still, if you can squeeze one or more of these into your Salish Sea adventure—or if you're a local looking for a fun day trip—there's plenty to be found in these pages.

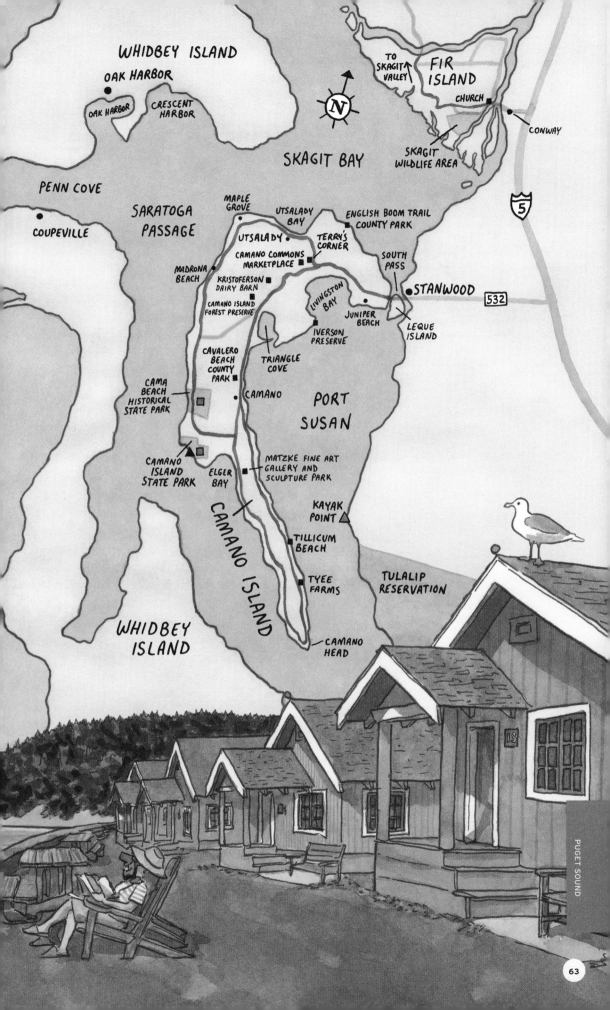

WHIDBEY ISLAND

OAK HARBOR

OAK HARBOR

CRESCENT HARBOR

PENN COVE

COUPEVILLE

SARATOGA PASSAGE

MAPLE GROVE

UTSALADY BAY

UTSALADY

CAMANO COMMONS MARKETPLACE

TERRY'S CORNER

MADRONA BEACH

KRISTOFERSON DAIRY BARN

CAMANO ISLAND FOREST PRESERVE

LIVINGSTON BAY

IVERSON PRESERVE

JUNIPER BEACH

CAVALERO BEACH COUNTY PARK

TRIANGLE COVE

CAMA BEACH HISTORICAL STATE PARK

CAMANO

PORT SUSAN

CAMANO ISLAND STATE PARK

ELGER BAY

MATZKE FINE ART GALLERY AND SCULPTURE PARK

KAYAK POINT

CAMANO ISLAND

TILLICUM BEACH

TYEE FARMS

CAMANO HEAD

WHIDBEY ISLAND

TULALIP RESERVATION

SKAGIT BAY

TO SKAGIT VALLEY

FIR ISLAND

CHURCH

CONWAY

SKAGIT WILDLIFE AREA

5

ENGLISH BOOM TRAIL COUNTY PARK

SOUTH PASS

STANWOOD

532

LEQUE ISLAND

N

Camano

Apostrophe-shaped Camano Island is sixteen miles long (and in places less than a mile wide), and connected by bridge to Stanwood, fifty miles north of Seattle. This is a feature, not a bug; island boosters tout Camano as a "ferry-free" destination, easy to fit into spur-of-the-moment plans.

▲ Though their shells seldom wash up on the beach here, a population of Pacific sand dollars makes their home at Camano Island State Park. You can sometimes spot live specimens during minus tides.

UFF DA! VELKOMMEN TIL STANWOOD

While Stanwood is not technically *on* Camano Island, you literally can't miss it, as you have to pass through it to reach the bridge. Founded in 1866, the town began as a collection of canneries, creameries, and lumber mills. Many of its original white settlers were of Norwegian heritage, and that Scandinavian flavor survives today. Points of interest include a number of historic buildings downtown, the Sons of Norway Hall, and the vintage neon sign at the historic Hamilton Lumber building. Stock up on Scandinavian souvenirs at the Uff Da Shoppe, located on (what else?) Viking Way.

▼ English Boom Trail County Park is a great place to watch rainbows emerge in the ever-shifting Pacific Northwest weather—particularly in the spring.

ENCLAVES AND SUMMER SPOTS

Camano Island itself, like so many others in the Salish Sea region, is a mix of farms and residential enclaves. Many of these house seasonal residents and vacation rentals. The oldest community, Utsalady, settled in the 1850s, was home to a large population of Chinese immigrants—until white locals formed a violent mob and forcibly removed their Chinese neighbors from the island in the 1880s. A resort settlement sprang up in the 1920s, and the area became a major transit point for rumrunners during the Prohibition era. Today the community is mostly a collection of private homes, but the historic Utsalady Ladies Aid building still stands and still houses meetings for the group.

The tiny enclave of Juniper Beach sits at the north end of Port Susan, inside the crescent of the eastern shore.

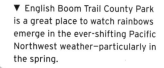

This part of the island is the only area that boasts sandy beaches. Juniper Beach was once home to an oyster farm that kept the island afloat (no pun intended) during the Great Depression. On the western shore is Madrona Beach, another neighborhood that began as a 1920s resort. Many of the original historic cottages remain, some as vacation rentals. At the southern tip of the island are the homes of Tyee Beach—if you're peckish, stop by Tyee Farms for a fresh deli sandwich, picnic provisions, or a bit of penny candy.

PLENTY OF PARK-ING

Camano Island has just two state parks, but they are both worthy of distinction. Camano Island State Park is a great choice for hikers, campers, or RV travelers. Cama Beach Historical State Park, just one mile up the shore, got its start as a Depression-era resort, and now rents both its historic beach cabins and a number of boat types at reasonable rates.

The island's many county parks are worth exploring as well. English Boom, a historic former log storage yard (called a log boom) belonging to the English Lumber Company, boasts island views and great bird-watching. The Iverson Preserve offers sandy beach access and year-round sturgeon fishing opportunities. Cavalero Beach, Utsalady Point, and Maple Grove all have boat launches (fees apply).

While the state parks require a Discover Pass or a daily use fee, all the county parks are free for day use, except for the boat launches. And fishing and shellfish opportunities abound at both types of parks—don't forget your licenses!

ISLAND INSPIRATION

Like Vashon Island (page 34), Camano is home to a vibrant artist community. Look for the Camano Island Studio Tour each May, or visit the Matzke Fine Art Gallery and Sculpture Park. And for an inspiring breakfast or lunch with a view, try the Cama Beach Café and Catering, open on weekends in the off-season and daily during the summer.

▲ A giant Dungeness crab silhouette welcomes shoppers to the Camano Commons Marketplace, home to a farmers' market on Tuesday afternoons in the summer.

▼ Keep an eye out for the nine nest boxes placed along the English Boom Trail to house purple martins—and sometimes offer a perch to much larger birds.

▲ The best moments for bird-watchers observing swans and snow geese are when the enormous flocks take off and land, obliterating the view with a fog of white wings.

▼ The historic Fir-Conway Lutheran Church, dedicated in 1916, is actually a "new" structure, as it replaced an older, smaller church built in 1888.

Fir

Fir Island, just a few miles north of Camano, is sometimes seen as an extension of the Skagit Valley (technically it is, as it lies within the Skagit Delta). Getting here from the mainland is so seamless that many visitors don't even realize it is an island. This low-lying isle—part agricultural community, part ecological reserve—is especially susceptible to flooding, so it is surrounded by a ten-foot earthen dike. A favorite spot for both bird-watchers and seasonal hunters, Fir is connected to the mainland by bridges at two points: from Conway to the east and La Conner to the north.

FOWL PLAY

Fir Island has been an important migratory bird habitat for millennia. The most famous visitors are the snow geese that migrate here by the tens of thousands every winter from Wrangel Island in Russia's part of the Arctic Sea. These are the only snow geese that migrate between Eurasia and North America (subsets of the group overwinter in British Columbia and California). The geese are easy to identify, with their bright white bodies, orange beaks, and black wing tips.

Trumpeter swans are the other winter stars of Fir Island. These comeback kids were once brought to the brink of extinction by overhunting; in 1933 fewer than seventy trumpeters existed in the wild. Aerial surveys found another population of them in Alaska, and wildlife agencies employed careful breeding and reintroduction programs until the population rebounded. Today there are around fifty thousand wild trumpeters in North America, and their official conservation status has been restored to "least concern."

If you pass a flock of trumpeters on your Fir Island sojourn, be sure to roll your windows down! The noisy birds really do sound like a jazz band warming up.

Though the snow geese and trumpeters understandably steal the show, there are plenty of other ways to satisfy your bird-watching urge. Throughout the year, 180 bird species have been recorded in the area, including bald eagles and other raptors, a host of shore and marsh birds, and song-birds. In the winter you'll also see many (seriously, many) ducks and other waterfowl gleaning tidbits from the stubbly fields—bonus beneficiaries of the Barley for Birds program, where local farmers plant subsidized winter grain to help fatten up the geese for their long flight north in the spring. The Audubon Society has conducted their annual Christmas Bird Count of species present in the area since 1900.

The best time to visit is in February, after the hunt-ing season has ended. Swans and geese are often visible from any roadside, and the Skagit Wildlife Area (Discover Pass required) maintains several bird-watching areas and platforms on the island. Commonsense rules apply: do not approach the birds; beware of hunting seasons, cyclists, and traffic; and respect private property boundaries.

▼ Travelers leaving Fir Island by its northern bridge will cross immediately into the lower Skagit Valley, home of the famous tulip fields that bloom every April.

THE WHEEL OF THE YEAR

When the snow geese have flown away, there is still plenty to see on and around Fir Island. Since the terrain is so flat, exploring the island by bicycle is a great option—at least in the summer. You'll pass berry and veggie farms, and in April the Skagit Valley Tulip Festival lies just over the northern bridge. Stop at the Snow Goose Produce farm stand, or visit an artisan fair at the Saltbox Barn, a former dairy. Or try the Nell Thorn Waterfront Bistro & Bar in La Conner for a meal sourced from Fir Island and Skagit Valley fields.

PUGET SOUND

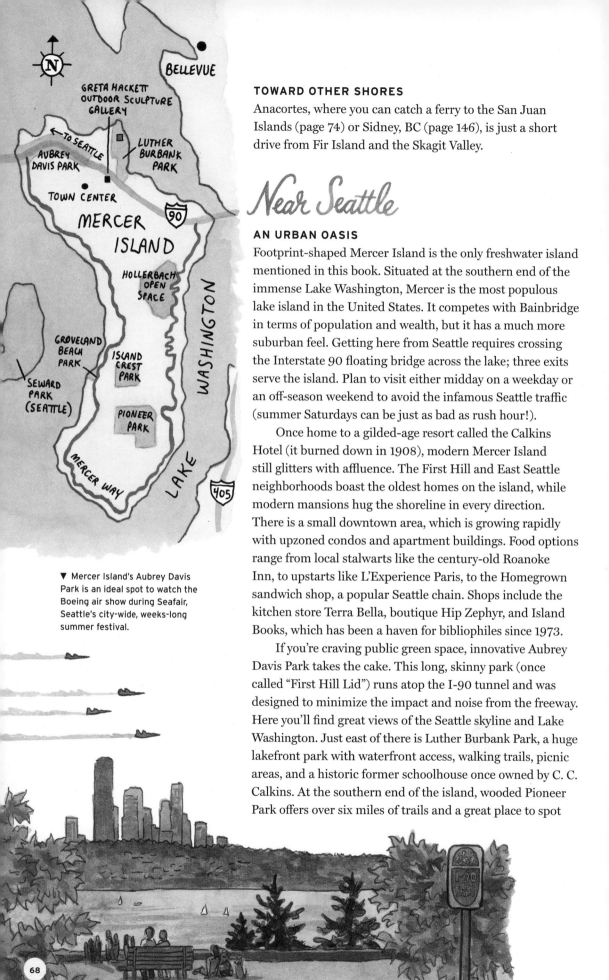

TOWARD OTHER SHORES

Anacortes, where you can catch a ferry to the San Juan Islands (page 74) or Sidney, BC (page 146), is just a short drive from Fir Island and the Skagit Valley.

Near Seattle

AN URBAN OASIS

Footprint-shaped Mercer Island is the only freshwater island mentioned in this book. Situated at the southern end of the immense Lake Washington, Mercer is the most populous lake island in the United States. It competes with Bainbridge in terms of population and wealth, but it has a much more suburban feel. Getting here from Seattle requires crossing the Interstate 90 floating bridge across the lake; three exits serve the island. Plan to visit either midday on a weekday or an off-season weekend to avoid the infamous Seattle traffic (summer Saturdays can be just as bad as rush hour!).

Once home to a gilded-age resort called the Calkins Hotel (it burned down in 1908), modern Mercer Island still glitters with affluence. The First Hill and East Seattle neighborhoods boast the oldest homes on the island, while modern mansions hug the shoreline in every direction. There is a small downtown area, which is growing rapidly with upzoned condos and apartment buildings. Food options range from local stalwarts like the century-old Roanoke Inn, to upstarts like L'Experience Paris, to the Homegrown sandwich shop, a popular Seattle chain. Shops include the kitchen store Terra Bella, boutique Hip Zephyr, and Island Books, which has been a haven for bibliophiles since 1973.

If you're craving public green space, innovative Aubrey Davis Park takes the cake. This long, skinny park (once called "First Hill Lid") runs atop the I-90 tunnel and was designed to minimize the impact and noise from the freeway. Here you'll find great views of the Seattle skyline and Lake Washington. Just east of there is Luther Burbank Park, a huge lakefront park with waterfront access, walking trails, picnic areas, and a historic former schoolhouse once owned by C. C. Calkins. At the southern end of the island, wooded Pioneer Park offers over six miles of trails and a great place to spot

▼ Mercer Island's Aubrey Davis Park is an ideal spot to watch the Boeing air show during Seafair, Seattle's city-wide, weeks-long summer festival.

owls swooping overhead. If you're looking for a more artistic experience, try the Greta Hackett Outdoor Sculpture Gallery, a downtown park that displays the city's public art collection.

Before you leave the island, be sure to drive the loop of Mercer Way, which winds you past stately neighborhoods, historic former farmhouses, many wooded areas and parks, and lots of peekaboo views of Seattle, Mount Rainier, and Lake Washington. It's sure to impart a sense of discovering a hidden world in the middle of the big city.

HISTORICAL HODGEPODGE

Located off the northern tip of Vashon, Blake Island is centrally located but far from the beaten path. The entire island is set aside as Blake Island Marine State Park. No cars are allowed on the island, and private, chartered, or human-powered vessels are the only transportation there and back.

Historically a camping location for the Suquamish people, oral tradition says Blake was the birthplace of Chief Si'ahl (page ix) in the 1780s. In the early twentieth century, the Trimble family purchased the island for their estate, then invited Seattle's Camp Fire Girls to set up a summer camp on the island. The camp was named Camp Sealth and later moved to its permanent location (page 39) on Vashon. The Trimbles abandoned the island in 1929, after a family death, and in 1959 the state bought it.

At one end of the island is Tillicum Village, a seasonal tourist attraction operated by Argosy Cruises. Founded in 1962 during the Seattle World's Fair by a white restaurant owner, it began as dinner theatre loosely based on a pastiche of Northwest Indigenous cultures. In recent years the owners have made an effort to make the experience more culturally sensitive and authentic, hiring Indigenous dancers, using stories with permission, and consulting tribal members from Coast Salish and Alaska Native communities.

Visitors catch the Argosy boat at Pier 54 in Seattle and enjoy views of Mount Rainier and Alki Point Lighthouse on their way. The four-hour excursion includes a buffet salmon dinner cooked on traditional cedar spits, followed by dancing

▼ Visitors to Tillicum Village are greeted with a cup of clams in broth and encouraged to crush the shells under their feet to help maintain the path up to the longhouse.

and storytelling. Boaters and campers on Blake can also visit Tillicum Village and partake of the dinner separately, without paying for the cruise portion.

Miscellaneous Islands

THE QUIET LIFE

Like Vashon-Maury (page 34), Marrowstone Island's name often refers to two connected isles (the other being Indian Island), rather than just one. This pair connects by bridge to Port Hadlock, a few miles south of Port Townsend. The two islands were conjoined by a man-made causeway, or isthmus, until 2019. In partnership with the Port Gamble S'Klallam Tribe, the land bridge was removed to restore the tidal estuary (and salmon migration routes). State Route 116 crosses through the southern end of Indian Island, but that's the extent of public access there. The rest of the island is owned by the US Navy.

Marrowstone has a single village, Nordland, and just one business, the general store. The shop bears a sign boasting that "all the beaches are clothing optional," but as the island's parks don't corroborate this claim, you might want to silence your inner nudist and leave your pants on. Fort Flagler Historical State Park is one of several historic military installations in the area (you can spy Fort Casey Historical State Park, page 48, directly across Admiralty Inlet), with beautifully restored officers' houses, a tiny lighthouse, and a military museum. Mystery Bay Marine State Park caters to boaters—its location on a protected cove is ideal—but car travelers can visit too. On your way back out, you might stop at Indian Island County Park and view the restored estuary between the islands.

From here it's easy to access Whidbey Island (page 42) from Port Townsend, which is a worthy stop in its own right. The entire downtown, with its many Victorian buildings, is on the National Register of Historic Places. Nearby Fort Worden Historical State Park is another restored military base and home to Point Wilson Lighthouse, the tallest on the Sound. Port Townsend has a large community of boaters and hosts the Wooden Boat Festival in September, as well as the Race to Alaska (R2AK), a 750-mile boat race for human-powered boats (page 60), each June.

▲ Marrowstone Island is a favorite haunt of harlequin ducks and other seabirds. Bring your binoculars, as there are good bird-watching spots all over the island.

STRAIT OF JUAN DE FUCA

N

FORT WORDEN HISTORICAL STATE PARK

POINT WILSON LIGHTHOUSE

ADMIRALTY INLET

PORT TOWNSEND

20

TO WHIDBEY ISLAND →
WASHINGTON STATE FERRIES

PORT TOWNSEND

MARROWSTONE POINT LIGHTHOUSE

INDIAN ISLAND

PORT HADLOCK

MYSTERY BAY MARINE STATE PARK

FORT FLAGLER HISTORICAL STATE PARK

SCOW BAY

116

NORDLAND

INDIAN ISLAND COUNTY PARK

OAK BAY

MARROWSTONE ISLAND

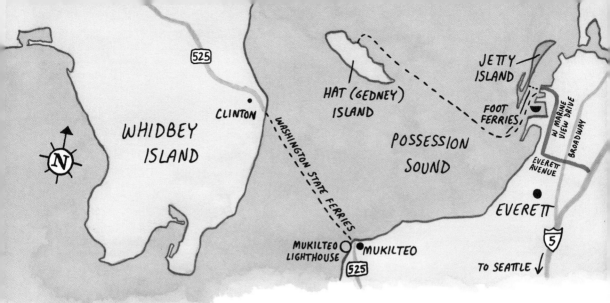

PUBLIC AND PRIVATE ESCAPES

Back on the Sound's eastern shore are two small islands between Whidbey and the port city of Everett. Jetty Island is a two-mile-long, man-made sandbar built as a jetty in the late-nineteenth century to protect navigation and moorage around the city. Every summer from July 5 through Labor Day, a free foot ferry runs daily from Everett. Jetty is an ideal spot for bird-watching or spying the occasional whale—or just finding a sandy spot to take in the sun and sea air. Expect crowds from Everett, especially on weekends. Bring everything you need with you, and pack out all trash when you leave—there are no services or camping here.

Athletes have another reason to love Jetty Island. Its location experiences gentle but near-constant breezes—about fifteen knots on average—which make it a favorite spot for kiteboarding, a fairly new sport that's sort of a cross between surfing and parasailing. You can try it yourself with gear and lessons from Urban Surf in Everett, or you can just pull up a beach chair and watch from the sand.

A second, private foot ferry connects Everett to Hat Island (its proper name is Gedney Island, but locals call it "Hat" because of its distinctive silhouette). Like some of the islands in the South Sound, this one is residential and private, open only to homeowners and their guests. However, there are a few vacation-rental properties on Hat Island, so keep it in mind if you're looking for an unusual alternative to Whidbey Island or Everett-area lodging.

▼ Just before Jetty Island opens to the public for the season, it hosts the annual Jetty Island Light Wind Olympics, a competition for kiteboarders.

Look Skyward

Birders will find plenty to occupy themselves on the islands. More than 150 bird species depend upon the marine ecosystem of the Salish Sea. Bring a notebook to keep track, as your list of sightings will grow quickly.

VIOLET-GREEN SWALLOW

DARK-EYED JUNCO

AMERICAN GOLDFINCH

BUSHTIT

WINTER WREN

RED-SHAFTED NORTHERN FLICKER

STELLER'S JAY

BLACK OYSTERCATCHER

▲ SMALL BIRDS. The region is home to an enormous number of songbirds, corvids, jays, and hummingbirds. Many of these are backyard denizens, making bird-watching easy from anywhere.

◀ SHOREBIRDS. Look for a diverse population of waders, rails, and divers on beaches and in marshes, particularly at low tide.

RUFOUS HUMMINGBIRD

GREAT BLUE HERON

SEMIPALMATED PLOVER

PACIFIC LOON

BONAPARTE'S GULL

BELTED KINGFISHER

▶ PELAGIC BIRDS. An island adventure can give you the chance to see pelagic (seabird) species not easily spotted from the mainland. Look along rocky shores and headlands, for a start.

BRANDT'S CORMORANT

SNOWY OWL

WESTERN SCREECH OWL

► BALD EAGLES. Washington has the most bald eagles in the lower forty-eight, and the San Juan Islands (page 74) have the most eagles in the state. If you're lucky, you might glimpse their balletic aerial courtship dance.

BALD EAGLE

◄ OWLS. These stealthy nocturnal raptors are difficult to observe visually, but you might just hear one overhead on an evening forest stroll.

NORTHERN SPOTTED OWL

AMERICAN KESTREL

COOPER'S HAWK

OSPREY

▲ OSPREYS. These "fish eagles" are the inspiration for the mascot of the Seattle Seahawks. The islands are an ideal place to look for ospreys.

▲ HAWKS. The many hawk species can be difficult for novices to tell apart, but these diurnal raptors are a common sight on lone tele-phone poles and treetops.

SNOW GOOSE

CANADA GOOSE

BRANT

BARROW'S GOLDENEYE

WOOD DUCK

TRUMPETER SWAN

HOODED MERGANSER

▲ DUCKS AND GEESE. These noisy birds are often easy to spot, particularly on marshes, freshwater ponds, or winter farm fields.

PART 2 SAN JUAN

ISLANDS

The San Juan Islands, the American counterpart of Canada's Southern Gulf Islands (page 158), are the jewels in Washington's crown. With more than 400 islands, islets, and rocks (128 of them named) in the archipelago, the San Juans are both a tourist haven and a diverse ecological wonder. Ever-shifting weather and complex waterways make the ferry ride alone an unforgettable journey—but getting there is only the beginning of the adventure.

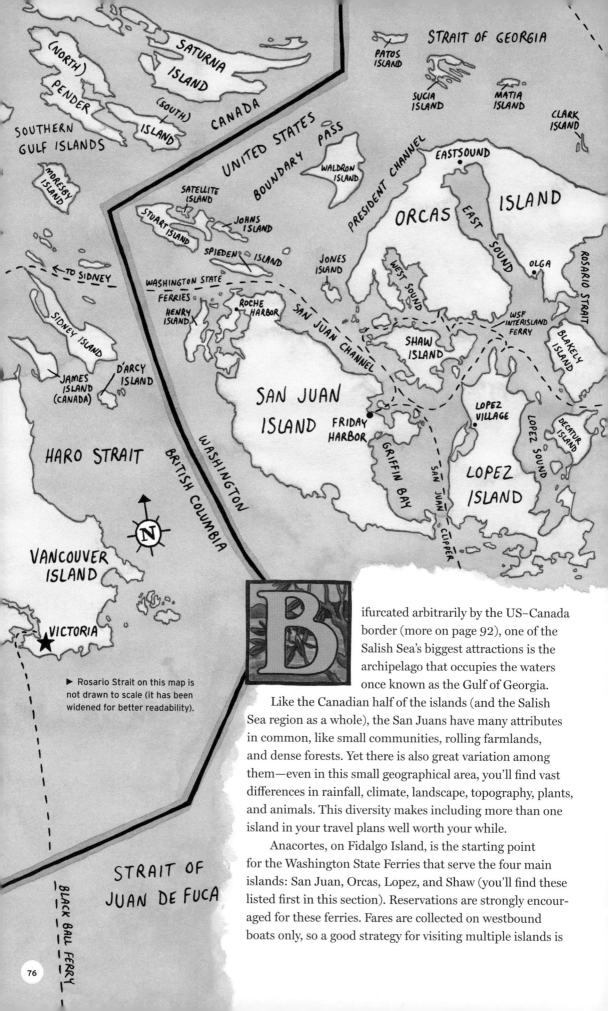

▶ Rosario Strait on this map is not drawn to scale (it has been widened for better readability).

ifurcated arbitrarily by the US–Canada border (more on page 92), one of the Salish Sea's biggest attractions is the archipelago that occupies the waters once known as the Gulf of Georgia.

Like the Canadian half of the islands (and the Salish Sea region as a whole), the San Juans have many attributes in common, like small communities, rolling farmlands, and dense forests. Yet there is also great variation among them—even in this small geographical area, you'll find vast differences in rainfall, climate, landscape, topography, plants, and animals. This diversity makes including more than one island in your travel plans well worth your while.

Anacortes, on Fidalgo Island, is the starting point for the Washington State Ferries that serve the four main islands: San Juan, Orcas, Lopez, and Shaw (you'll find these listed first in this section). Reservations are strongly encouraged for these ferries. Fares are collected on westbound boats only, so a good strategy for visiting multiple islands is

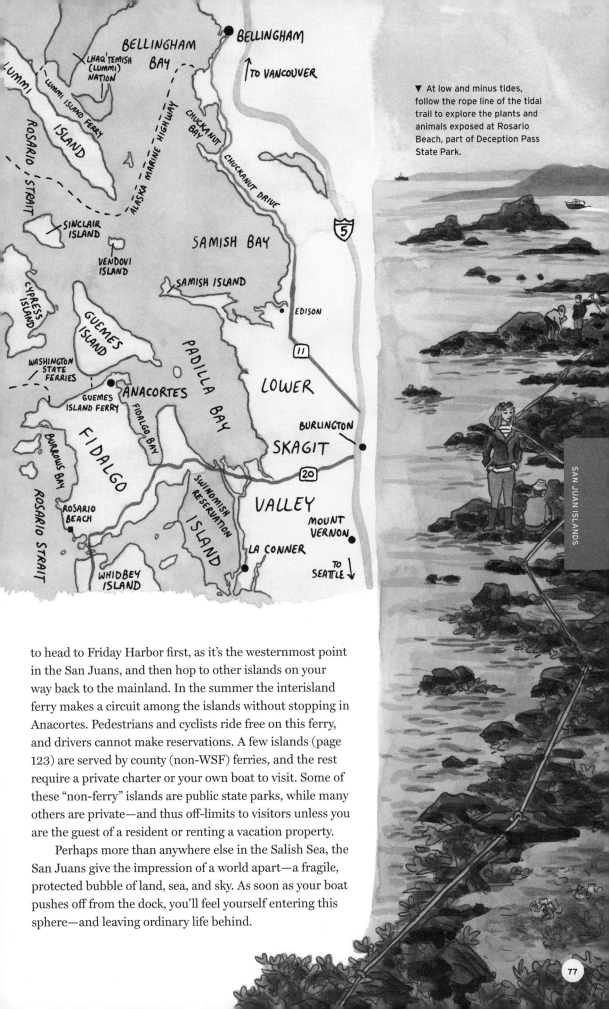

Map labels:

BELLINGHAM BAY
BELLINGHAM
LHAQ'TEMISH (LUMMI) NATION
↑ TO VANCOUVER
LUMMI ISLAND FERRY
LUMMI ISLAND
ROSARIO ISLAND
ALASKA MARINE HIGHWAY
CHUCKANUT BAY
CHUCKANUT DRIVE
ROSARIO STRAIT
SINCLAIR ISLAND
VENDOVI ISLAND
SAMISH BAY
SAMISH ISLAND
EDISON
5
11
CYPRESS ISLAND
GUEMES ISLAND
WASHINGTON STATE FERRIES
GUEMES ISLAND FERRY
ANACORTES
PADILLA BAY
FIDALGO BAY
LOWER
BURLINGTON
SKAGIT
20
BURROWS BAY
FIDALGO
ROSARIO BEACH
ROSARIO STRAIT
SWINOMISH RESERVATION
ISLAND
LA CONNER
VALLEY
MOUNT VERNON
TO SEATTLE ↓
WHIDBEY ISLAND

▼ At low and minus tides, follow the rope line of the tidal trail to explore the plants and animals exposed at Rosario Beach, part of Deception Pass State Park.

SAN JUAN ISLANDS

to head to Friday Harbor first, as it's the westernmost point in the San Juans, and then hop to other islands on your way back to the mainland. In the summer the interisland ferry makes a circuit among the islands without stopping in Anacortes. Pedestrians and cyclists ride free on this ferry, and drivers cannot make reservations. A few islands (page 123) are served by county (non-WSF) ferries, and the rest require a private charter or your own boat to visit. Some of these "non-ferry" islands are public state parks, while many others are private—and thus off-limits to visitors unless you are the guest of a resident or renting a vacation property.

Perhaps more than anywhere else in the Salish Sea, the San Juans give the impression of a world apart—a fragile, protected bubble of land, sea, and sky. As soon as your boat pushes off from the dock, you'll feel yourself entering this sphere—and leaving ordinary life behind.

FIDALGO

This gateway island is not, technically, part of the San Juan and Gulf Islands (instead it is more closely connected to Whidbey Island and the mainland). But since it is the main point of entry for—and culturally connected to—the San Juans, it makes sense to include it in this chapter. Fidalgo Island is truly the threshold between mainland Western Washington and the Salish Sea—and if you're embarking on a San Juans sojourn from here, it's also the last place you'll see a traffic light for quite some time.

Historically the territory of two Indigenous cultures, Fidalgo's eastern lobe is home to the Swinomish Reservation. The Samish Indian Nation, overlooked by the 1855 Treaty of Point Elliott and thus never given a reservation, have spent recent decades buying land for themselves in the area. They now own two-hundred-some acres on Fidalgo, Lopez, and Huckleberry Islands, plus an administrative center in Anacortes.

Since the 1890s Fidalgo has been the working port of the San Juans, with Anacortes running the canneries, fisheries, shipbuilding operations, and transportation hub upon which the other islands relied. In the 1950s this expanded to oil refining—two of Washington's five oil refineries are still located near March Point, just across Fidalgo Bay from downtown Anacortes.

If you're continuing on from Whidbey Island (page 42), you'll arrive via the Deception Pass Bridge. If coming from the lower Skagit Valley, you'll cross the Swinomish Channel Bridge and be treated to a sweeping view of Padilla Bay and several smaller islands. Either way, it's worth spending some time on Fidalgo (and in Anacortes) before you ship out to your next port of call.

▼ The residential neighborhoods of Anacortes are filled with historic Victorian and Craftsman homes, many of them perched on the cliff's edge and overlooking Rosario Strait and the San Juan Islands.

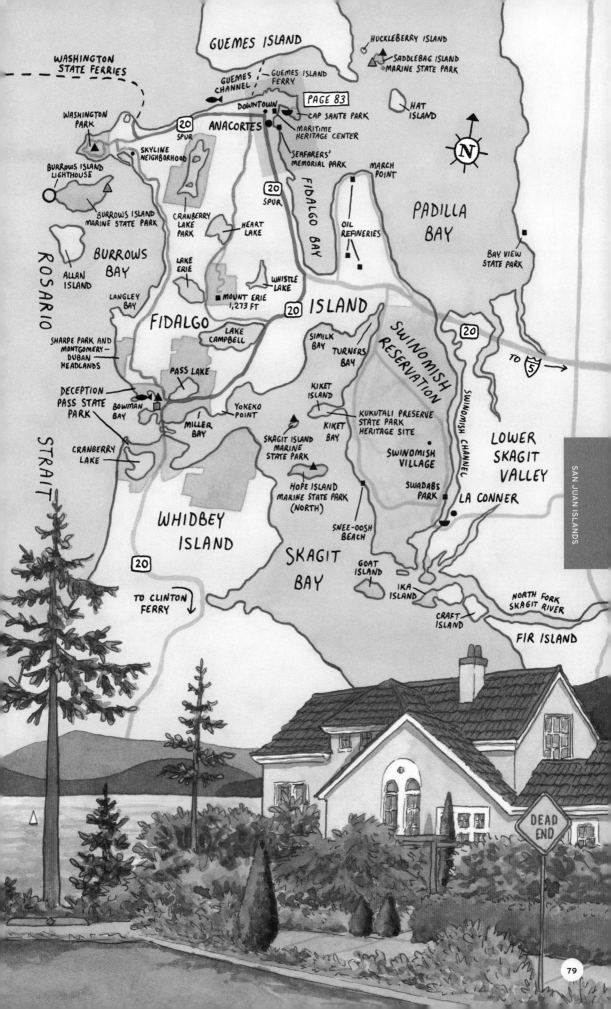

SAN JUAN ISLANDS

▲ Mount Erie's distinctive silhouette makes Fidalgo Island recognizable from afar, in every direction.

▼ Swadabs Park contains three large pavilions built in the shape of traditional Coast Salish woven cedar hats. They were built in 2011, when the Swinomish hosted the annual Tribal Canoe Journeys.

THE OTHER SIDE OF DECEPTION PASS

While most tourists seem to flock to the Whidbey side (page 50), Deception Pass State Park spills onto the southern shore of Fidalgo. Most of the amenities here lie around Bowman Bay, where you'll find a campsite, boat launch, and tiny museum dedicated to the Depression-era Civilian Conservation Corps's (CCC) role in building the park's infrastructure.

Just west of Bowman Bay is Rosario Beach, which includes a loop of hiking trails and a rocky, roped trail along a series of tide pools (illustration on page 77). Above the beach you'll find a large cedar statue depicting the story of Ko-Kwal-Alwoot (the Maiden of Deception Pass), carved in 1983 by local (non-Indigenous) artist Tracy Powell to honor the Samish people.

A PUBLIC-PRIVATE PARTNERSHIP

Other parks and preserves dot Fidalgo Island, and some of them are emblematic of how the San Juans handle land conservation. While some parcels become full-blown, publicly owned parks, others benefit from conservation easements—where private property owners (or the neighbors of an existing public park) put all or part of their land in a public trust for environmental or historical preservation. You'll find many of these "land bank" preserves around the region and mentioned throughout these pages. Note that not all of them are open for public recreation—the local land trust organizations usually have good websites with maps and trail information for visitors (you'll find some of these on page 13).

Nearly three thousand acres comprise the Anacortes Community Forest Lands, a public-private network of protected lands around Cranberry, Whistle, and Heart Lakes, as well as Mount Erie, the highest point on the island. The highlands contain tree species not found in many other places in the region, and there's also a small amount of old-growth lowland forest, preserved by the Skagit Land Trust. There are many public access points and trails within these areas, though parking is extremely limited—making the preserves more of a draw for local residents than for tourists.

On the western shore is county-run Sharpe Park, which includes the Montgomery-Duban Headlands and several rocky promontories. The trails here are rugged but well marked, and the views are worth the exertion.

THE EASTERN LOBE

Much of eastern Fidalgo Island comprises the Swinomish Reservation. Not much is open to the public here, but you'll find Swadabs Park across the channel from La Conner, at the site of the ancestral village of Txiwuc. Pro tip: if you're coming from the lower Skagit Valley, this is a great scenic back way onto the island! You can skip the highway speeds of the Swinomish Channel Bridge, and take the beautiful Rainbow Bridge from downtown La Conner instead. Checking out Swadabs Park is a fun side jaunt if you're in the area for the Tulip Festival (page 67).

Kukutali Preserve, a tribally managed day-use park on Skagit Bay, includes Kiket Island. In 2018 the Swinomish restored the tidal estuary by removing the roadbed on the tombolo (a sandy isthmus), so now visitors can walk to Kiket at low tide. The preserve includes two miles of trails on both Kiket and Fidalgo, but Kiket's north shore and Flagstaff Island (connected by yet another tombolo) are habitat preserves and closed to visitors. Seafood harvesting and other foraging are available to tribal members only. Remember your tide chart and plan your visit accordingly to avoid getting stranded.

OFF-ISLAND ISLANDS

Several other small islands lie offshore from Fidalgo, in just about every direction. Besides Kiket, Skagit Bay is also home to Hope and Skagit Island Marine State Parks, which are best accessed from Cornet Bay, on the Whidbey side (page 51) of Deception Pass State Park. Farthest south are Goat, Ika, and Craft Islands, located at the mouth of the Skagit Delta. Ika is private, but Goat and Craft are both state managed as part of the Skagit Wildlife Area. Goat Island, which boasts the ruins of a 1909 military fort, requires sailing or paddling from La Conner. Craft Island can be reached on foot with

▲ The Fidalgo side of Deception Pass State Park has a number of 1930s-era picnic shelters built by the CCC. Some offer stunning views of the shore and islands.

▼ Ko-Kwal-Alwoot married a sea spirit to save her village from famine. As she joined him, her hair became seaweed in the waters of the pass.

an extremely muddy, low-tide hike from the tip of Fir Island (page 66). The marine state parks have campsites, but Craft and Goat are for day use only.

In Padilla Bay, Hat Island (not to be confused with Gedney Island's nickname, page 71) is managed by the Washington Department of Natural Resources as a conservation area and has no public access points.

Off the western shore of Fidalgo, in Burrows Bay, are a pair of sizeable hilly islands. Allan Island is private but Burrows Island is an undeveloped marine state park. At the time of this writing, the small lighthouse at the western tip (illustration on page 185) is being restored for eventual tours and even lodging, but for now you can get a good view of it from your own boat, or take a paddle tour there from Anacortes Kayak Tours, which leave from the Skyline Marine Center. Pro tip: this outfit also offers bioluminescence tours, which leave at sunset.

ANACORTES: THE BIG CITY

No matter which direction you're coming from, you'll eventually be dumped out in Anacortes. Many visitors stop just long enough to gas up the car and do a bit of grocery shopping before the ferry loads, but Anacortes has enough history, interesting architecture, and open spaces of its own that it's worth exploring here, even if just for a few hours.

UNA ROSA BY ANY OTHER NAME

You'll have noticed by now that many islands and waterways around here carry Spanish names. In 1791 Spanish mariner Francisco de Eliza explored and charted the region, in part to find the legendary Northwest Passage. He named many of the places he surveyed for his employer, Juan Vicente de Güemes Padilla Horcasitas y Aguayo, the viceroy of Mexico.

▲ Anacortes has several registered historic residential and commercial buildings, as well as a self-guided walking tour that includes interpretive signs and information about the city's history.

▼ The *W.T. Preston* was used as a snagboat, removing log jams and debris from rivers around Puget Sound. She is the last surviving US Army Corps of Engineers snagboat on the West Coast.

(Many of the English names here come from a 1792 British naval survey of the area.) However, the name Anacortes is meant to *look* Spanish, but it is actually adapted from "Anna Curtis," the wife of fellow settler Amos Bowman—hence its Americanized pronunciation (page 188).

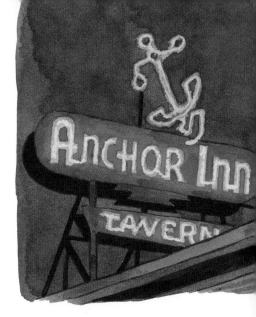

A SEAFARER'S CITY

The area around the state ferry terminal has exploded with new homes and condos in recent years, but the historic downtown is filled with turn-of-the-century homes and storefronts. Anacortes is steeped in maritime and canning history (check out the vintage seafood labels on the municipal trash cans), and is still very much a working port. Stop by Seafarers' Memorial Park on Fidalgo Bay, or visit the Maritime Heritage Center—this includes the *W.T. Preston*, a 1929 paddle steamer moored across the street and now a public museum. You can spruce up your boat after shopping the new-old stock of tools at Marine Supply & Hardware (image on page 6). Or come for Shipwreck Fest in July—a giant outdoor community flea market of antiques, yard art made from old fishing gear, and other flotsam and jetsam.

Afterward, grab a cuppa and a novel at Pelican Bay Books & Coffeehouse. Or, if you're there on a weekend morning, snag a coveted table at Dad's Diner. If you're staying overnight before a morning sailing, the Majestic Inn & Spa offers rooms with a view in a restored 1890 store building. And right next to the ferry is the Ship Harbor Inn, with suites and cabins perched right above Rosario Strait.

KNOCKOUT PARKS

Across the marina from downtown is Cap Sante, a rocky headland that protects the harbor. At the top is a small city park that offers enormous views of downtown, Mount Baker, and a whole bunch of islands.

At the west end of town, Washington Park is the city's most spectacular green space. Here you'll find a scenic loop road, a network of forested hiking trails, water views in three directions, and a sizable campground. Nearby is the suburban Skyline neighborhood, where you can catch a whale-watching or other boat tour.

MAKE SURE YOU CATCH THE RIGHT BOAT

If you're taking a ferry on from here, double-check that you're at the right terminal! All WSF vessels leave from the terminal on the western side of town, near Washington Park. Guemes Island (page 123), however, is accessible by a small county ferry that leaves from a terminal off Sixth Street.

▲ You won't find many neon signs on other Salish Sea islands, so get your vintage neon fix on Commercial Avenue in downtown Anacortes.

SAN JUAN ISLANDS

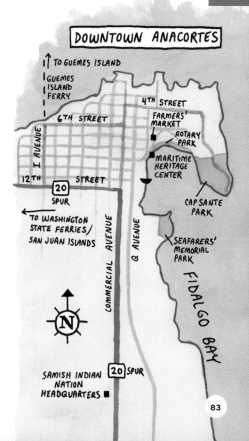

DOWNTOWN ANACORTES

TO GUEMES ISLAND
GUEMES ISLAND FERRY
4TH STREET
6TH STREET
FARMERS' MARKET
ROTARY PARK
I AVENUE
MARITIME HERITAGE CENTER
12TH STREET
20 SPUR
CAP SANTE PARK
TO WASHINGTON STATE FERRIES/ SAN JUAN ISLANDS
COMMERCIAL AVENUE
Q AVENUE
SEAFARERS' MEMORIAL PARK
FIDALGO BAY
N
SAMISH INDIAN NATION HEADQUARTERS
20 SPUR

THE Working Waterfront

The islands might attract tourists and pleasure boaters, but they also are home to active, working ports—hubs of marine cargo, fishing, and transportation. Below are some of the tools and trappings of the industrial waterfront.

SHIPPING CONTAINER

Surge Marine

CONTAINER SHIP

▶ **CARGO.** The region hosts a large number of deepwater ports with the capacity to handle ocean-crossing container ships. These behemoths are a common sight on the Strait of Juan de Fuca.

▶ **REPAIRS.** Every vessel needs maintenance and occasional repairs, whether on the water (wet dock) or on land (dry dock).

LINKSPAN (APRON)

CAR FERRY

DRY DOCK

STERN FENDER

PILINGS

FERRY SLIP

HALYARD SHACKLE

TURNBUCKLE

RIVET

SPAR VARNISH

▲ **SEA TRAVEL.** Public ferries, commercial charters, and private boats sometimes use the same facilities, and working ports help manage traffic from every source.

▶ **AIR TRAVEL.** Passenger and cargo planes are essential services for the non-ferry islands. These small planes are novelties for tourists, but a part of workaday life for residents.

SEAPLANE (FLOATPLANE)

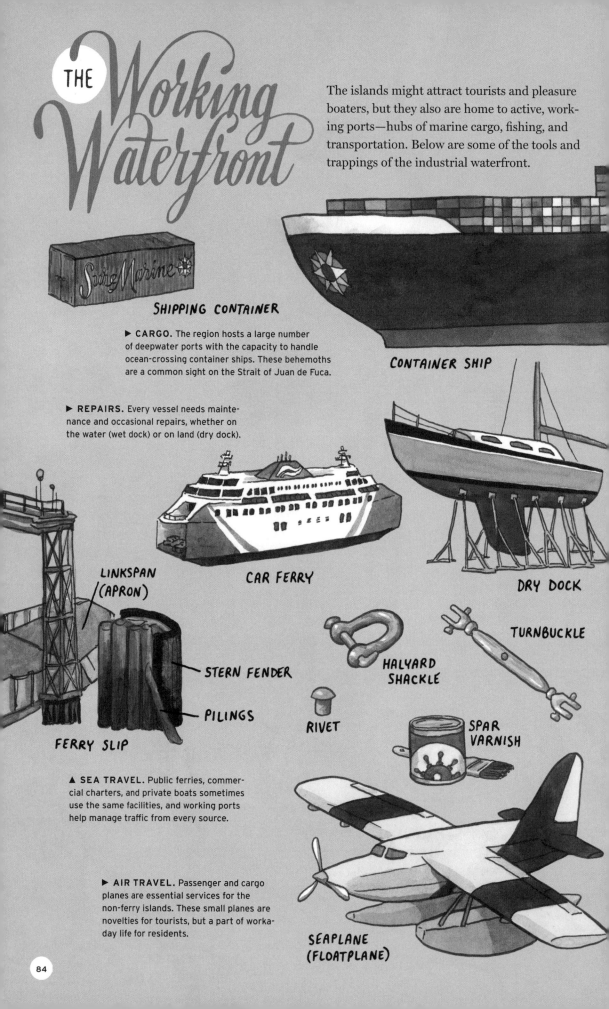

GILLNETTER

▶ **FISHING.** Some ports specialize in commercial fishing vessels—both local ones that cruise the Salish Sea and long-haul boats that travel down seasonally from Alaska.

TRAWLER

SureMarine

TROLLER

◀ **TRAPS AND TRAPPINGS.** A common sight at commercial fishing terminals are towering stacks of crab pots, tangled nets, and discarded buoys.

TWISTED ROPE

BRAIDED ROPE

SHIP-TO-SHORE CRANE (CONTAINER CRANE)

MONOFILAMENT

TRAP FLOAT OR BUOY

GLASS FISHING FLOAT

NET

CRAB POT

▲ **RARE FINDS.** Japanese fishing boats once used handblown glass floats to buoy their nets. For decades stray floats washed ashore on the Northwest coast—though nowadays it's easier to find them at antique stores.

PINK SALMON

SMOKED SALMON   **SALT COD**   **SALTED CODFISH**

PRESERVED SEAFOOD

◀ **EPHEMERA.** Look for antique cannery labels and other working-port ephemera at local museums or on public trash cans in Anacortes!

CANNERY

▲ **SHIP TO SHORE.** Huge port cranes transfer shipping containers off cargo ships and into holding areas on the land—where they're then transferred to tractor trailers for overland transport.

▶ **FOOD PROCESSING.** The Salish Sea has a long history of processing its seafood bounty for commercial sale. You can still find old cannery buildings up and down Northwest shorelines.

SAN JUAN

Second largest in the archipelago (just two square miles smaller than Orcas), San Juan is the most populous. It's also the main transit hub and connecting point to Vancouver Island, BC (page 140), and the Gulf Islands (page 158). Seasonally, Island Express Charters runs a Friday Harbor foot ferry from Port Townsend, and Victoria Clipper runs daily trips (also passenger-only) out of Seattle.

The island has been a crossroads for millennia. Many Coast Salish peoples have shared it as their ancestral fishing and gathering grounds: the Samish, Lummi, Swinomish, Mitchell Bay, and Semiahmoo from what is now Washington, and the Saanich, Cowichan, Songhees, and T'Sou-ke from the now-Canadian side of the Strait. Hudson's Bay Company ran a mid-1800s outpost here, and both Britain and the United States have claimed it (more on page 92).

San Juan Island is forested in patches, with many conifers and red-barked madrone trees. Part of the island lies within the Olympic rain shadow, giving it a number of treeless prairies and a drier, sunnier climate than others in the chain. This climate allows for plenty of open pastureland and farms, and lots of good-weather options for outdoor enthusiasts. San Juan devotees love its sheer variety of attractions and activities for every interest and age level— plan to spend at least a few days here, if you can.

San Juan has a good number of transit options, including public roads—but there are also options for walk-on ferry travelers, including taxis, bike and moped rentals, trolley tours, and public transit buses (peak season only). Also like many other islands, San Juan is bike friendly, but take care on the narrow roads. Expect huge crowds in the summer, particularly on the Fourth of July, and Memorial and Labor Day weekends.

▼ Many nature lovers come to Cattle Point for the foxes (page 94), but in June the prairies blaze orange with California poppies, introduced here many decades ago.

N

TO SIDNEY, BC
SPIEDEN ISLAND

POSEY ISLAND
MARINE
STATE PARK
PEARL
ISLAND
ROCHE HARBOR
ROCHE
HARBOR
HENRY
ISLAND

LONESOME COVE RESORT
ROCHE HARBOR
AIRPORT
REUBEN
TARTE
COUNTY
PARK

JONES ISLAND
MARINE STATE PARK

ORCAS
ISLAND

WEST
SOUND

DEER HARBOR
CRANE
ISLAND

YELLOW
ISLAND

WASP
ISLANDS

WASP
PASSAGE

WSF INTERISLAND FERRY

SHAW
ISLAND

WESTCOTT BAY
VISITOR CENTER

SAN JUAN
ISLAND
NATIONAL
HISTORICAL
PARK
(ENGLISH CAMP)

ROCHE

DUCK
SOUP

SPORTSMAN
LAKE

HARBOR

SAN JUAN CHANNEL

WASHINGTON STATE FERRIES

ROAD

UNIVERSITY OF
WASHINGTON FRIDAY
HARBOR
LABORATORIES

TO LOPEZ, ANACORTES

HARO

SNUG
HARBOR
RESORT

CADY
MOUNTAIN
894 FT

WEST VALLEY ROAD

MOUNT
GRANT PRESERVE

BEAVERTON VALLEY ROAD

SAN JUAN

ISLAND

FRIDAY HARBOR
SEAPLANE
BASE

FRIDAY
HARBOR

FRIDAY
HARBOR
AIRPORT

TURN ISLAND
MARINE STATE PARK

TURN
POINT PARK

SAN JUAN
CLIPPER

PAGE 96

SAN JUAN
COUNTY PARK

TROUT
LAKE

KING
SISTERS
PRESERVE

SAN JUAN VALLEY ROAD

FAIRGROUNDS

JACKSON
BEACH

WEST SIDE ROAD

LIME KILN
LIGHTHOUSE

MOUNT DALLAS
1090 FT

ZYLSTRA
LAKE

DOUGLAS ROAD

GRIFFIN
BAY

LIME KILN
POINT
STATE PARK

DEADMAN BAY
PRESERVE

WOLD ROAD

PELINDABA
LAVENDER

BAILER HILL ROAD

CATTLE POINT ROAD

WESTSIDE
SCENIC PRESERVE

FALSE
BAY

FRAZER
HOMESTEAD
PRESERVE

PAGE 92

SAN JUAN ISLAND
NATIONAL HISTORICAL
PARK (AMERICAN
CAMP)

BRITISH COLUMBIA (CANADA)

WASHINGTON (USA)

STRAIT

VISITOR CENTER

SOUTH
BEACH

CATTLE POINT
LIGHTHOUSE

TO SEATTLE

SAN JUAN ISLANDS

87

▲ The Gallery of Whales occupies the second floor of the Whale Museum and includes several actual skeletons.

▼ Friday Harbor partially inspired David Guterson's novel *Snow Falling on Cedars*, which depicts a community loosely based on a pastiche of San Juan and Bainbridge (page 26) Islands.

THE ONE AND ONLY

Arriving by ferry is a visual treat, as you are greeted by Friday Harbor's picturesque historic waterfront. This is the seat of, and only incorporated town in, San Juan County, with about 2,500 year-round residents. When the town was incorporated in 1909, fish canneries, lumber mills, and agricultural products drove the economy. These industries dwindled after World War II, and in the 1970s real estate and tourism started to dominate. Now, in the summer Friday Harbor sees thousands of tourists arrive each day.

Friday Harbor's other claim to fame is scientific research. In 1904 the University of Washington established a marine biology field station here. The Friday Harbor Laboratories (in the background of the illustration at top right) are not open to the public, but UW students, faculty, and visiting scientists study there and conduct marine research around the islands.

Friday Harbor is also leading the research on orcas (page 98) and other cetaceans. Since 1976, after a public outcry finally ended the practice of capturing live orcas from local waters for aquariums and theme parks around the United States, local scientists have been studying orca behavior and monitoring the regional populations. Both the Center for Whale Research and the Whale Museum have their headquarters in Friday Harbor. The Whale Museum is open to the public and also runs a hydrophone (underwater microphone) at Lime Kiln Point State Park (page 97).

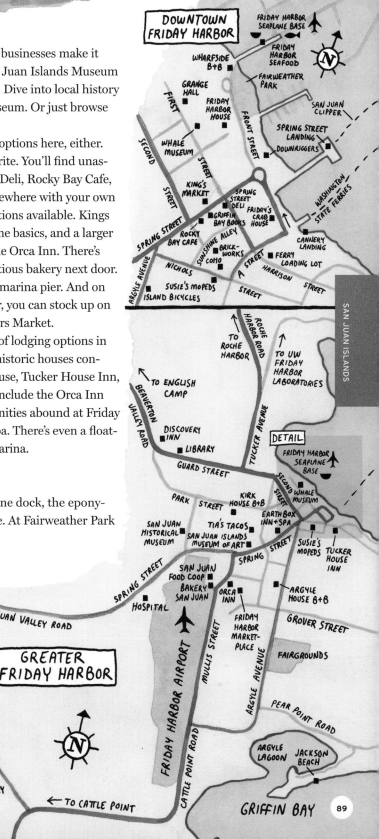

The state of Washington requires every public port to have an "official seal," meaning an ink stamp—but Friday Harbor took it literally and designated Popeye as theirs in 2005!

IN THE HEART OF TOWN

Friday Harbor's walkability and many businesses make it easy to spend a day here. Visit the San Juan Islands Museum of Art for rotating fine-art exhibitions. Dive into local history at the nearby San Juan Historical Museum. Or just browse the shelves at Griffin Bay Bookstore.

There's no shortage of restaurant options here, either. Friday's Crabhouse is a perennial favorite. You'll find unassuming but solid fare at Spring Street Deli, Rocky Bay Cafe, and Tina's Place. If you're staying somewhere with your own kitchen, there are plenty of market options available. Kings Market on Spring Street has most of the basics, and a larger grocery store is tucked away behind the Orca Inn. There's also a small food co-op with a scrumptious bakery next door. Friday Harbor Seafood is right on the marina pier. And on Saturdays from April through October, you can stock up on produce at the San Juan Island Farmers Market.

San Juan has the greatest variety of lodging options in the islands. In town there are several historic houses converted to B and Bs, including Kirk House, Tucker House Inn, and Argyle House. Economy options include the Orca Inn and Discovery Inn, and swankier amenities abound at Friday Harbor House and Earthbox Inn & Spa. There's even a floating inn aboard a boat docked at the marina.

ON THE WATERFRONT

From the ferry landing to the floatplane dock, the eponymous harbor is an active, vibrant place. At Fairweather Park

you'll find a statue of Popeye, the milky-eyed harbor seal who has returned to Friday Harbor every summer since 1995. Adjacent is *Interaction*, a sculptural portal of Coast Salish house poles by Musqueam artist Susan Point. She created the piece in 2004 to reestablish the island's link to its Indigenous heritage—which has been largely erased from the archipelago by white settlement and tourist culture. Spring Street Landing, the "clock dock" adjacent to the ferry terminal, is where the Victoria Clipper and several whale-watching tours dock. Inside the clock building is a tank displaying marine animals native to the waters under your feet. And you can book a sunset sailing aboard the *Spike Africa*, a wooden schooner named for a legendary West Coast sailor.

ON THE OUTSKIRTS

Outside the downtown core are a few outdoor points of interest. Farthest out is the Gothic-style Valley Church similar in age and style to one on Lopez Island. South of the fairgrounds is Jackson Beach, with a sandy lagoon and relatively few beachgoers. And from tiny Turn Point County Day Park, kayakers can paddle across to Turn Island Marine State Park and its handful of tent campsites (map on page 87).

BUNTING AND BLUE RIBBONS

Friday Harbor hosts an impressive Fourth of July parade down Spring Street. Later are a public barbecue (page 93), a live Music at the Port event, and fireworks over the harbor. (Charmingly, the last ferry of the evening waits until the fireworks are finished to push off from the dock.) The nostalgic fun continues in August with the San Juan County Fair, with cooking and craft competitions, 4-H events for kids, livestock judging, vendor booths, and carnival rides.

The other big August event is the Friday Harbor Fly-In, a celebration of historic small aircraft (and other vehicles) held at the airport. Autumn brings the Friday Harbor Film Festival, as well as Savor the San Juans, a weekend

▲ Susie's Mopeds rents the island's ubiquitous cherry-red mopeds or two-seater "scoot-coupes." This is a great option for walk-on ferry passengers who want to tour the back roads at their own pace.

farm-to-table extravaganza with farm tours on the three largest islands, wine tastings, and yet another parade in Friday Harbor. Finally, the holiday season begins with Friday Harbor Winterfest, which includes a tree-lighting ceremony in front of Cask & Schooner, and the Old Fashioned Christmas Market at the Brickworks building.

HAPPILY HOMEGROWN

San Juan Island's agricultural roots have much in common with those of adjacent Lopez (page 112). Both have the ideal "banana belt" (rain shadow) growing climate, and in recent years San Juan producers have created a small agritourism industry throughout the island. Visit a roadside, honor-system farm stand, call ahead to arrange a farm tour, or just enjoy a farm-to-table meal at Duck Soup.

The biggest agritourism magnet is Pelindaba Lavender's farm, where you can walk the fields and cut your own bouquet. The farm holds a lavender festival with harvesting and culinary demonstrations on the third weekend in July, when the blossoms are at their peak. You can also purchase lavender products like teas, soaps, dried wreaths, and herb blends. And if you can't make it out to the farm, there's a year-round Pelindaba Lavender shop in Friday Harbor.

Fiber fans will find a rich and woolly history. In 1853, a Hudson's Bay Company employee brought 1,369 sheep to

▲ The Pelindaba Lavender shop is festooned with drying lavender bundles hanging from the rafters.

▼ At the Fourth of July parade, look for pirate ships, orca-dogs and salmon-toddlers, brass bands, equestrians, and classic car floats.

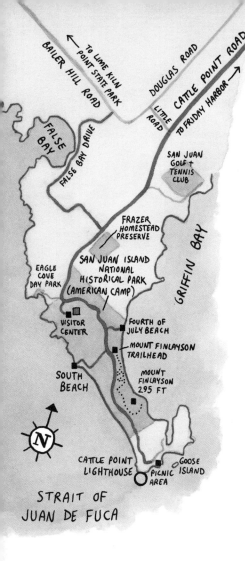

graze the treeless hills at the southern tip of the island. Wool became a big business here after that. Shepherds isolated rams on smaller, uninhabited islands, and then rowed them ashore (no, really!) to San Juan and other large islands when their services were required. This is a similar strategy to the one practiced for centuries by Coast Salish peoples for their "wool dogs" (more on page 123). Today there are far fewer sheep being raised on the island, but San Juan Woolworks produces small-batch yarns from a heritage flock established in the 1970s. Knitters who want to meet their yarn donor in person can flock to the Farm at Krystal Acres, home of fifty huacaya alpacas.

San Juan's well-paved roads make all your farm stops easy. Follow the San Juan Islands Scenic Byway, a network that also includes Orcas Island, part of Anacortes, and—in a nod to traditional Coast Salish canoe routes—the ferry route itself. Distinctive signs (page 5) help to keep you on the right path. Drive safely and with patience—blind curves, deer, farm dogs, cyclists, and other hazards abound.

A FIELD OF MUD, TWICE A DAY

If you're heading south from the interior of the island, take the back road along False Bay (see map, left), the shallow inlet that empties completely at low tide (hence the name: don't anchor here!). The area below the high-tide line is a biological reserve that's open to the public, so the mudflats are an excellent place for a low-tide hike or nature lesson. You can park where False Bay Drive hugs the shore and access the beach there. No harvesting or disturbing of tide creatures is allowed. And don't stray too far—when the tide comes back in, the bay floods fast!

A PIGHEADED STANDOFF

The Treaty of Oregon in 1846 settled the US-British (now Canadian) border along the forty-ninth parallel. That latitude bisects Vancouver Island (page 140) and many of the

islands in what was then called the Gulf of Georgia, so the treaty assigned most of them to Britain and put the border "in the middle of the channel" between the islands. The treaty was unclear as to *which* channel it meant, however, so San Juan Island became ground zero for the dispute.

On June 15, 1859, thirteen years to the day after the Treaty of Oregon's signing, an American farmer on San Juan Island found a stray pig eating his tubers. He shot the pig—which turned out to belong to an Irishman employed by Hudson's Bay Company. Each man demanded compensation for the loss of pig and potatoes, taking his complaint to his respective nation's military. The conflict quickly escalated, resulting in both sides building military outposts to prevent one another from claiming the island by force. No shots were ever fired (the pig's demise excluded), but the military stand-off resulted in a tense, twelve-year joint occupation—and an international embarrassment. Finally, Swiss arbitration settled the border dispute, awarding the San Juans to America in 1872. Today, San Juan commemorates the "Pig War" with a reenacctment at English Camp (page 96) and the Fourth of July Pig War Barbecue in Friday Harbor.

A STUDY IN CONTRASTS

Most of the southern tip of the island is set aside as San Juan Island National Historical Park. American Camp, the southern half of this park (the other unit is English Camp), preserves the US military base from the Pig War conflict. The two camps highlight the sharp contrasts in landscape and climate at opposite ends of the island—and they mirror the wildly different culture and state of morale at each outpost. The American Camp was notoriously disorganized and

▲ The split rail fencing clearly visible at American Camp is a hallmark of San Juan as a whole. You'll find it along roadsides and property boundaries all over the island.

▼ If you visit False Bay at the right time, you might find biologists studying the tidal and shorebird species there. Respect their work, and don't touch any markers or instruments you might find!

devolved into a hotbed of drinking and even suicide as the conflict dragged on. The treeless balds (prairies) near Cattle Point seemed to exacerbate these problems, as the soldiers battled harsh weather and frequent storms. Today the park preserves several historic structures, and the visitor center displays camp artifacts. Best of all are the sweeping views of the Strait and the Olympic Mountains. Hike the Mount Finlayson trail loop, or build a driftwood hut at South Beach. Admission is free, but the park is day use only.

West of American Camp is a tiny county day park at Eagle Cove, one of the island's best "secret" beaches. The lighthouse and picnic area at Cattle Point are managed by Washington State Parks. Back northward, off Cattle Point Road, is a land bank preserve at the historic Frazer Homestead. You can hike along it on a public trail from the American Camp visitor center, but the farm itself is leased to a private grower and is off limits.

OF FOXES AND RABBITS

Starting around 1870, lighthouse keepers are thought to have introduced European rabbits to the San Juans for food. The population, predictably, spiraled out of control. Enter the red fox: settlers brought non-native foxes to control the rabbits, and an endless predator-prey cycle was born. Periodic population crashes tend to make one or the other species dominant (and thus easier to spot) for a time. American Camp is one of the best places to spot foxes—and unfortunately, thanks to locals and tourists alike, they're also bold as brass. As with all wild animals, do not feed or touch them!

▼ The Roche Harbor marina also hosts a seafood market, boat and kayak rentals, charter services, and whale-watching and fishing tours.

HISTORY MEETS THEME PARK

At the opposite end of the island is Roche Harbor—part hotel, part village, part pleasure port. The site was originally home to Wh'lehl-kluh, a large, multitribal Indigenous community. From 1886 to the 1930s, it was the site of the

largest lime works—limestone quarry and lime kilns—on the West Coast. The company town was converted into a resort and "boatel" (hotel for boaters and yacht owners) in 1956. Its Victorian-era aesthetic may be a bit twee for some tastes, but there's plenty of real history to discover too. Don't miss the historic bricks that pave the walkways around the hotel.

The resort includes historic lodging, including the Hotel de Haro and the original company town cottages. Or you can rent an ersatz-historic luxury house. The resort also features three restaurants, a spa, a tiny post office, retail shops, and the only privately owned Catholic chapel in the country. In the summer a line of vintage wooden bathing huts turns into a daily artist's fair, and there's a nightly colors (flag-lowering) ceremony. The marina is an official customs checkpoint for boaters arriving from British Columbia, and a launch point for Stuart Island (page 129) as well as Posey Island Marine State Park (map on page 130), which offers campsites for human-powered boaters.

IN CASE YOU BROUGHT A OUIJI BOARD
A favorite haunt of Gothic novel fans and goth teenagers alike, the Afterglow Vista is San Juan Island's spookiest tourist attraction. This mausoleum was built to house the remains of Tacoma & Roche Harbor Lime Company owner, robber baron capitalist, and devout Freemason John S. McMillin—along with his immediate family and one of his employees. Its grandiose, symbolic architecture has inspired a lot of artsy photo shoots over the years.

To get there, park at the small lot west of the airport and follow the wooded path. The trail passes other historic gravesites for many of McMillin's other employees, several of whom were of Japanese descent. If you visit remember that the mausoleum, though it includes a literal table and set of chairs, is still someone's grave: respect those interred here, and leave no trace of your presence.

▲ The gardens that surround the Hotel de Haro are a popular wedding venue. If you visit during the summer, expect to share the grounds with a bridal party or two.

▼ The Afterglow Vista includes one intentionally broken column, representing life's brevity—that "man dies before his work is completed."

SAN JUAN ISLANDS

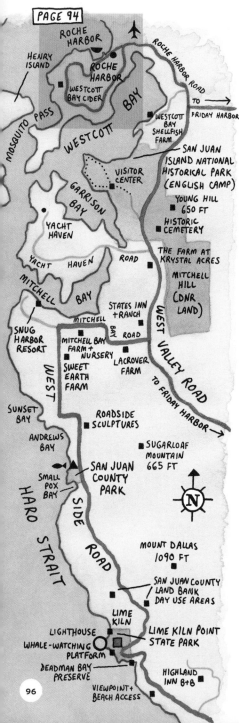

PAGE 94

HENRY ISLAND

ROCHE HARBOR

ROCHE HARBOR

WESTCOTT BAY CIDER

WESTCOTT BAY

ROCHE HARBOR ROAD

TO → FRIDAY HARBOR

MOSQUITO PASS

WESTCOTT BAY SHELLFISH FARM

WESTCOTT

SAN JUAN ISLAND NATIONAL HISTORICAL PARK (ENGLISH CAMP)

VISITOR CENTER

GARRISON BAY

YOUNG HILL 650 FT

HISTORIC CEMETERY

YACHT HAVEN

THE FARM AT KRYSTAL ACRES

MITCHELL HILL (DNR LAND)

YACHT HAVEN ROAD

MITCHELL BAY

STATES INN + RANCH

MITCHELL BAY ROAD

SNUG HARBOR RESORT

MITCHELL BAY FARM + NURSERY

LACROVER FARM

WEST VALLEY ROAD

WEST

SWEET EARTH FARM

TO FRIDAY HARBOR →

SUNSET BAY

ROADSIDE SCULPTURES

ANDREWS BAY

SUGARLOAF MOUNTAIN 665 FT

SMALL POX BAY

SAN JUAN COUNTY PARK

N

HARO STRAIT

SIDE ROAD

MOUNT DALLAS 1090 FT

SAN JUAN COUNTY LAND BANK DAY USE AREAS

LIME KILN

LIGHTHOUSE

WHALE-WATCHING PLATFORM

LIME KILN POINT STATE PARK

DEADMAN BAY PRESERVE

HIGHLAND INN B+B

VIEWPOINT + BEACH ACCESS

96

THE NOOKS AND CRANNIES

This end of the island has many small attractions to round out your visit. Next to Roche Harbor is the San Juan Islands Sculpture Park, featuring an easy walking path and picnic area among the artwork. Carve your name (it's encouraged!) on the Friendship Totem, a contemporary sculpture created by Kwakwaka'wakw artist Winadzi (Simon Daniel James). Nearby Westcott Bay Cider produces several traditional ciders from its orchards and offers tastings on Saturday afternoons in the tourist season. Tiny Reuben Tarte Park (map on page 87) provides a protected beach for launching a kayak and a rocky knoll with views of Jones Island (page 129). It's easy to miss the side road down to Westcott Bay Shellfish Farm—in the summer, grab an oyster lunch at one of their Tide Tables (lunch comes with a free oyster shucking lesson). Snug Harbor Resort's cabins and boat launch are a favorite of kayakers. Finally, San Juan County Park crams a lot of public amenities onto a tiny parcel of land. You'll find the island's only tent campground here (the fairgrounds in Friday Harbor offer RV camping)—sites are available year-round, but reservations for the summer are hard to get.

WALK IN AN ENGLISH COUNTRY GARDEN

The English Camp unit of San Juan Island National Historical Park is located just south of Roche Harbor. This is where British Royal Navy set up their garrison, displacing the multicultural Indigenous gathering place called Pe'pi'ow'elh, without a treaty. The historic buildings and replica formal garden here point to the completely different experience the British had, compared to their American peers. The harbor protected the camp from the worst of the weather, and soldiers enjoyed the company of civilian society, as they hosted balls and parties to keep isolation at bay.

◄ English Camp's formal garden replicates an 1867 design planted by Captain William Addis Delacombe in order to bring a little bit of England to the island for his wife.

ENDING ON A HIGH NOTE

Finish your adventure at Lime Kiln Point State Park, named for the nineteenth-century kilns that fired local limestone into lime for producing mortar. You can see a preserved kiln up close by hiking a short trail to the northern tip of the park. At Lime Kiln Point is a 1919 lighthouse, perched just across Haro Strait from Vancouver Island. The park is open year-round for day use only (though the campsites at San Juan County Park are just up the road), and the main loop trail is accessible, though not paved. The small interpretive center and gift shop is open, and park rangers are on hand to answer questions during the peak season.

BUST OUT THOSE BINOCULARS

In the summer the park's main event is the chance to see orcas come right up to shore to feed. The famous J, K, and L pods of the Southern Resident orcas historically hunt salmon along San Juan's western shore, making them a living icon of the islands. The Lhaq'temish (Lummi) people call them the Qwe 'lhol mechen, which roughly translates to "our relations under the sea," and honor the orcas as part of their extended family. As the whales' food supply dwindles, sightings in the area have become more and more rare, and the Southern Resident pods have been slowly starving to death. In 2019 Lummi tribal members performed a ceremony in which they offered twelve live Chinook salmon to the sea and bestowed a new family name of Sk'aliCh'elh on the resident pods to renew their pledge to protect them.

Lime Kiln Point State Park maintains a whale-viewing platform on the shoreline trail and a research station inside the lighthouse, with a whiteboard updated with recent sightings. In recent years transient orcas (page 98) have been spending more time in local waters, thanks to increased sea lion populations. These aren't often spotted at Lime Kiln Point but are frequent cash cows these days for the daily whale-watching boats that leave from Friday Harbor and Anacortes.

▲ Orca-spotting from Lime Kiln Point requires a lot of patience and luck, but even if you don't see any whales, a long day of searching is often rewarded with a spectacular sunset.

▼ Don't miss the kooky roadside sculptures and fruity "cabins" located along the roadside on West Side Road.

Thar SHE Blows

Orcas, or killer whales, are the Salish Sea's most famous living attraction. Whether you catch a glimpse of the critically endangered Southern Residents or spot a more common transient orca, you'll experience a thrill of a lifetime.

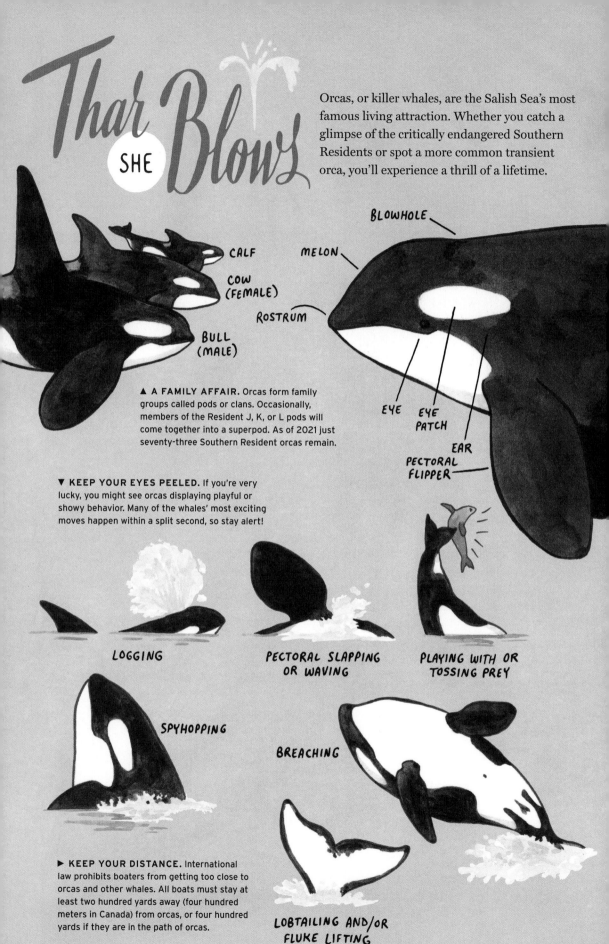

CALF

COW (FEMALE)

ROSTRUM

BULL (MALE)

BLOWHOLE

MELON

EYE

EYE PATCH

EAR

PECTORAL FLIPPER

▲ **A FAMILY AFFAIR.** Orcas form family groups called pods or clans. Occasionally, members of the Resident J, K, or L pods will come together into a superpod. As of 2021 just seventy-three Southern Resident orcas remain.

▼ **KEEP YOUR EYES PEELED.** If you're very lucky, you might see orcas displaying playful or showy behavior. Many of the whales' most exciting moves happen within a split second, so stay alert!

LOGGING

PECTORAL SLAPPING OR WAVING

PLAYING WITH OR TOSSING PREY

SPYHOPPING

BREACHING

▶ **KEEP YOUR DISTANCE.** International law prohibits boaters from getting too close to orcas and other whales. All boats must stay at least two hundred yards away (four hundred meters in Canada) from orcas, or four hundred yards if they are in the path of orcas.

LOBTAILING AND/OR FLUKE LIFTING

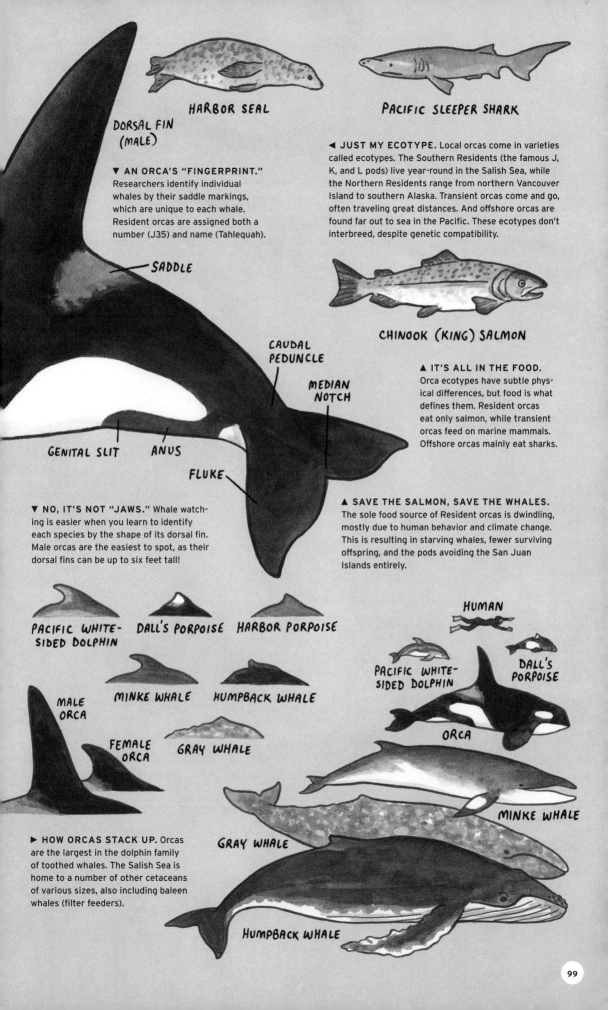

HARBOR SEAL

PACIFIC SLEEPER SHARK

DORSAL FIN (MALE)

▼ AN ORCA'S "FINGERPRINT." Researchers identify individual whales by their saddle markings, which are unique to each whale. Resident orcas are assigned both a number (J35) and name (Tahlequah).

SADDLE

◄ JUST MY ECOTYPE. Local orcas come in varieties called ecotypes. The Southern Residents (the famous J, K, and L pods) live year-round in the Salish Sea, while the Northern Residents range from northern Vancouver Island to southern Alaska. Transient orcas come and go, often traveling great distances. And offshore orcas are found far out to sea in the Pacific. These ecotypes don't interbreed, despite genetic compatibility.

CHINOOK (KING) SALMON

CAUDAL PEDUNCLE

MEDIAN NOTCH

▲ IT'S ALL IN THE FOOD. Orca ecotypes have subtle physical differences, but food is what defines them. Resident orcas eat only salmon, while transient orcas feed on marine mammals. Offshore orcas mainly eat sharks.

GENITAL SLIT   ANUS

FLUKE

▼ NO, IT'S NOT "JAWS." Whale watching is easier when you learn to identify each species by the shape of its dorsal fin. Male orcas are the easiest to spot, as their dorsal fins can be up to six feet tall!

▲ SAVE THE SALMON, SAVE THE WHALES. The sole food source of Resident orcas is dwindling, mostly due to human behavior and climate change. This is resulting in starving whales, fewer surviving offspring, and the pods avoiding the San Juan Islands entirely.

PACIFIC WHITE-SIDED DOLPHIN

DALL'S PORPOISE

HARBOR PORPOISE

HUMAN

MINKE WHALE

HUMPBACK WHALE

PACIFIC WHITE-SIDED DOLPHIN

DALL'S PORPOISE

MALE ORCA

ORCA

FEMALE ORCA

GRAY WHALE

► HOW ORCAS STACK UP. Orcas are the largest in the dolphin family of toothed whales. The Salish Sea is home to a number of other cetaceans of various sizes, also including baleen whales (filter feeders).

MINKE WHALE

GRAY WHALE

HUMPBACK WHALE

ORCAS

The San Juans' largest island has a devout following. It attracts both outdoorsy types and hippies, with its down-to-earth feel and informal culture. Orcas's name comes from "Horcasitas" (page 82), not the whale, so is pronounced differently (page 188). The island is shaped a bit like a pair of lungs or a life vest, with long, fjordy East Sound nearly cutting the landmass in two, and the left lobe further split into three smaller ones. The ferry terminal is at the bottom of the left lobe, and there are no public roads along the outer shore.

Orcas has a totally different climate than its island neighbors. It is far wetter, with Mount Constitution receiving forty to sixty inches of rain a year (southern Lopez gets an average of just nineteen). Orcas is also downright mountainous—the highest peak in the archipelago, Mount Constitution, towers (with a literal stone tower) at 2,398 feet. Both it and Turtleback Mountain (with the "head" of the turtle at Orcas Knob) are visible from all over the region.

Buses are rare and rental cars expensive here—unless you are a cyclist in very good shape, you'll want to bring your own motorized transport. Orcas is also much more private than San Juan or Lopez, with many roads and enclaves that are off-limits to lookie-loos, or sometimes unfriendly to visitors ambling by on the county roads. Be especially mindful of public-private boundaries here, as the change can happen quite abruptly. And keep your paper map handy—wrong turns are easy to make, and cell service is spotty at best. Boaters can access many public stretches of beach, but most of these are not accessible by road or hiking trail.

▼ The front porch of the Orcas Hotel is the perfect place to sit with a cup of coffee and watch the ferries arrive and depart.

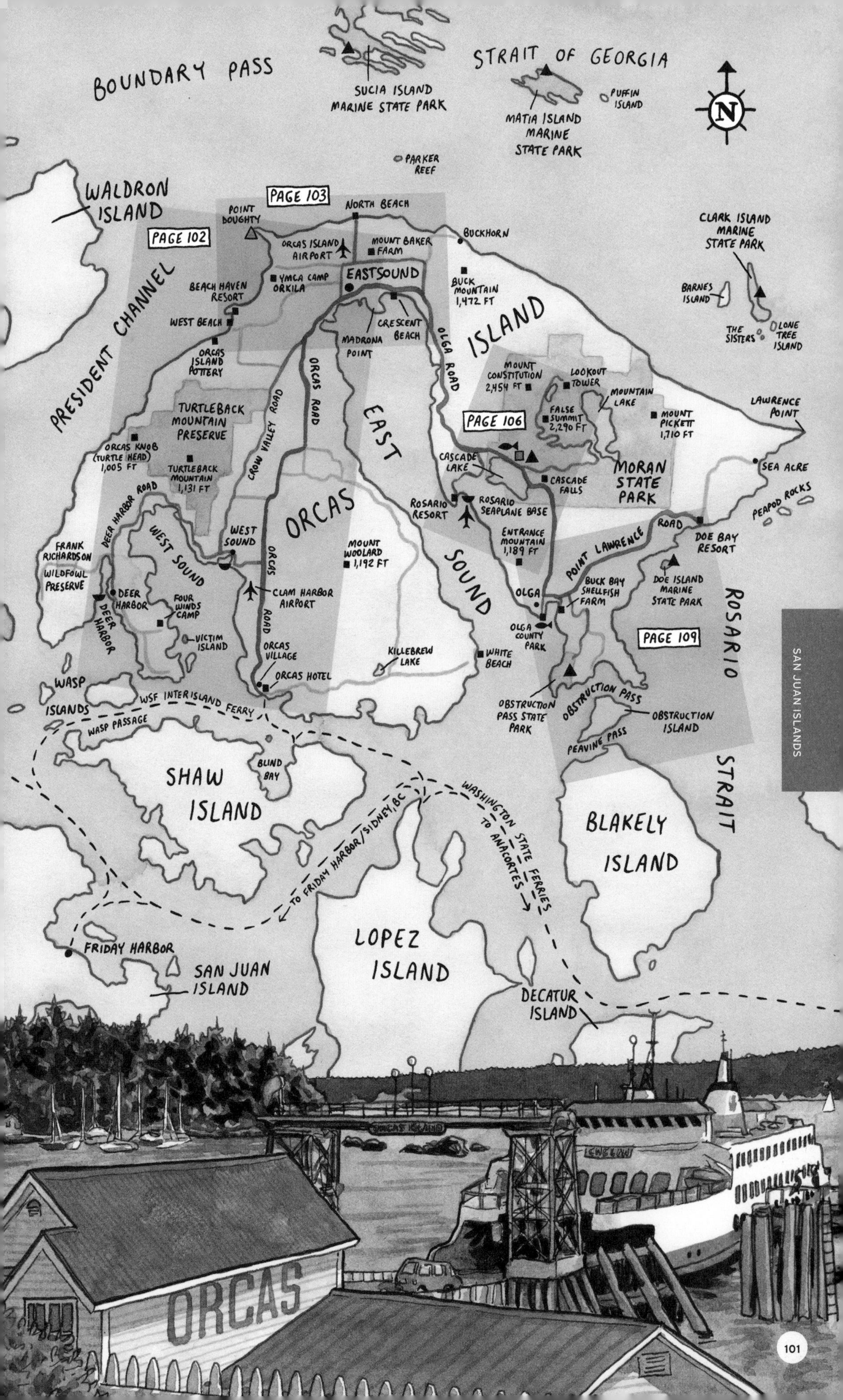

BOUNDARY PASS

STRAIT OF GEORGIA

SUCIA ISLAND MARINE STATE PARK

MATIA ISLAND MARINE STATE PARK

PUFFIN ISLAND

PARKER REEF

N

WALDRON ISLAND

PAGE 103

PAGE 102

POINT DOUGHTY

NORTH BEACH

ORCAS ISLAND AIRPORT

MOUNT BAKER FARM

BUCKHORN

CLARK ISLAND MARINE STATE PARK

EASTSOUND

YMCA CAMP ORKILA

BUCK MOUNTAIN 1,472 FT

BARNES ISLAND

BEACH HAVEN RESORT

CRESCENT BEACH

ISLAND

THE SISTERS

LONE TREE ISLAND

WEST BEACH

MADRONA POINT

OLGA ROAD

PRESIDENT CHANNEL

ORCAS ISLAND POTTERY

MOUNT CONSTITUTION 2,454 FT

LOOKOUT TOWER

MOUNTAIN LAKE

LAWRENCE POINT

TURTLEBACK MOUNTAIN PRESERVE

PAGE 106

FALSE SUMMIT 2,290 FT

MOUNT PICKETT 1,710 FT

ORCAS ROAD

EAST

ORCAS KNOB (TURTLE HEAD) 1,005 FT

TURTLEBACK MOUNTAIN 1,131 FT

CROW VALLEY ROAD

CASCADE LAKE

MORAN STATE PARK

SEA ACRE

CASCADE FALLS

PEAPOD ROCKS

WEST SOUND

ROSARIO RESORT

ROSARIO SEAPLANE BASE

SOUND

FRANK RICHARDSON WILDFOWL PRESERVE

DEER HARBOR ROAD

WEST SOUND

ORCAS

MOUNT WOOLARD 1,192 FT

ENTRANCE MOUNTAIN 1,189 FT

POINT LAWRENCE

ROAD

DOE BAY RESORT

DEER HARBOR

FOUR WINDS CAMP

ORCAS ROAD

CLAM HARBOR AIRPORT

BUCK BAY SHELLFISH FARM

DOE ISLAND MARINE STATE PARK

DEER HARBOR

VICTIM ISLAND

OLGA

ROSARIO

WASP ISLANDS

ORCAS VILLAGE

KILLEBREW LAKE

OLGA COUNTY PARK

PAGE 109

STRAIT

ORCAS HOTEL

WHITE BEACH

WSF INTER ISLAND FERRY

WASP PASSAGE

OBSTRUCTION PASS STATE PARK

OBSTRUCTION PASS

OBSTRUCTION ISLAND

PEAVINE PASS

BLIND BAY

SHAW ISLAND

BLAKELY ISLAND

TO FRIDAY HARBOR/SIDNEY, BC

WASHINGTON STATE FERRIES TO ANACORTES

FRIDAY HARBOR

SAN JUAN ISLAND

LOPEZ ISLAND

DECATUR ISLAND

ORCAS

SAN JUAN ISLANDS

101

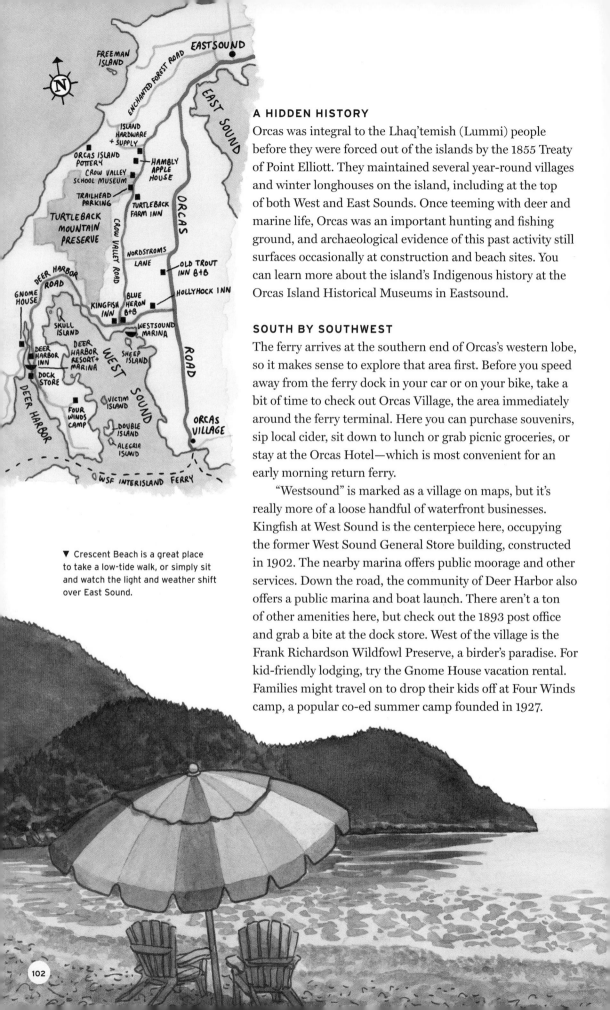

A HIDDEN HISTORY

Orcas was integral to the Lhaq'temish (Lummi) people before they were forced out of the islands by the 1855 Treaty of Point Elliott. They maintained several year-round villages and winter longhouses on the island, including at the top of both West and East Sounds. Once teeming with deer and marine life, Orcas was an important hunting and fishing ground, and archaeological evidence of this past activity still surfaces occasionally at construction and beach sites. You can learn more about the island's Indigenous history at the Orcas Island Historical Museums in Eastsound.

SOUTH BY SOUTHWEST

The ferry arrives at the southern end of Orcas's western lobe, so it makes sense to explore that area first. Before you speed away from the ferry dock in your car or on your bike, take a bit of time to check out Orcas Village, the area immediately around the ferry terminal. Here you can purchase souvenirs, sip local cider, sit down to lunch or grab picnic groceries, or stay at the Orcas Hotel—which is most convenient for an early morning return ferry.

"Westsound" is marked as a village on maps, but it's really more of a loose handful of waterfront businesses. Kingfish at West Sound is the centerpiece here, occupying the former West Sound General Store building, constructed in 1902. The nearby marina offers public moorage and other services. Down the road, the community of Deer Harbor also offers a public marina and boat launch. There aren't a ton of other amenities here, but check out the 1893 post office and grab a bite at the dock store. West of the village is the Frank Richardson Wildfowl Preserve, a birder's paradise. For kid-friendly lodging, try the Gnome House vacation rental. Families might travel on to drop their kids off at Four Winds camp, a popular co-ed summer camp founded in 1927.

▼ Crescent Beach is a great place to take a low-tide walk, or simply sit and watch the light and weather shift over East Sound.

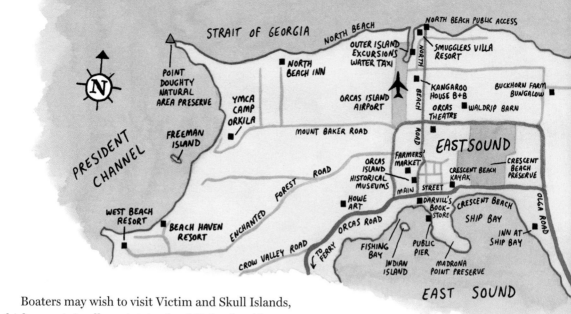

Boaters may wish to visit Victim and Skull Islands, which are minimally maintained public lands with no camping or services. The islands are so named to memorialize the Lummi people killed in 1858 by Haida raiders from what is now the northern British Columbia coast.

HEADING UP-ISLAND

On your way to the village of Eastsound, take the scenic alternate route of Crow Valley Road. Here you'll find historic farms and the trailhead parking for Turtleback Mountain Preserve (there are no roads here—hiking only). Just past the trailhead is the 1888 Crow Valley School, now a one-room museum open on summer weekends. If you find yourself in need of tools or supplies for your trip, stop by Island Hardware & Supply, an Orcas institution for fifty-odd years.

Toward the western shore is Orcas Island Pottery, a working studio and tourist destination that features functional pieces by several local ceramic artists. Established in 1945, it was purchased by potter Julia Crandall in 1953. She trained her daughter in the business, and now Syd Exton, Julia's granddaughter, is the current owner and lead artist. During open hours, you'll find the merchandise set out onto outdoor picnic tables around the property.

MEETING IN THE MIDDLE

The two lobes of Orcas Island converge at the top, at a narrow strip of land less than two miles wide—barely more than an isthmus. Here is where East Sound (the waterway) and Eastsound (the village) come together, at the site of the Lummi village called Ts'el-xwi-sen or Chulxwesing. Eastsound was a transit hub for the historic Mosquito Fleet (page 10) from the 1850s to the 1930s.

The village of Eastsound is home to most of the island's shops and cultural attractions. Check out the line of galleries along North Beach Road, do some shopping at Smörgåsbord or Darvill's Bookstore, or bring the kids to the Orcas W.I.L.D. nature museum. On the outskirts of the village is Howe Art, home of the giant kinetic chrome sculptures of artist Anthony Howe. Occasionally the grounds are open to the public, but call ahead to ask and avoid trespassing.

For a taste of Orcas fare, visit Brown Bear Baking, the Barnacle, or Island Skillet. You can take home some preserves from Girl Meets Dirt or a bottle from Doe Bay Wine Company. Then you can lay your head at one of many inns around Eastsound, or rent the bungalow at Buckhorn Farm.

If parades are your thing, Orcas is the place. The Solstice Parade marks the longest day of the year, but best of all is the Pet Parade in May—where you can vote for the "Mayor" of Eastsound. Past mayoral candidates have included Butters the French bulldog, Rainbow the rooster, April the cow, and Tokitae (Lolita), the last living captive Southern Resident orca. She remains at Miami Seaquarium, but Lummi activists are lobbying to return her to the San Juans.

THE UPPER SHORES

West of town, there are a pair of shoreline resorts that offer cabin rentals and private beaches. Nearby, the YMCA runs both day and overnight camps for kids at Camp Orkila. At the top of the island is Point Doughty Natural Area Preserve,

▲ The view from the Moran State Park observation tower is wonderful, of course, but there's an equally jaw-dropping vista point about halfway up the road.

▼ Visitors enter Moran State Park from the north via the original park entrance—a magnificent concrete arch built in 1928 and later enlarged to accommodate a wider road.

MORAN STATE PARK

▶ The Cascade Lake Trail is a mostly flat, easy scenic loop favored by families and beginner hikers.

containing a few trails and a marine campsite minimally maintained by the Bureau of Land Management. From Brandt's Landing Marina, a water taxi departs for Sucia and other islands (page 132). Back in the village, roadside Crescent Beach is the perfect spot to launch, and you can even rent a kayak across the road. Adjacent is a lesser-known preserve that continues into the woods with a great walking trail. Madrona Point protects a historic Lummi burial ground that continued to be used even after white settlement of the island. This area is off-limits—obey the marked boundary out of respect for the dead, and do not trespass. Indian Island, just offshore, is now also closed to protect wildflowers and nesting birds.

THE CAPTAIN OF INDUSTRY

Past Eastsound, the eastern lobe of Orcas becomes densely wooded and even more mountainous. All the islands were heavily logged in the nineteenth century, but the additional rainfall on Orcas has made the secondary-growth forests grow thick and fast. The logging days here are over, and the focus has shifted to recreation and conservation.

Perhaps the person most emblematic of Orcas's shift from industry to preservation is Robert Moran. A gilded-age business magnate who made his fortune in Seattle's ship-building industry, Moran moved to Orcas Island in 1905, ostensibly to retire (though he lived until 1943). An economic downturn began shortly afterward, and he began buying up homestead plots around Mount Constitution, ending up with about a third of the eastern portion of the island.

While he initially thought only of preserving water rights and the scenery for himself and his heirs, Moran eventually joined the conservation movement that wealthy Americans like President Theodore Roosevelt helped build. He began to push the state to establish a park, promising to donate land if they matched it with additional parcels.

MORAN STATE PARK

The Washington State Board of Park Commissioners was established in 1913, and Moran donated 2,731 acres in 1921. He continued to donate land and fund improvements throughout Moran State Park until 1933, and then the CCC (page 80) spent another decade developing park amenities and infrastructure. Today's park is more than 5,000 acres in size and is one of the most visited in the state.

UP AND DOWN THE MOUNTAIN

The largest portion of Moran State Park encompasses Mount Constitution, which includes most of the park's thirty-eight miles of trails. A paved road ends at a parking area near the top, and from there a short trail brings you to a stone observation tower with 360-degree views. The tower was built by the CCC in 1935, in the style of medieval watchtowers found in the Caucasus Mountains in eastern Europe. Inside are interpretive displays about the natural and human history of the park. There's also a small campground on Mountain Lake, but most of the rest of the mountain is designated as backcountry. The trails here are open year-round to hikers and in the off-season to mountain bikers.

The rest of the park surrounds lowland Cascade Lake. Here you will find about a hundred campsites—this is one of only two state-park campgrounds in the San Juans (the other is Spencer Spit, page 114), and it fills up fast. Save your sanity and make a campsite reservation ahead of time—you'll also find an up-to-date sign with the number of remaining campsites at the ferry ticket booth in Anacortes. In the peak season you'll find many park amenities around the lake, including boat rentals, accessible restrooms, and a snack bar. The lake is stocked with trout for fishing, and Camp Moran offers cabin rentals for families.

Don't miss the trail down to Cascade Falls, which is located below Mount Constitution Road. At forty feet tall,

▼ In addition to employing Arts and Crafts principles to the mansion's architecture, Moran also hired the famous Olmsted Brothers—who created Seattle's park system—to design the grounds of his estate.

it is the largest falls in the San Juans. Cross the footbridge to the lower viewpoint for the best vantage point. Nearby are trails connecting to three other waterfalls.

THE GRAND DAME

The best place to learn more about Robert Moran and his legacy—plus catch some of the best views on Orcas—is to see where he lived. The Rosario, now a sprawling forty-acre resort, contains the original Moran Mansion, built between 1906 and 1909. The mansion was styled as a nautical retreat for the Moran family and their guests, with brass fittings, built-in fixtures that resemble ship staterooms, and marine-theme decor. An indoor basement pool was designed for spa treatments, as Moran moved to Orcas on his doctor's orders, in order to benefit from the climate and sea air. Before his death, Moran sold the property to a San Francisco business-man, who then sold it to Texas oil baron Ralph Curtain in 1958. Curtain turned it into a high-end yacht resort. The property changed hands several more times over the years, but the resort still provides lodging, meals, conference space, and marina facilities to guests.

The mansion itself no longer includes guest rooms, but there is still a bar and restaurant here, and the eastern portion of the building is open as a self-guided, free museum. In the basement pool area, spa treatments are still available. Don't miss the Roundhouse suite, which sits apart from the mansion and was built in 1913 as a playhouse for children in the Moran family.

Most of the current resort lodging occupies newer buildings on the hillside.

▲ Doe Bay Resort's open-air soaking tubs are perched on a secluded cove, protected from the rain, and hidden from view by outsiders.

► The Moran Mansion includes a two-story pipe organ and a 1900 Steinway piano. The Rosario Resort still offers free music concerts here in the summer.

▼ The Olga Public Dock is a favorite of recreational crabbers. Even if that's not your thing, you can stand and watch the crustaceans scuttling on the bay floor below your feet.

There's also a bar and grill near the water, and a full-service marina and seaplane base. The lawn along the marina provides a nice place to stroll along the other historic buildings on the complex. For more affordable lodging alternatives, there are a handful of B and Bs in the residential neighborhood up the hill.

THE ÜBER-SANCTUARY

The other major resort on Orcas Island is Doe Bay. More than a hotel, it has an array of accommodations and ever-growing site plan that give it the feeling of a village. You can choose from guesthouse rooms, rustic cabins, yurts, tent campsites—even a tree house. The amenities and setting are the draw here—though there is also a range of quality among the accommodations and scenery, so choose your lodging carefully. All guests have access to (clothing-optional) saltwater soaking pools fed by natural hot springs. There's also a spa, kayak rentals, and a network of hiking trails. Doe Bay's mission isn't just relaxation, but also inner peace and personal improvement—giving it a loyal fan base of new-age types. In the fall there's also a writers' retreat called Write Doe Bay, offering workshops and plenty of focused time to get your thoughts down on paper.

DOWN TO THE TIP

At the bottom of the eastern lobe, you'll find the small hamlet of Olga. The area is pretty sleepy, but be sure to check out Olga Pottery and Orcas Island Artworks. The Olga Public Dock is a great landing place for travelers arriving by boat or kayak. Adjacent to the dock is a small park and picnic area.

A handful of side roads traverse the southeastern tip of the island. Just past Olga is Buck Bay Shellfish Farm, a third-generation family aquaculture business that began in the early 1940s. Here you can grab fresh oysters, clams, spot prawns, salmon, and crab to go—or, a recent development, you can dine in and slurp oysters just feet from where they were harvested. There's also a vacation rental unit available on the property.

Continuing south, don't miss Obstruction Pass State Park, your last chance at beach access for overland travelers. This small, mostly undeveloped park is not ADA-accessible—but if you can manage it, you can follow a fairly long trail through the woods to a pebbled beach near the southernmost tip of Orcas Island. Wear sturdy shoes with some grip to navigate the uneven trail—or better yet, arrive by boat and relax at one of the handful of campsites.

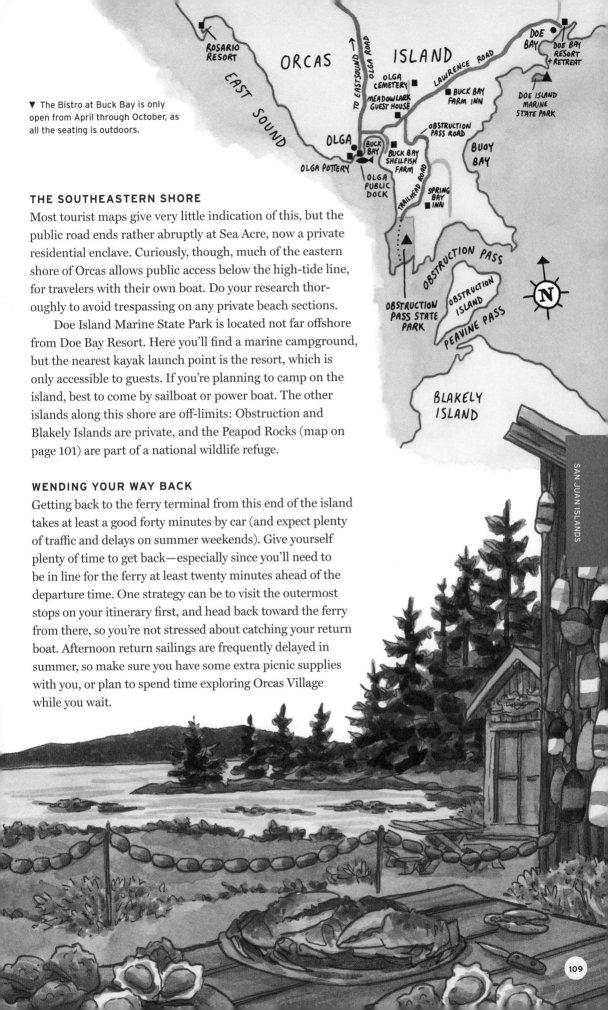

▼ The Bistro at Buck Bay is only open from April through October, as all the seating is outdoors.

THE SOUTHEASTERN SHORE

Most tourist maps give very little indication of this, but the public road ends rather abruptly at Sea Acre, now a private residential enclave. Curiously, though, much of the eastern shore of Orcas allows public access below the high-tide line, for travelers with their own boat. Do your research thoroughly to avoid trespassing on any private beach sections.

Doe Island Marine State Park is located not far offshore from Doe Bay Resort. Here you'll find a marine campground, but the nearest kayak launch point is the resort, which is only accessible to guests. If you're planning to camp on the island, best to come by sailboat or power boat. The other islands along this shore are off-limits: Obstruction and Blakely Islands are private, and the Peapod Rocks (map on page 101) are part of a national wildlife refuge.

WENDING YOUR WAY BACK

Getting back to the ferry terminal from this end of the island takes at least a good forty minutes by car (and expect plenty of traffic and delays on summer weekends). Give yourself plenty of time to get back—especially since you'll need to be in line for the ferry at least twenty minutes ahead of the departure time. One strategy can be to visit the outermost stops on your itinerary first, and head back toward the ferry from there, so you're not stressed about catching your return boat. Afternoon return sailings are frequently delayed in summer, so make sure you have some extra picnic supplies with you, or plan to spend time exploring Orcas Village while you wait.

Fresh AND Foraged

To eat like an islander, choose one of the Pacific Northwest's signature dishes—these delicacies often feature local produce and seafood. Or visit a farmers' market to find wild-foraged or farm-fresh seasonal ingredients to cook yourself.

PENN COVE MUSSELS

DUNGENESS CRAB MAC-N-CHEESE

SALMONBERRY

HUCKLEBERRY

▲ **SIMPLE SHELLFISH.** The best island restaurants prepare fish and shellfish simply, allowing the flavors of the seafood itself to shine through.

BERRY PIE

▶ **WILD BERRIES.** These summer treasures grow in abundance around the islands. While blackberries are invasive pests, the other berries are traditional Indigenous foods.

MORELS

CHANTERELLES

ROSE HIPS

▶ **MUSHROOMS.** Wild edible fungi are prized ingredients and iconic finds at local farmers' markets. Look for morels in the spring or chanterelles in the autumn.

◀ **BEACH INGREDIENTS.** Sea beans provide crunchy texture and natural salt to cooked and raw dishes, and wild rose hips are prized for adding vitamin C and tart flavor to teas and jellies.

▼ **RAW AND LOCAL.** Many island sushi bars feature locally fished and foraged ingredients, such as geoduck sashimi, seaweed salad, and grilled black cod.

SEA BEANS

SUSHI

FIDDLEHEADS

CEDAR-PLANK GRILLED SALMON

◄ **FOREST GREENS.** Lady ferns are the West Coast's edible fiddlehead species. These tender shoots, tasty in soups and stir-frys, are available in early spring.

► **SALMON.** The Northwest's most famous fish is a tourist draw all by itself. Try it grilled on cedar planks or dried into a sweet jerky called salmon candy.

SALMON CANDY

SALAL

► **EMBELLISHMENTS.** Ordinary dishes become extraordinary when island-raised or Salish-Sea-caught ingredients are added to bring their flavors to the next level.

HIMALAYAN BLACKBERRY

RAMEN

LAVENDER ICE CREAM

APPLE CIDER DOUGHNUTS

◄ **HERBS.** Whether cultivated or foraged from the roadside, the islands are home to a number of herbs and other botanical garnishes.

► **ISLAND BEVERAGES.** You can find good coffee all over the Pacific Northwest, but cider and perry (alcoholic fruit beverages) are local specialties that come in sweet, dry, sour, or ale-like varieties.

CHICORY

▼ **TRY IT GRILLED.** While many love raw oysters, grilling them is a Northwest tradition. Many local "sea farms" boast outdoor oyster bars—or grill your own with your favorite sauce.

CIDER

PACIFIC OYSTERS

ESPRESSO

LOPEZ

If you're looking for a San Juan Islands experience somewhere in between the tourist bustle of Friday Harbor and the utter solitude of an outer island (page 126), Lopez might be just the thing. The attractions here mainly revolve around the island scenery itself—and the joys of slowing down enough to enjoy it. The (relative) lack of crowds gives you more breathing room and a glimpse of what "normal" island living is like. The laid-back pace of life here has given the place the loving nickname of "Slow-pez."

Lopez's other moniker is "the friendly isle." After all the keep-out signs on Orcas, this is a breath of fresh air. Get your waving arm ready, because from the moment you disembark the ferry, Lopezians (yes, they really are called that) are determined to say hello to you. You'll find local drivers giving their signature index-finger hello from the steering wheel, residents waving from their front porches, even pedestrians raising a coffee cup to toast you as you pass.

There is no public transit system on Lopez, so you'll need your own mode of transportation to see the island. And if you're coming from Friday Harbor by car, know that you will likely have to reverse onto the boat from the ferry landing. (Don't worry, the ferry crew will guide you!) But if you're a cyclist, you've come to the right place. The island's gentle rolling landscape, paved roads, rain-shadow climate, and open spaces are beloved by bikers of all ages and skill levels—but for safety's sake, wear a helmet and stick to the side roads. If you're a driver, stay alert, share the road, and take it slow(pez). And if you need wheels, you can easily rent a bike in Lopez Village (page 114).

▲ Goats are effective at nibbling away noxious weeds. In 2010 San Juan County began a test program to rent out goats for clearing tough bracken around the islands.

▼ The noncompetitive Tour de Lopez has run every April since 2004. The event is open to cyclists of all ages and also features food, live music, and fundraising for local facilities.

BLAKELY
ISLAND

N

CANOE
ISLAND

UPRIGHT
CHANNEL

UPRIGHT
HEAD
PRESERVE

LOPEZ
ISLAND
SHELLFISH
FARM

HUMPHREY
HEAD

WASHINGTON STATE FERRIES TO ANACORTES

FLAT
POINT

UPRIGHT
CHANNEL
PARK

ODLIN
COUNTY
PARK

FLOWER
ISLAND

← TO FRIDAY HARBOR

SWIFTS
BAY

ROY PRESTHOLT
TURKEY BARN

PORT
STANLEY

FROST
ISLAND

THATCHER
PASS

PAGE 114

LOPEZ
VILLAGE

WEEKS
WETLAND
PRESERVE

BARN
OWL
BAKERY

PORT
STANLEY
SCHOOL-
HOUSE

SPENCER SPIT
STATE PARK

THE SPIT
PRESERVE

LIBRARY

HUMMEL
LAKE
PRESERVE

DECATUR
ISLAND

OTIS
PERKINS
PARK

FISHERMAN
BAY

FISHERMAN BAY ROAD

BEECHER
PRESERVE

TRUMP
ISLAND

CENTER
ISLAND

JAMES
ISLAND
MARINE
STATE PARK

SAN JUAN CLIPPER

LOPEZ
SOUND

KIMBALL
PRESERVE

RIM
ISLAND

SAN JUAN ISLAND

LOPEZ

ISLAND

CENTER

ROAD

LOPEZ HILL

RAM
ISLAND

FORTRESS
ISLAND

SPERRY
PENINSULA

ROSARIO

STRAIT

LOPEZ
ISLAND
AIRPORT

CENTER
CHURCH

LOPEZ
UNION
CEMETERY

HISTORIC
TELEPHONE OFFICE

SKULL
ISLAND

HUNTER
BAY

TO SEATTLE

GRANGE
HALL

MUD BAY

ROAD

PAGE 117

SHARK REEF
SANCTUARY

DAVIS
BAY

CHARLES
ISLAND

RICHARDSON

MACKAYE
HARBOR

MUD
BAY

MUD BAY
PARK

SOUTHEND
MARKET

GEESE
ISLETS

LONG
ISLAND

WATMOUGH
BAY PRESERVE

OUTER
BAY

AGATE
BEACH
COUNTY
PARK

ALECK BAY

ICEBERG
POINT

BLACKIE
BRADY
COUNTY PARK

POINT
COLVILLE

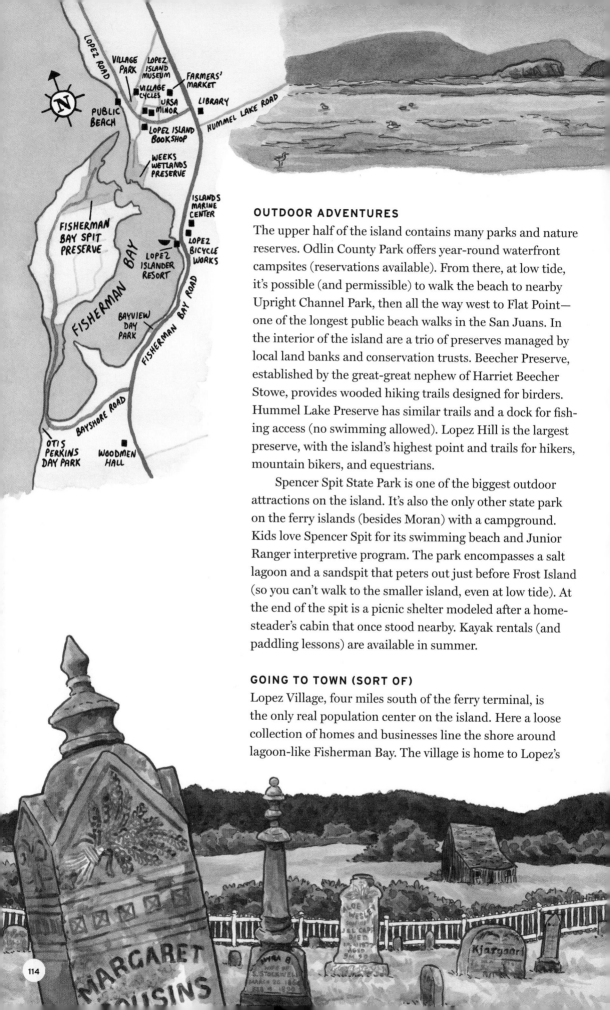

Map labels:

N

LOPEZ ROAD

VILLAGE PARK

LOPEZ ISLAND MUSEUM

FARMERS' MARKET

VILLAGE CYCLES

URSA MINOR

LIBRARY

PUBLIC BEACH

HUMMEL LAKE ROAD

LOPEZ ISLAND BOOKSHOP

WEEKS WETLANDS PRESERVE

ISLANDS MARINE CENTER

FISHERMAN BAY SPIT PRESERVE

FISHERMAN BAY

LOPEZ ISLANDER RESORT

LOPEZ BICYCLE WORKS

FISHERMAN BAY ROAD

BAYVIEW DAY PARK

BAYSHORE ROAD

OTIS PERKINS DAY PARK

WOODMEN HALL

OUTDOOR ADVENTURES

The upper half of the island contains many parks and nature reserves. Odlin County Park offers year-round waterfront campsites (reservations available). From there, at low tide, it's possible (and permissible) to walk the beach to nearby Upright Channel Park, then all the way west to Flat Point—one of the longest public beach walks in the San Juans. In the interior of the island are a trio of preserves managed by local land banks and conservation trusts. Beecher Preserve, established by the great-great nephew of Harriet Beecher Stowe, provides wooded hiking trails designed for birders. Hummel Lake Preserve has similar trails and a dock for fishing access (no swimming allowed). Lopez Hill is the largest preserve, with the island's highest point and trails for hikers, mountain bikers, and equestrians.

Spencer Spit State Park is one of the biggest outdoor attractions on the island. It's also the only other state park on the ferry islands (besides Moran) with a campground. Kids love Spencer Spit for its swimming beach and Junior Ranger interpretive program. The park encompasses a salt lagoon and a sandspit that peters out just before Frost Island (so you can't walk to the smaller island, even at low tide). At the end of the spit is a picnic shelter modeled after a homesteader's cabin that once stood nearby. Kayak rentals (and paddling lessons) are available in summer.

GOING TO TOWN (SORT OF)

Lopez Village, four miles south of the ferry terminal, is the only real population center on the island. Here a loose collection of homes and businesses line the shore around lagoon-like Fisherman Bay. The village is home to Lopez's

▲ The walk along Spencer Spit affords panoramic views of the lagoon; Frost, Orcas, and Blakely Islands; and Lopez Sound.

two main lodging options (Lopez Islander Resort and Edenwild Boutique Hotel), but there are also a few vacation rental options and cabins around the island. And you can rent a bike from either Village Cycles or Lopez Bicycle Works—the latter also offers free paper maps of the island.

All around the village you'll see tall tapered wooden structures—some with windows and doors, some without. They are historic water towers (or "tank houses" as some locals call them), though most no longer have holding tanks inside. Potable water is carefully conserved on all the islands, but Lopez and San Juan, with their drier climates, are especially vulnerable to both drought and saltwater intrusion on freshwater wells.

There is little shopping in Lopez Village—though Lopez Bookshop is small but mighty, and the village somehow supports two apothecary shops. There are, however, plenty of good things to eat. Snack on a cinnamon roll from Holly B's Bakery or, if you can find it, a pint of Lopez Island Creamery's seasonal huckleberry ice cream (they're now based out of Anacortes, but Lopez Village Market still carries tubs). Or grab a farm-to-table meal at Ursa Minor, or foodtruck fried potatoes at Poutine Your Mouth. And stock up on sandwich bread for your picnic by visiting the Barn Owl Bakery, located in the former Grayling Gallery (bread is also available for pickup at the Grayling farmstand).

Throughout the year, arts lovers can catch a performance at the Lopez Center for Community and the Arts or at the performance space at historic Woodmen Hall. In the spring you can attend a concert from the Salish Sea Early Music Festival or see the outdoor Shakespeare Under the Stars play, which rotates performances among the ferry

▼ The ornate historic gravestones at Lopez Union Cemetery sketch out the island's immigrant history, with many English and Scandinavian family names.

CHRISTEN JENSEN
BORN IN DENMARK
1852
DIED ON LOPES
JUNE 4

SAN JUAN ISLANDS

▲ The island's many historic barns and buildings mean a whole lot of barn swallows. You'll find them swooping all over the place in the summertime.

▼ One of the water towers in Lopez Village once housed a milk separator, part of the island's once-booming dairy industry.

islands in July and August. Or drop in on the monthly square dances held at the Grange Hall (south of Lopez Village), which include free lessons and a potluck dinner.

THE SPIT AND THE LAGOON

Fisherman Bay is hemmed in by a long tombolo, or sandspit, and a number of wetlands. Boaters entering the bay must take care and heed all nautical markers, as the entrance is narrow and requires skilled navigation at low tide. Weeks Wetland Preserve, at the edge of Lopez Village, is a good introduction to Fisherman Bay. A short path leads to an observation platform for bird-watching—to protect nesting sites, no dogs are allowed here. Just across the way (or a four-mile drive by road) is Fisherman Bay Spit Preserve, featuring trails and lovely views of Lopez Village. Finally, Otis Perkins Day Park lies at the south end of the tombolo (which is also preserve land), offering public beach access on the Upright Channel side of the spit. Cyclists beware: this is a wind-whipped spot. Look for the occasional kiteboarder here, like on Jetty Island (page 71).

A SHORELINE LIKE SWISS CHEESE

Southern Lopez is a labyrinth of beaches, bays, reefs, and rocks—a danger to boaters (so sail or paddle with care). Overland visitors can also access many beaches and waterfront parks. And in 2013 President Obama created San Juan Islands National Monument, which protects many offshore reefs and rocks, both here and on other islands. The monument is managed by the Bureau of Land Management (instead of the National Park Service), so there's little fanfare or tourist-facing info as of yet. But keep in mind that many offshore preserves are off-limits to boaters.

There are few services down here, but for snacks or a tide table (or a taco truck!), stop by Southend Market & Café. If they're closed, you'll have to head back to Lopez Village. The main public road ends at a narrow isthmus connecting to Sperry Peninsula. Formerly the long-time home of a summer camp, the entire peninsula was bought by Microsoft cofounder Paul Allen in 1996, displacing the camp. In 2000 Camp Nor'wester reopened on Johns Island (page 129), and Sperry Peninsula is still very much private.

GET THEE TO A BEACH

Shark Reef Sanctuary is a small park on the western shore. A short trail takes you to a shore jagged with rocks and natural jetties. Bring your binoculars to spot harbor seals up close and San Juan Island across the water.

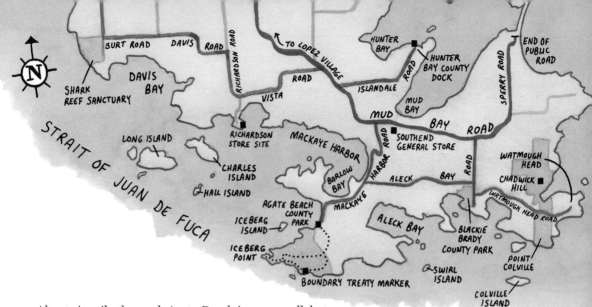

About six miles by road, Agate Beach is very small, but a great spot for a windswept walk. Hikers rave that the outhouse here is the cleanest in the state (a luxury when you've been hiking all day!). Blackie Brady beach is another tiny "pocket park," with a lovely beach at the bottom of a steep wooden staircase. Warning: storms have eroded the beach below, so dismounting the steps now requires either a jump or hanging from the rope that someone helpfully tied at the bottom (yikes).

The two largest preserves require a real hike to explore. Best known is Iceberg Point—close to the very bottom of the archipelago—which offers views of the Strait of Juan de Fuca and the Olympic Mountains. To get here, park at Agate Beach and follow the trail, the entrance to which is marked by a hand-lettered rusty sawblade. Be careful not to trespass, as the trail crosses and abuts private property.

Finally, sprawling Watmough Bay Preserve includes sections of old-growth forest and stunning shoreline views. There's a parking lot here, but the network of trails is a bit complicated and surrounded by private property. You can find a map for this and some other Lopez preserves on the San Juan County Conservation Land Bank website.

TO OTHER SHORES (AND BACK)

The Hunter Bay County Dock provides access to offshore islands like Decatur (page 126). Note that if you're hoping to leave your car there while you paddle, parking may be hard to find. Many Decatur residents keep a car there full-time, either for themselves or for their teenagers who attend high school on Lopez.

▼ The Treaty of 1908 marked the Canadian border with a series of obelisks. Since the border marker would be offshore here, it's marked at the trail to Iceberg Point, the nearest spot on land.

Flipper AND Fin

The Salish Sea is teeming with marine life, both above and below the waterline. Keep a sharp eye out and your binoculars handy, and the wildlife you spot might just become the highlight of your island adventure.

SEA OTTER

RIVER OTTER

▲ **OTTERS.** The region is home to both river and sea otters. River otters are quite elusive—though sometimes found nesting under a waterfront porch! And once in a while it's possible to glimpse an endangered sea otter from the shoreline or ferry.

DALL'S PORPOISE

HARBOR PORPOISE

PACIFIC WHITE-SIDED DOLPHIN

▶ **CETACEANS.** The islands are home to several toothed whale species, including orcas, dolphins, and porpoises (special section about orcas on page 98). Gray, minke, and humpbacks are baleen (filter-feeder) whales.

SEAL PUPS

▲ **LEAVE 'EM BE.** Harbor seal mothers leave their newborn pups ashore for up to several hours at a time while they hunt. These pups are not abandoned! Never touch or try to move them.

HARBOR SEAL

STELLER SEA LION

CALIFORNIA SEA LION

▲ **PINNIPEDS.** A common sight in many spots, seals and sea lions are some of the most entertaining denizens of the Salish Sea.

PINK SALMON

HUMPBACK WHALE

GRAY WHALE

▶ **EXTREME FEEDING.** Every spring, along their migration route, gray whales risk the shallow shoreline waters of northern Puget Sound to gorge themselves on ghost shrimp.

OTHER ISLANDS

OTHER ISLANDS

▲ The Pacific tree frog, also called the Pacific chorus frog, is common throughout the San Juans. Their familiar "ribbit" calling is the iconic noise used in movie sound effects.

Though San Juan, Orcas, and Lopez are the top tourist attractions in the San Juans, there are many other islands to explore. Their lack of amenities often leave them overshadowed by the big three, but if you like the peace and quiet of ordinary island life, this can be a major draw. A few of these smaller islands are accessible by public car ferries. All the others require your own boat, a water taxi, or charter out of a larger island (you'll find some listed on page 14), or air service, if available. Some of these islands are immediately adjacent to the big three and are easily reached by kayak. You'll find those mentioned in the chapters for each main island (for instance, you'll find Doe Island Marine State Park in the Orcas chapter, page 109).

Within these islands you'll find many marine state parks, several private preserves, and a few private islands that you'll pass on your way to somewhere else. Also included are notes on a few "residential islands," in case you find yourself the guest of a property owner or staying at a vacation rental there. Some private islands include small sections of public beach. However, "public" shorelines are only public to the mean high-tide line! Anything above that is private property, so keep out. Note that at most anchorages, boaters will be charged a moorage fee (some for all stops, some for overnight moorage only).

▼ The Shaw Island Classic sailboat race makes a circuit around its namesake island every summer.

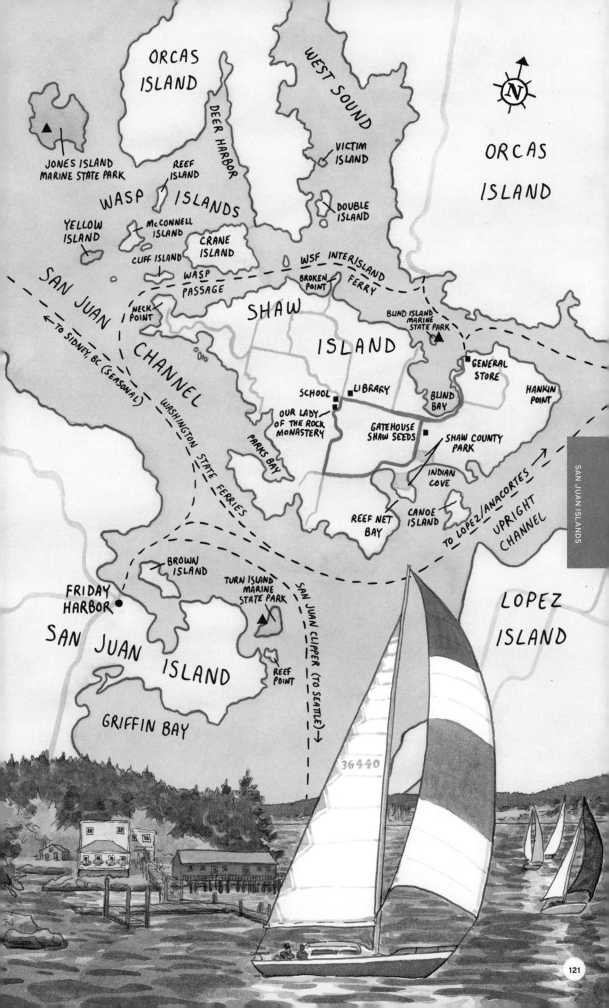

ORCAS
ISLAND

WEST SOUND

ORCAS
ISLAND

VICTIM
ISLAND

DOUBLE
ISLAND

DEER HARBOR

REEF
ISLAND

JONES ISLAND
MARINE STATE PARK

WASP ISLANDS

YELLOW
ISLAND

McCONNELL
ISLAND

CUFF ISLAND

CRANE
ISLAND

WASP
PASSAGE

WSF INTERISLAND
FERRY

BROKEN
POINT

BLIND ISLAND
MARINE
STATE PARK

NECK
POINT

SHAW

ISLAND

GENERAL
STORE

HANKIN
POINT

SAN JUAN

To SIDNEY, BC (SEASONAL)

CHANNEL

WASHINGTON STATE FERRIES

SCHOOL

LIBRARY

BLIND
BAY

OUR LADY
OF THE ROCK
MONASTERY

GATEHOUSE
SHAW SEEDS

SHAW COUNTY
PARK

PARKS BAY

INDIAN
COVE

REEF NET
BAY

CANOE
ISLAND

To LOPEZ/ANACORTES

UPRIGHT
CHANNEL

BROWN
ISLAND

TURN ISLAND
MARINE
STATE PARK

SAN JUAN CLIPPER (TO SEATTLE)

LOPEZ

ISLAND

FRIDAY
HARBOR

SAN JUAN ISLAND

REEF
POINT

GRIFFIN BAY

36440

▲ Look for Shaw's distinctive hand-carved wayfinding signage all over the island. You'll find examples nailed to the wall of the Shaw Island Library.

Other Ferry Islands

You can still take your car to Shaw, Guemes, and Lummi Islands—and you'll definitely need it if you want to visit all three on the same trip. Each relies on a completely separate ferry system with a long distance between terminals, so plan to space them out over different days or legs of your journey. Each would be great for a half-day trip, a quiet base for a vacation rental, or a jumping-off point for kayaking to one of the marine state parks in the archipelago.

A PEACEFUL RETREAT

Shaw Island, the smallest on the WSF San Juans route, is known to the Lummi people as Sq'emenen, and is part of their traditional territory. Shaw distinguished itself in the twentieth century by becoming a holy haven for Catholic religious orders. Three communities of nuns have been established here over the years. Benedictine nuns still run an active monastery and farm, and the Sisters of Mercy keep an "unofficial" retreat property here. Most well-known were the Franciscan Sisters of the Eucharist, who until 2004 ran the ferry terminal and the general store. Our Lady of the Rock Monastery does still accept visitors and farm volunteers (including overnight guests) from all faiths, on a donation basis and with notice.

While "hot spot" might be too generous a term, Shaw does have a few attractions and points of interest. Shaw General Store—the only shop on the island—has been selling local groceries and marine supplies since 1898. Adjacent Silver Bay Cottage, built in 1902, is now available for vacation rentals. At the center of the island is the public library, which also has a small historical museum onsite. Shaw County Park provides the only public beach access and boat launch—there's also a small campground here. On your way to catch your return ferry, stop at the Gatehouse Shaw Seeds stand to buy seeds for your garden.

Just offshore is three-acre Blind Island Marine State Park, a great place for a picnic and ferry watching. The small campsite here is reserved for human-powered boaters (page 60). Students can have their own private-island experience at Canoe Island French Camp, which offers immersion-style language instruction in the summer.

▼ The Shaw Island school, like those on other small islands like Waldron, Lummi, or Decatur, is still very much alive. This school educates about a dozen students in two multiage classrooms.

AN EASY JAUNT

Guemes Island, once also called Dog Island, was home to skéxe—the extinct Salish wool dog, raised for its thick, woolly fur, which was shorn for blanket weaving. Five minutes across the channel from Anacortes (via the Guemes Island Ferry), Guemes is another favorite of cyclists, without Lopez's crowds. Guemes is sleepy like Shaw, but just making a figure-eight bike loop around the island is a pleasant side trip. Here, too, the only services are at the general store, near the ferry landing.

On your loop, consider a hike up the Guemes Mountain trail for sweeping views of Padilla Bay and Mount Baker. You'll find public beach access at a handful of points, including Peach Preserve, Young's Park, and the end of Edens Road. Kelly's Point and nearby Yellow Bluff are popular landing spots for kayakers and a great place to search for agates (colorful, translucent rocks containing quartz). Guemes Island Resort, at the northern tip of the island, offers lodging with a view, free loaner kayaks and paddle boards for guests, and often better availability than shoreline resorts on the bigger islands.

CASTING A WIDER NET

At the northeastern boundary of the San Juans lies Lummi Island, connected to the mainland by its own ferry, run by Whatcom County. At just nine square miles, Lummi Island isn't exactly a tourist wonderland. But a trio of natural preserves are open to the public: Otto and Curry provide easy wooded walking trails, and the Baker Preserve offers a steep 1.6-mile hike to an overlook a thousand feet above Rosario Strait. Public beach access can be found at Church, Sunset, and Lummi Island Beaches.

The island's namesake, the Lhaq'temish (Lummi) people, have long employed a technique of open-water salmon fishing they call sxʷálə?, or reef nets. This method is unique to the Salish Sea and was invented by Coast Salish peoples at least 1,800 years ago. By anchoring canoes in pairs and suspending a large rectangular net between them in a *V* shape, the fishers create a trap that resembles a natural reef to the fish. Spotters on tall ladders help the fishers, waiting for a flood (rising) tide to bring a shoal (school) of salmon toward the boats, and signaling when to raise the nets at just the right moment to catch the fish.

Canada outlawed reef netting in 1916 and Washington imposed limits in the 1970s that forced reef netting into decline. But restrictions have eased, and some Coast Salish and even white fishers have revived reef netting. The low-tech, high-yield, passive method is considered a sustainable

▲ Like most island shops, the Guemes Island General Store has a bit of everything, plus a small cafe.

▼ Guemes Island's beaches still yield the occasional agate, while many others in the San Juans have long since been picked over by beachcombers.

and cruelty-free form of wild salmon fishing. Proponents hope it will preserve both fish populations and an ancient way of life—while still meeting consumer demand for local seafood. From Lummi you can see an example of a commercial reef netting operation offshore in Legoe Bay. You'll also find a replica reef netter canoe at the Shaw Island Library, and a reef net "graveyard" in Fisherman Bay on Lopez.

Willows Inn, once the main attraction on Lummi Island, served locally-sourced prix fixe dinners by star chef Blaine Wetzel. However, in 2021 the *New York Times* broke the story that employees had reported years of abuse, wage theft, and sexual harassment—as well as faked ingredient origins. Wetzel settled a class-action wage-theft lawsuit after a federal investigation confirmed the accusations, and the restaurant closed for good in late 2022. For a more authentic locavore experience, shop for produce at Full Bloom Farm, then stay at their loft vacation rental. You can find more island produce at the Saturday Market, and sample some of Lummi's reef-netted salmon at the Beach Store Cafe.

▲ Perhaps because of the Lummi's fishing history, buoys are a popular piece of decor on the island. Look for buoy-bedecked shacks, posts, and fences along the roadside.

OFF ON A TANGENT

Around Lummi and Guemes are a handful of small islands and related mainland attractions. Saddlebag Island Marine State Park requires a motorized boat or a strenuous kayak trip from Anacortes (camping overnight is recommended for paddlers). The Samish Nation owns and manages nearby Huckleberry Island for public day use. Undeveloped Vendovi Island is set aside as a 217-acre preserve with several hiking trails. Sinclair Island is almost entirely private, but charter services out of Anacortes offer transportation for guests and residents. Samish Island, connected to the lower Skagit Valley by road, is part of the ancestral Samish homelands. The tribe maintains a private cemetery there, as well as a multigeneration tribal summer camp. The Washington Department of Fish and Wildlife operates a small public park there called Samish Island Recreation Area. And if you *really* want to extend your adventure, you might try a trip along the Alaska Marine Highway, a ferry route with its southernmost terminus in Bellingham. From here it's possible to connect to a network of ferries bound for Juneau, Ketchikan, Glacier Bay, and beyond.

▼ Once practiced throughout the Salish Sea, reef netting in the San Juans is now done only at Lummi Island, a few seasonal spots, and at Cherry Point, near Blaine, Washington.

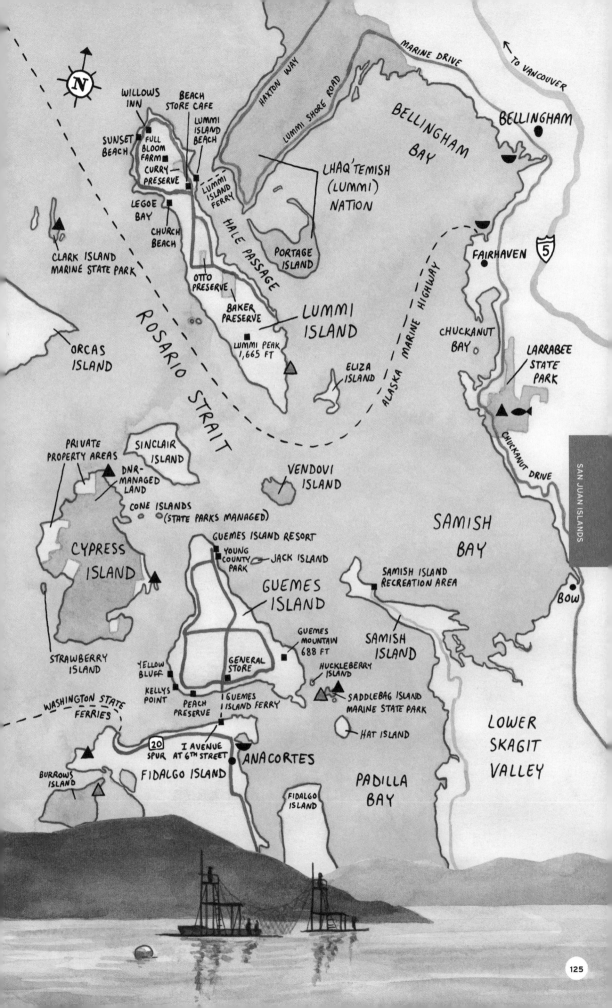

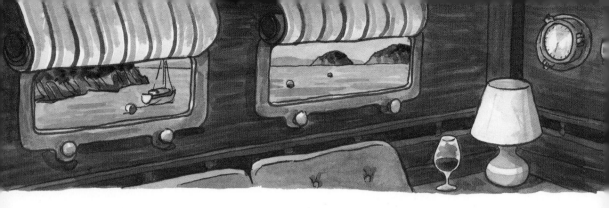

The Outer Islands

If you have the time, punctuate your San Juans adventure with a visit to what the locals call the "outer" or "non-ferry" islands. Quite a few of these are fully public, set aside as state parks or ecological preserves. Others are secluded communities carved up into small farms and housing plats. In some cases, a single party owns the entire island.

THE LOST WORLD

Cypress Island, just west of Guemes, is one of the last largely untouched islands in the San Juans. It's rarely mentioned in tourist brochures, but frequent ferry passengers know its silhouette well. Much of Cypress is open to the public as a state conservation area, managed by the Washington Department of Natural Resources (DNR). The mountainous island features pristine forests, miles of hiking trails, and the third-highest peak in the San Juans. Strawberry Island, off the western shore, and the tiny Cone Islands, just east of Cypress, are also public lands. You'll find several mooring sites, boat launches, and campsites around the island, but no potable water. There are also residents on Cypress, so be careful of public-private boundaries. Trespassing could result in the DNR revoking public access privileges.

AN ISLAND CO-OP

Decatur Island is an insulated rural enclave, but still connected to the outside world with electricity, running water, and internet. The few dozen year-round residents enjoy a laid-back, rural lifestyle and have created a community founded on mutual aid and resourcefulness. Residents even share responsibility for the island's feral sheep, organizing communal roundups for shearing and veterinary care.

If you have a reason to be here, you'll find Decatur festooned with homemade art and down-to-earth charm. The island is mostly private (including the airstrip), but there are a few amenities here for off-islanders. The sole shop on

▲ Some boaters visiting the outer islands prefer to anchor offshore, hike during the day, then return to the comfort of their vessel for eating and sleeping.

▼ The one-room Decatur Island School educates just a handful of students through the eighth grade. The fence around the school garden features a driftwood alphabet.

▶ Kimball Preserve includes Rim Island and its tombolo, as well as the rocky headlands of southern Decatur Island.

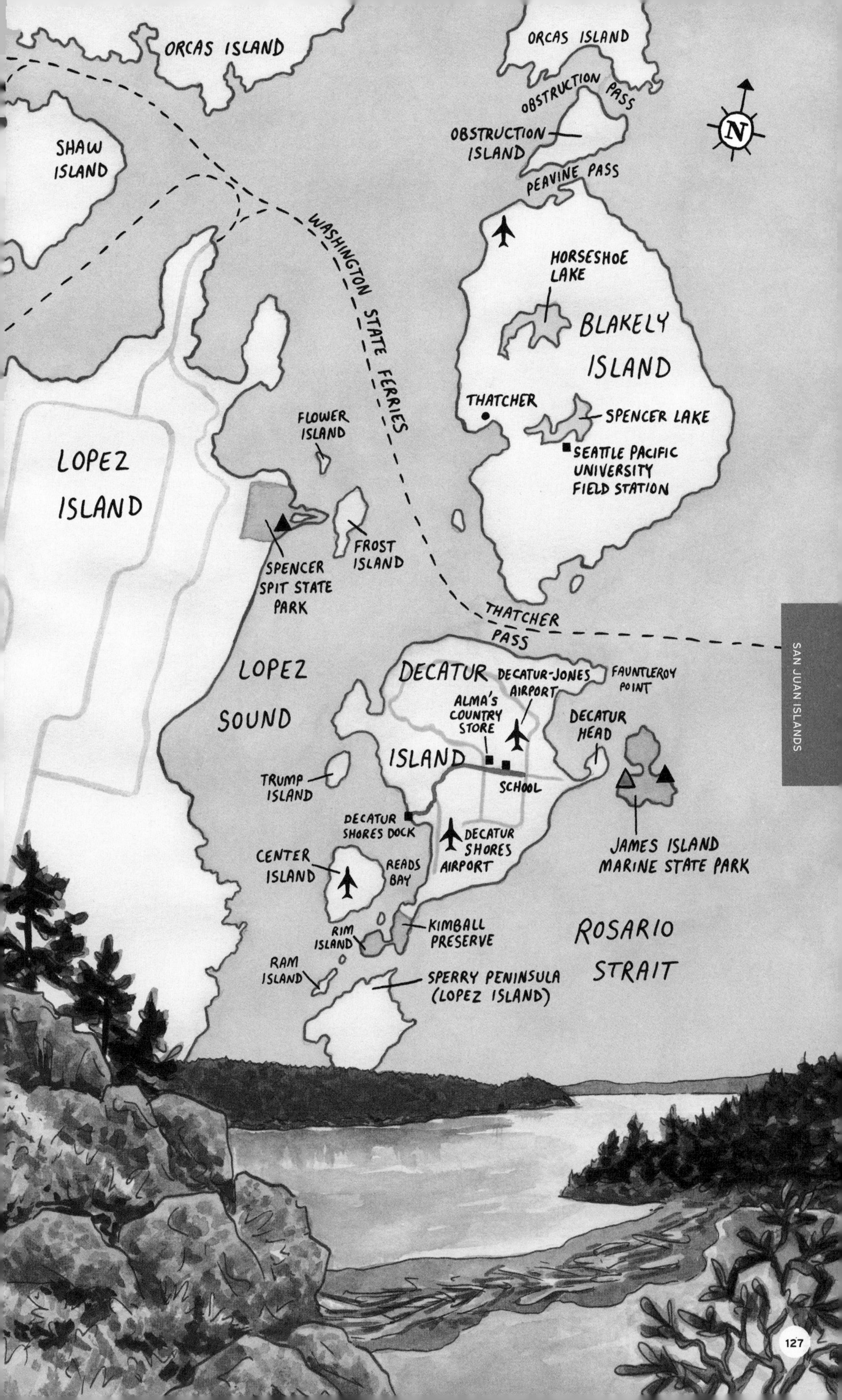

ORCAS ISLAND

ORCAS ISLAND

OBSTRUCTION PASS

OBSTRUCTION
ISLAND

PEAVINE PASS

SHAW
ISLAND

WASHINGTON STATE FERRIES

BLAKELY
ISLAND

HORSESHOE
LAKE

THATCHER

SPENCER LAKE

SEATTLE PACIFIC
UNIVERSITY
FIELD STATION

LOPEZ
ISLAND

FLOWER
ISLAND

FROST
ISLAND

SPENCER
SPIT STATE
PARK

THATCHER
PASS

LOPEZ

SOUND

DECATUR

DECATUR-JONES
AIRPORT

FAUNTLEROY
POINT

ALMA'S
COUNTRY
STORE

DECATUR
HEAD

ISLAND

TRUMP
ISLAND

SCHOOL

DECATUR
SHORES DOCK

DECATUR
SHORES
AIRPORT

JAMES ISLAND
MARINE STATE PARK

CENTER
ISLAND

READS
BAY

ROSARIO

RIM
ISLAND

KIMBALL
PRESERVE

RAM
ISLAND

SPERRY PENINSULA
(LOPEZ ISLAND)

STRAIT

127

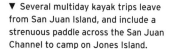

▲ Indigenous people historically did controlled burns on Yellow Island to encourage camas growth (page 175). The island was never opened to grazing—thus preventing invasive species from taking root.

▼ Several multiday kayak trips leave from San Juan Island, and include a strenuous paddle across the San Juan Channel to camp on Jones Island.

the island, Alma's Country Store, hosts an outdoor market on summer weekends and vacation-rental lodging upstairs. At the southern tip of the island is the Kimball Preserve, which offers public access for human-powered boaters (day use only; no road access). Paraclete and Island Express offer water taxi service for residents and guests.

THE LIGHT THAT NEVER WAS

What is now James Island Marine State Park was set aside as a light station in 1875, but no lighthouse was ever built. Today you'll find a few mooring buoys and campsites, and recreational fishing is a popular activity off the eastern shore. The island boasts two white-sand beaches and tranquil coves, but the hiking trails provide the only interior access to the island—everything else is an off-limits forest preserve.

ONLY FOR THE FEW

Blakely Island (not to be confused with Blake, page 69) is absolutely private and fiercely guarded by residents. However, certain Washington students and researchers might gain access here. The University of Washington Friday Harbor Laboratories monitor several sites around the island for research. And Seattle Pacific University operates a small biology field station here, with a residence hall and facilities for about two dozen students and faculty.

INTERSTITIAL ADVENTURE

A small cluster of small islands and narrow passes occupies the Wasp Passage (see the Shaw-area map on page 121). Almost all the islands are private, but the journey itself is the fun for boaters. Skilled sailors like to go "gunkholing" (cruising through shallow waters) here, but enough boaters have been been left high and dry on rocks that most are advised to steer clear. The summer interisland ferry goes this way between Friday Harbor and Orcas, giving passengers a good look—from a safe distance—at many of the islands.

ENVIRONMENTAL MICROCOSM

Another favorite of campers, Jones Island Marine State Park's varied microclimates and landscapes give it the feel of San Juan Island—in miniature. Here you'll find rare brittle prickly pear cacti, mossy nurse logs, a small heritage orchard, and a tiny "library" located in—no, really—the restroom. One trail here is ADA accessible, and there's potable water available in the summer for your convenience.

A CARPET OF COLOR

The only other Wasp Passage island with public access (but no water or restrooms!) is Yellow Island, owned by the Nature Conservancy as a wildflower and native grassland preserve. Caretakers estimate that fully a quarter of all flower species native to the San Juans can be found here. Paddle out in May for peak blooms; landing is allowed on the south shore only. Overnight visits and pets are prohibited; groups of more than six people need written permission to visit.

ALMOST CANADA

Stuart Island lies at the very northwestern edge of the archipelago, just three miles from the nearest shore of the Canadian Gulf Islands (page 158). Experienced kayakers may overcome the tidal currents and rocky shoals to get here from Roche Harbor on San Juan Island, but everyone else should arrive by water taxi.

Here you'll find Stuart Island Marine State Park, which occupies part but not all of the island's acreage—be especially mindful of public and private land boundaries. Roads and trails wind around an old schoolhouse called the Teacherage Museum, a historic cemetery, and Turn Point Lighthouse (whose mule barn is illustrated on page 135). There's also a fairly large campground, plus an excellent sheltered bay for anchorage. Just offshore, Satellite Island is owned by the YMCA, and Johns Island is home to Camp Nor'wester, a four-week summer youth camp.

▼ Boating in Haro Strait provides stunning views of Lover's Leap, the sheer cliffs located near the northwestern tip of Stuart Island.

SAN JUAN ISLANDS

PRIVATE SAFARI

Nearly treeless Spieden Island—called Safari Island in the 1970s and '80s—is easily recognized from northern San Juan Island. Its owners introduced herds of exotic game here for hunting. Today it is owned by James Jannard, founder of Oakley sunglasses, as a private wildlife sanctuary. There is no public access to Spieden, but you might just glimpse a ram climbing its grassy slopes from your boat as you pass.

THE MINI VEGGIE BASKET

Off-grid Waldron Island has about a hundred residents and a few farms that supply the bigger islands. To visit the interior, you'll need to be a guest of a resident. There is a post office and public dock in Cowlitz Bay, and Point Disney is now a preserve—prospective visitors must contact the San Juan Preservation Trust for access permission. Nearby Skipjack and Bare Islands are part of the San Juan Islands National Wildlife Refuge—landing there is prohibited.

THE NORTHERN BOUNDARY

A necklace of small islands forms the northern frontier of the San Juans in the Strait of Georgia—the largest of these are marine state parks. Though North Beach on Orcas is just a few nautical miles away, tidal currents make for a very long paddle. Most opt to sail, motor, or hire a water taxi out to these islands, and then take small kayak outings from there.

▲ A trio of exotic game species still survive on Spieden Island: sika deer from Asia, fallow deer from Europe, and mouflon sheep from the Eurasian Caspian region.

▼ Orcas Island is not drawn to scale on this map—it has been widened.

▲ Patos Island Lighthouse is the northernmost point in the San Juan Islands. Its still-active beacon has a sibling on the Canadian side of the border—East Point Lighthouse (page 164) on Saturna Island.

PATOS ISLAND LIGHTHOUSE

LITTLE PATOS ISLAND

PATOS ISLAND
MARINE STATE PARK

STRAIT OF GEORGIA

SUCIA ISLAND
MARINE STATE PARK

WATER TAXI

PARKER REEF

ROLFE COVE

PUFFIN ISLAND

MATIA ISLAND
MARINE STATE PARK

N

POINT DOUGHTY

NORTH BEACH

BRANDT'S LANDING MARINA

ORCAS ISLAND AIRPORT

EASTSOUND

ORCAS ISLAND

BARNES ISLAND

LONE TREE ISLAND

CLARK ISLAND
MARINE STATE PARK

THE SISTERS

(Pro tip: water taxis often cost the same for one passenger as for five or six, so travel in a group!) Parker Reef, located partway between Orcas and Sucia, is a popular recreational fishing spot for immature ("blackmouth") Chinook salmon.

THE ODD DUCK OUT

The name for Patos Island, the outermost of the San Juans, comes from the Spanish word for "duck." The 1893 light-house at Alden Point provides picture-postcard views from the water. Landing on Patos Island Marine State Park is a bit tricky, as there is no dock and only two mooring buoys— any approaching craft must land directly onshore. This remote park, like many others, features trails, campsites, and pit toilets, but no potable water. As at all marine state parks, pack in everything you need, and pack out all trash.

HERE BE DRAGONS

Horseshoe-shaped Sucia Island gets its name from the Span-ish word for "dirty," referring to the mess of reefs and jagged rocks that fouled up eighteenth-century shore landings. In the nineteenth century, the island was a haven for human traffickers smuggling Chinese laborers to the mainland, and rumrunners sneaking booze in from Canada during Prohibi-tion in the 1920s and '30s.

Today, Sucia is a hands-down favorite among weekend sailors, beginner kayakers, geology buffs, and painters. It is also one of the most popular of Washington's state parks, with more than 100,000 visitors a year. People flock here for the nautical fun and the views, and especially the spec-tacular Chuckanut sandstone formations that line the bays all over the island. These include wind-sculpted holes and hollows, curling rock waves, dragon-like silhouettes, and golden stone honeycombs. And in 2012 scientists found a "dragon" when they dug up a dinosaur femur there.

Sucia Island Marine State Park is spread around six bays and several small finger islands, and offers many campsites and mooring buoys (first-come, first-served;

▲ Most of the marine state parks are unmanned, so boaters and campers must self-register. Carry cash with you to pay for moorage and campsite fees more easily.

▼ Sucia Island's sandstone was once quarried for cobblestones for Seattle's streets. In many places the stone is weathered into a series of round hollows called tafoni.

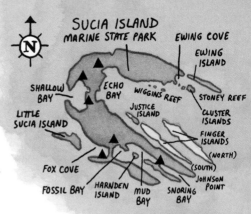

▶ Everything shown in beige on this map is outside the boundaries of Sucia Island Marine State Park. These areas are privately owned and off-limits to the public.

"saving spots" is illegal). Sucia is the only island in this chain that has potable water available. If you don't have your own boat, Outer Island Excursions runs a daily water taxi here from Brandt's Landing Marina on Orcas Island.

CONSULT THE RULE BOOK

Windswept Matia Island's name, which means "no protection" in Spanish, is well earned. Now uninhabited, it (along with Sucia) was once used for fox farming. And from the 1890s until 1921 it was home to recluse and mail-order mystic Elvin Smith, the "Hermit of Matia." At the age of eighty-six, he was lost at sea returning from a regular supply run from Orcas, where he picked up letters from his long-distance faith-healing customers.

In 1959 Matia Island Marine State Park was established, in part to protect a grove of old-growth trees. Due to its protected habitat areas, Matia has more rules and restrictions than its neighbors. The campground on Rolfe Cove has just a handful of sites, and fires are prohibited. In addition to the campsites, the park includes a loop trail, picnic area, and the beaches below the mean high tide mark. The rest of the island is "wilderness area" and closed to visitors. Puffin Island, just offshore, is also out of bounds.

BEACHY-KEEN

Clark Island Marine State Park boasts some of the only sandy beaches in the San Juan Islands. This popular weekend spot, which is also a favorite stopover point for long-haul kayakers, features a number of mooring spots for boats, and several campsites. Nearby Barnes Island is private, and Lone Tree Island and the Sisters are off-limits as parts of the national wildlife refuge. You can sometimes hear the cacophony of their nesting seabirds from Clark Island.

SAN JUAN ISLANDS

Barn Beauty

Some of Washington's best architecture can be found not in cities, but down on the farm. Most of the state's islands were farmed beginning in the mid-nineteenth century, and many historic or unusual barn structures still stand. Several are protected as state heritage landmarks.

▼ NO TRESPASSING. Nearly all of the islands' barns are on private property—make sure you stick to public roads. Some, like the Biendl Barn, can be best viewed by boat or kayak!

CROCKETT BARN (1895), WHIDBEY ISLAND

▲ REPURPOSED FOR SURVIVAL. Many barns have been converted for nonagricultural uses, like wedding venues, event centers, or even private homes.

JOHN BIENDL BARN (c. 1910), SHAW ISLAND

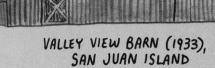

VALLEY VIEW BARN (1933), SAN JUAN ISLAND

▼ ROOFLINES GALORE. Historic barns come in a number of distinctive architectural styles. Not every form is represented in the Salish Sea region, but you'll find many different types here, often within the same island.

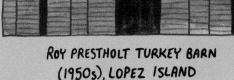

ROY PRESTHOLT TURKEY BARN (1950s), LOPEZ ISLAND

GABLE

BROKEN GABLE

GAMBREL

HIP

MONITOR (WESTERN)

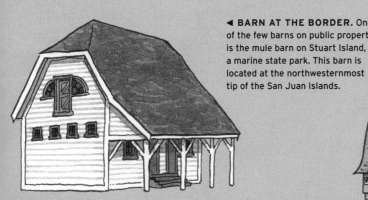

◀ BARN AT THE BORDER. One of the few barns on public property is the mule barn on Stuart Island, a marine state park. This barn is located at the northwesternmost tip of the San Juan Islands.

TURN POINT LIGHTHOUSE MULE BARN (c. 1891), STUART ISLAND

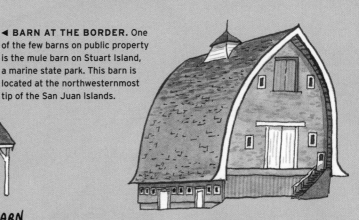

WALDRIP BARN (1918), ORCAS ISLAND

▼ CHECK THE LIST. Washington State maintains the Heritage Barns Register, a list of more than seven hundred historic structures statewide. More than sixty of these barns reside in the islands.

▼ USEFUL BEAUTY. Barns are often red because farmers once made cheap, long-lasting barn paint with lime and iron oxide. The rust killed fungi and moss and was an effective sealant.

KRISTOFERSON DAIRY BARN (1914), CAMANO ISLAND

NASHI ORCHARDS BARN (1970s), VASHON ISLAND

BARN TURNED INTO RESIDENTIAL HOME (1905, CONVERTED 2005), BAINBRIDGE ISLAND

HAMBLY APPLE HOUSE (1900), ORCAS ISLAND

GABLE-ON-HIP

GOTHIC

BANK

SALTBOX

ROUND

DUTCH

PART 3 BRITISH

Canada's west-coast province is home to more than forty thousand islands—the most populous and accessible of these lie in or around the Salish Sea. While BC's island world is too vast for any one chapter to contain, you'll find ideas here to inspire a bonus or side trip to your Salish Sea adventure. The Canadian islands have much in common with Washington's, so to avoid redundancy, this section focuses on natural and cultural attractions that are unique or iconic BC experiences.

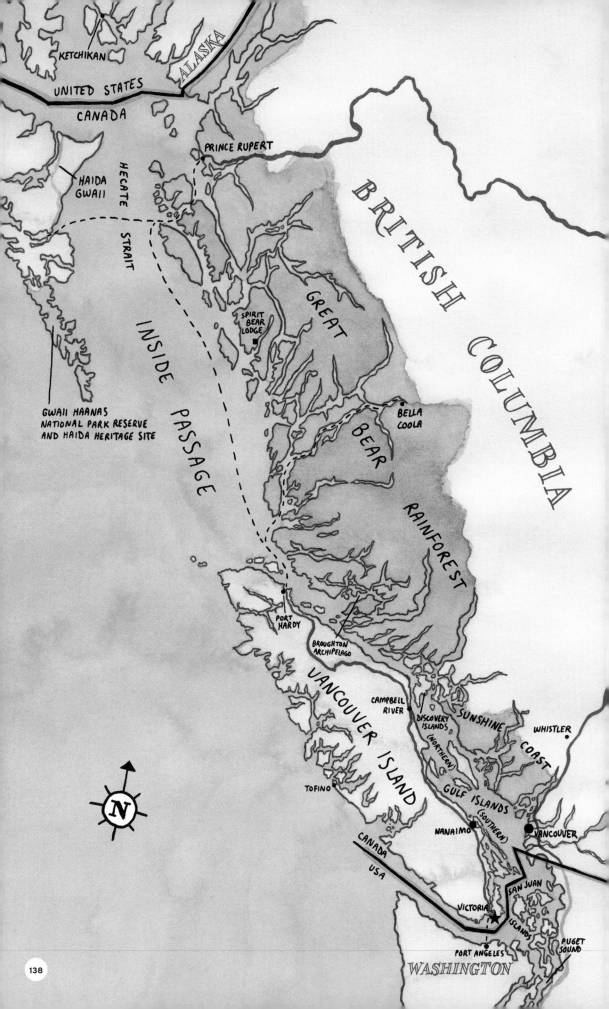

KETCHIKAN

ALASKA

UNITED STATES

CANADA

PRINCE RUPERT

HAIDA
GWAII

HECATE

STRAIT

BRITISH COLUMBIA

GREAT

SPIRIT
BEAR
LODGE

BELLA
COOLA

INSIDE

PASSAGE

BEAR

RAINFOREST

GWAII HAANAS
NATIONAL PARK RESERVE
AND HAIDA HERITAGE SITE

PORT
HARDY

BROUGHTON
ARCHIPELAGO

CAMPBELL
RIVER

SUNSHINE

DISCOVERY
ISLANDS

(NORTHERN)

COAST

WHISTLER

VANCOUVER ISLAND

GULF ISLANDS

(SOUTHERN)

TOFINO

NANAIMO

VANCOUVER

N

CANADA

USA

SAN JUAN

VICTORIA

ISLANDS

PUGET
SOUND

PORT ANGELES

WASHINGTON

Over the past two centuries, colonialism and capitalism put the Salish Sea on the world stage. Spanish explorers, English tycoons, Asian laborers, ancient coastal trade routes, and European settlers all left their mark. Local Indigenous peoples (or "First Nations," as they are called in Canada), for a time, grew their own wealth through these relationships, before disease and land theft turned the outsiders' presence into a curse. Even today, BC's global influences are everywhere. You'll find Kwakwaka'wakw carvings beside English lawn bowlers, bagpipers under Chinese dragon gates, and rodeos near Hawaiian food trucks. This cultural mix has even attracted Hollywood—BC has been a film and television backdrop for many years, and you might find yourself experiencing a bit of déjà vu because of it.

American travelers will note several cultural and functional differences in BC, beginning with a spelling lesson. As a Commonwealth nation, Canada uses British English. Local signage often includes Indigenous names, sometimes spelled without capital letters. Calendar differences may also affect your holiday plans: Canada Day is July 1, and Canadian Thanksgiving is the second Monday of October.

Unlike Washington State, every inch of shoreline (15,985 miles of it!) in British Columbia is public land, to just above the high-water mark. However, that doesn't mean that *access* from land is guaranteed. Steep staircases and rough trails down to the beach are common. Boaters will also find many public marine provincial parks (like marine state parks, labeled "Marine P.P." on maps) to choose from.

Ferries have their own rules and restrictions. Like WSF, many BC Ferries routes allow reservations and some fares are collected one way only. However, with huge demand and many destinations, the BC Ferries reservation system tends to be complicated and expensive—plan for delays too. Those crossing into Canada in their own boats will need to clear customs at their chosen port of entry.

And, of course, Canada has its own currency, so you'll need to decide your strategy for handling cash, ATMs, credit cards, and foreign transaction fees. The exchange rate is often favorable for American travelers, but still, get ready to spend some serious cash. Costs in BC tend to run high, particularly in Victoria and remote areas.

▶ The Big Tree Trail on Meares Island, just a ten-minute water taxi ride from Tofino (page 151), is home to some of the largest old-growth evergreens in British Columbia.

VANCOUVER ISLAND

Even if you're just passing through, a BC sojourn will likely introduce you to Vancouver Island. At 456 kilometers (283 miles) long, it is home to both large cities and remote wilderness landscapes. Mountain ranges divide the island into different climate zones, from sodden temperate rain forests along the west coast to mild Mediterranean regions. Many areas, even a "short" (as the crow flies) distance from a city, are sparsely populated or uninhabited, and cell coverage is inconsistent. Also, tourist bureaus love to tout BC's wild animal population—but some also advertise destinations *safe* from it. Plan ahead to know what to expect where.

PAGE 154

BC FERRIES

QUEEN CHARLOTTE STRAIT

BROUGHTON ARCHIPELAGO

JOHNSTONE STRAIT

SAYWARD

PORT HARDY

CAPE SCOTT

CAPE SCOTT PROVINCIAL PARK (P.P.)

COAL HARBOUR

19

PORT McNEILL

TELEGRAPH COVE

NIMPKISH LAKE

LITTLE HUSON CAVE PARK

WOSS

PORT ALICE

VANCOUVER ISLAND

GOLD RIVER

28

MQUQWIN/ BROOKS PENINSULA PROVINCIAL PARK

N

NOOTKA ISLAND

HESQUIAT PENINSULA P.P.

PACIFIC OCEAN

MAQUINNA MARINE P.P.

There are no bridges to Vancouver Island, so water and air travel provide the only access. Entry points from the United States are Sidney (page 146) and Victoria (page 142), while BC Ferries arrive at Swartz Bay (page 160), Nanaimo (page 149), Comox (page 176), or Port Hardy (page 155).

Once you get here, you'll find that getting from point A to B might have to include stops at X, Y, and Z. Island regions are not generally contiguous to one another, and many routes are long spurs, rather than loops. Be prepared for a lot of doubling back if you'd like to explore each coast of the island. You'll find public bus transit and ride-hailing services only between Victoria and Nanaimo, and on the Saanich Peninsula (page 146). For all other destinations, you'll need your own transportation. Roads here twist around rugged coastlines and steep slopes. Gravel logging and park roads are seldom maintained and notorious for frequent potholes that can disable a low-clearance vehicle. Drive slowly, take safety precautions, plan to be self-sufficient when necessary, and pack accordingly (page 16)!

▲ Vancouver Island is home to rare "sea wolves." Coastal wolves are smaller and leaner than their mainland cousins, thanks to their penchant for swimming and their mostly seafood diet.

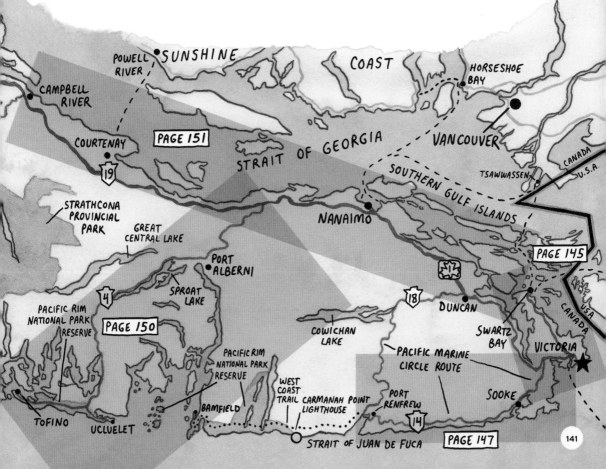

▲ What many tourists now call "high tea" is historically a laborer's meal served at a high table or counter. The Empress Hotel actually serves "afternoon tea," which is traditionally a more formal, elegant affair.

▼ The Empress Hotel (below) and BC Parliament Buildings (opposite) were designed by architect Francis Mawson Rattenbury, when he was just twenty-five and thirty-six years old, respectively.

A CULTURAL PASTICHE

Victoria, the provincial capital, includes a sizable city core and a sprawling ring of suburbs and parklands. The historic, walkable downtown surrounds the picturesque Inner Harbour. You'll find a world of dining options here, and a great way to explore both the city and its global delicacies is to take a food tour. A Taste of Victoria offers on-foot tasting tours of the city, starting at the Victoria Public Market.

OLDE-ENGLISH STYLE

In the nineteenth century Victoria was a trading outpost for the English corporation Hudson's Bay Company (HBC), which still exists today. Victoria's architecture provides a visual link to England, especially the BC Parliament Buildings, Abigail's Hotel, and Craigdarroch Castle. Two cornerstones of local cuisine are also British: pubs and tea. Garrick's Head, Irish Times, and—BC's oldest—Six Mile Pub & Eatery offer some of the best pub fare, and the Empress Hotel hosts the city's most famous teatime. Traditionally served around four o'clock, afternoon tea service here runs all day. Reservations are highly recommended.

POUTINE ON THE RITZ

Here you'll find one uniquely Canadian dish: poutine, a hot mess of French fries, cheese curds, and gravy. This Quebecois treat is now ubiquitous throughout Canada. In Victoria you'll find food-truck fare at Red Fish Blue Fish, or a fancy version with duck confit at Heron Rock Bistro. You'll even find vegan poutine at Very Good Butchers. For the most authentic head to La Belle Patate in nearby Esquimalt. Or scarf your fries for charity each autumn at the annual Poutine with Purpose festival.

TRADITION AND TRAGEDY

What is now Victoria is the homeland of several Coast Salish peoples, who today strive for recognition and inclusion after two centuries of erasure and genocide. In 1862, while a

ELK LAKE

17A

↑ TO SIDNEY/SWARTZ BAY

DOMINION ASTROPHYSICAL OBSERVATORY

← TO BUTCHART GARDENS

HORTICULTURE CENTRE OF THE PACIFIC

MOUNT DOUGLAS PARK

17

SAANICH

← TO GOLDSTREAM P.P./NANAIMO

PORTAGE INLET

VIEW ROYAL

1

ESQUIMALT GORGE PARK

SELKIRK WATER

UPPER HARBOUR

14

ESQUIMALT HARBOUR

SONGHEES FIRST NATION

ESQUIMALT

ESQUIMALT FIRST NATION

SONGHEES WALKWAY

CHINATOWN

INNER HARBOUR

OAK BAY

BICKFORD TOWER

MIDDLE HARBOUR

BERENS ISLAND LIGHTHOUSE

FISHERMAN'S WHARF

CRAIGDARROCH CASTLE

ABKHAZI GARDEN

HATLEY PARK

ESQUIMALT LAGOON

FISGARD LIGHTHOUSE

FORT RODD HILL NATIONAL HISTORIC SITE

OUTER HARBOUR

JAMES BAY

DETAIL

BEACON HILL PARK

GOVERNMENT HOUSE

ROSS BAY

CHINESE CEMETERY

COBURG PENINSULA

STRAIT OF JUAN DE FUCA

OGDEN POINT BREAKWATER LIGHTHOUSE

HOLLAND POINT PARK

CLOVER POINT PARK

TRIAL ISLANDS LIGHTHOUSE

COLWOOD

VICTORIA

BLACK BALL FERRY

TO PORT ANGELES ↓

DETAIL:

UPPER HARBOUR

CHINATOWN

FAN TAN ALLEY

VICTORIA PUBLIC MARKET

BASTION SQUARE

DOUGLAS STREET

JOHNSON STREET

INNER HARBOUR

WHARF STREET

GOVERNMENT STREET

EAGLE FEATHER GALLERY

JAMES BAY

MARITIME MUSEUM OF BC

EMPRESS HOTEL

ABIGAIL'S HOTEL

BC PARLIAMENT BUILDINGS

ROYAL BC MUSEUM

THUNDERBIRD PARK

1

DETAIL

JAMES BAY NEIGHBORHOOD

HOLLAND POINT PARK

EMILY CARR HOUSE

BEACON HILL PARK

"MILE ZERO" TERMINUS OF TRANSCANADA HIGHWAY

N

WELCOME TO VICTORIA

▲ Built in 1981, the Gate of Harmonious Interest at the east entrance to Chinatown is one of Victoria's most famous landmarks.

▶ The twelve-pointed Star Pond at the Butchart Gardens was once used to show off Robert Butchart's prize menagerie of exotic waterfowl.

▼ Visit Hatley Park in the spring to see its many bulbs in bloom.

smallpox epidemic raged in Victoria, white authorities forcibly relocated infected Indigenous people—decimating populations all the way up the coast to Haida Gwaii (page 155) by as much as 70 percent. You can begin tracing this history in the collections at the Royal BC Museum. (The museum also houses paintings of Haida Gwaii's famous totem poles by white Canadian artist Emily Carr.) Nearby Thunderbird Park contains a number of historic totem and house poles. And in June, which is National Indigenous History Month, visit the annual Victoria Indigenous Cultural Festival for food tastings, performances, artisan demonstrations, and more.

RED LANTERNS AND GOLDEN GATES

Chinese immigrants have lived and worked on Vancouver Island since the late eighteenth century, and Victoria is home to Canada's oldest Chinatown. For a (literal) taste, start with dim sum at Don Mee. Stroll down Fan Tan Alley (originally a gambling district named for a Chinese game of chance), the narrowest street in Canada. Then check out the beautiful Chinese Public School building, built in 1909. If you visit in late winter, don't miss the lion dances held to ring in the lunar new year. In August you can catch a race at the Victoria Dragon Boat Festival. Or visit a summer night market—an evening food or artisan fair with roots in medieval China—located downtown or in Oak Bay, which is also home to a historic Chinese cemetery.

HOW DOES YOUR GARDEN GROW?

The local rain-shadow climate (page 44) has blessed Victoria with perfect flower-growing conditions, earning it the nickname of the Garden City. You'll find lush estate gardens at Government House and Abkhazi Garden. Beacon Hill Park features native wildflower meadows, and gardeners will love the nine-acre Horticulture Centre of the Pacific. Make time for Hatley Park National Historic Site in Colwood. The Edwardian estate is divided into a series of formal gardens

SALT SPRING ISLAND

PAUQUACHIN FIRST NATION

PIERS ISLAND

BC FERRIES

SWARTZ BAY

COAL ISLAND

MORESBY ISLAND

BRETHOUR ISLAND

COMET ISLAND

GOOCH ISLAND

DOMVILLE ISLAND

LITTLE GROUP ISLANDS

FORREST ISLAND

ISLE-DE-LIS

TURN POINT LIGHTHOUSE

STUART ISLAND

SAN JUAN ISLANDS

WASHINGTON (USA)

BRITISH COLUMBIA (CANADA)

HENRY ISLAND

(SEASONAL)

TSEYCUM FIRST NATION

VICTORIA INTERNATIONAL AIRPORT

SIDNEY

WASHINGTON STATE FERRIES

SIDNEY SPIT

SAANICH INLET

MILL BAY

MALAHAT FIRST NATION

NORTH SAANICH

PAUQUACHIN FIRST NATION

SAANICHTON

PRIVATE FERRY

JAMES ISLAND

SIDNEY ISLAND

BC FERRIES

TSARTLIP FIRST NATION

TSAWOUT FIRST NATION

GULF ISLANDS NATIONAL PARK RESERVE

DARCY ISLAND

BAMBERTON PROVINCIAL PARK

BRENTWOOD BAY

BUTCHART GARDENS

FINLAYSON ARM

GOWLLAND TOD PROVINCIAL PARK

MOUNT WORK REGIONAL PARK

ELK LAKE

17A

CORDOVA BAY

N

HARO STRAIT

MALAHAT SUMMIT

SQUALLY REACH

17

MOUNT DOUGLAS PARK

THETIS LAKE REGIONAL PARK

SAANICH

CADBORO BAY

CHATHAM ISLANDS

GOLDSTREAM PROVINCIAL PARK

UNIVERSITY OF VICTORIA

UPLANDS PARK

1

OAK BAY

PACIFIC MARINE CIRCLE ROUTE

14

TO SOOKE

ESQUIMALT

DISCOVERY ISLAND MARINE P.P. AND LIGHTHOUSE

VICTORIA

COLWOOD

▲ "Rail trails" like the Galloping Goose are flat and smooth enough to allow cyclists to enjoy the scenery as well as the ride. Keep a sharp eye out for a rare sighting of the northern flying squirrel.

SOOKE DETAIL

SOOKE POTHOLES PROVINCIAL PARK

GALLOPING GOOSE TRAIL

17 MILE HOUSE PUB

MILNES LANDING

14

TRIANGLE ISLAND LIGHTHOUSE

T'SOU-KE FIRST NATION

SOOKE BASIN

BOARDWALK

SOOKE

EAST SOOKE

WHIFFIN SPIT LIGHTHOUSE

SOOKE HARBOUR HOUSE

EAST SOOKE REGIONAL PARK

PARKING AREA

T'SOU-KE FIRST NATION

N

SEAL PETROGLYPH

begun in 1908. Or start your own garden or urban farm with supplies from Buckerfield's in Saanichton.

The jewel in Greater Victoria's floral crown is the Butchart Gardens on the Saanich Peninsula. This UNESCO World Heritage Site and motherlode of formal gardens was shaped by one woman's vision. Jennie Butchart turned her husband's exhausted limestone quarry into a feat of landscape design, land reclamation, and horticulture. In 1908 the Butcharts named their attached family estate Benvenuto (Italian for "welcome"), and Jennie's hospitality became legend. She reportedly served eighteen thousand cups of tea to visitors before her family convinced her to charge admission. Today the gardens are open year-round and are spectacular in every season. Plan to spend a whole day here, and stick around for afternoon tea or an illuminated night tour.

PORTS OF CALL

Waterways dominate Victoria's geography and culture. Tour the Inner Harbour on one of the tiny "pickle boats" (page 10) run by Harbour Ferries, take a guided kayak paddle with Victoria Waterfront Tours, or visit the Maritime Museum of British Columbia. In August see the Victoria Symphony perform on the water at the Symphony Splash free concert (pro tip: kayakers get the best seats!). Or stroll along the three-mile scenic waterfront boardwalk called the Songhees Walkway, which starts near the Johnson Street Bridge.

The Saanich Peninsula flanks the first of many fjords you might encounter in BC. Along the eastern shore is sprawling Gowlland Tod Provincial Park. At the head is Goldstream Provincial Park, a wonderland of woods and waterfalls. On the western shore is tiny Bamberton Provincial Park, accessible by ferry from Brentwood Bay, near the Butchart Gardens.

OF BOOKS AND BOATS

At the other end of the Saanich Peninsula is the town of Sidney, which, along with nearby Swartz Bay, offers ferry access to the Gulf Islands (page 158), the BC mainland, and Friday Harbor (page 88). Before you board your boat, check out the Shaw Centre for the Salish Sea—part aquarium, part cultural center. Stroll the Waterfront Walkway and look for sea glass on the tiny beach nearby. Or visit one of many bookstores and reading-friendly cafes that earned Sidney its designation as one of Canada's two official "Book Towns" (the other is St. Martins, New Brunswick).

ISLANDS GALORE, JUST OFFSHORE

A few marine parks in the southernmost Gulf Islands are most easily reached from Sidney or Greater Victoria. From Sidney a summer ferry runs to Sidney and Portland (page 168) Islands. If you have your own boat, you can access D'Arcy and Discovery Islands. D'Arcy was a leper colony for Chinese laborers from 1894 to 1924 and has a haunted reputation. Half of Discovery Island is a Songhees First Nation reserve, so respect tribal property rights and heed the park boundary.

THE SOUTHERN LOOP

The easiest way to see southern Vancouver Island is to follow the Pacific Marine Circle Route out of Victoria. This well-marked, 260-kilometer (160-mile) network of connected highways takes you past worthwhile coastal sights. Take a short detour (map on page 143) to Fort Rodd Hill National Historic Site, which preserves an 1890s Royal Navy fort. Adjacent is Fisgard Lighthouse, one of BC's oldest beacons (illustration on page 185).

At the bottom of the island is historic Sooke, the traditional home of the T'Sou-ke people. After white settlement, the area was a hub for gold miners, loggers, and the railroad—whose tracks have become the Galloping Goose bike trail. Stop for a pint at the 17 Mile House Pub, built in 1894 and named for its distance from Victoria. Then stroll along the Sooke Marine Boardwalk Trail or dine at Sooke Harbour House. Explore nearby Sooke Potholes Provincial Park, home to a series of deep freshwater pools carved into rock by glaciers. Across the bay is East Sooke Regional Park, offering hikes with views of the Strait of Juan de Fuca.

A STRING OF BEACHES

Continue along the road to Port Renfrew, and stop at any number of scenic beaches along the way. French Beach Provincial Park is a popular choice for a seaside picnic spot. Mystic, China, and Botanical Beaches are all worth the hike required to reach them—the former features a rope

▲ Follow East Sooke Regional Park's Coast Trail to Alldridge Point to find a cluster of petroglyphs. This ancient seal may have been carved up to three thousand years ago. As a Provincial Heritage Site, touching and taking rubbings of the image are prohibited.

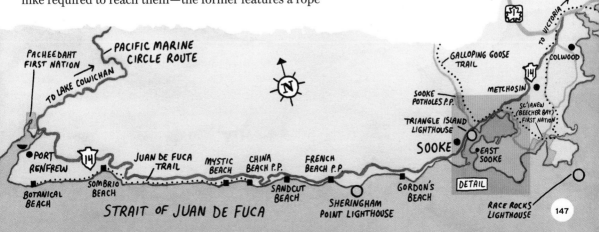

swing over the sand, a favorite selfie spot for visitors. Visit Botanical Beach at low tide to explore the many tide pools that pockmark the sandstone shore. Port Renfrew itself is the last stop before the Pacific Marine Circle Route turns inland. The tourist infrastructure here is Wild Renfrew, offering both suites and cottage lodging, whale-watching tours, and meals at Renfrew Pub and Coastal Kitchen Cafe.

▲ Cowichan Bay was the first town in North America to become a designated Cittaslow community, part of a worldwide movement dedicated to local cuisine and a slower pace of life.

WALKING THE WEST COAST

Thanks to the geography, you can't simply drive up the whole west coast of the island. But if you're an experienced backpacker, you can hike from Port Renfrew to Bamfield (map on page 141). The West Coast Trail is one of the most popular (and difficult, and expensive!) of several long-distance hiking trails on Vancouver Island. Running seventy-five kilometers (forty-seven miles), it has thirteen campsites and several lighthouses along the way—as well as many wooden ladders you must climb. Carry everything you need, as there are no services. The trail is open in summer only, and reservations are required and limited in number. If you're looking for a more beginner-friendly hike, try the Juan de Fuca Marine Trail between China and Botanical Beaches.

▼ Traditional Cowichan sweaters are known for their bold, nature-inspired motifs and their use of handspun, undyed wool in contrasting shades.

If you want to explore more of the west coast by car, you'll have to zigzag up to Port Alberni (page 150). For this reason, west coast destinations are broken up throughout this chapter, based on the routes that connect them to the rest of Vancouver Island.

HERE COMES THE SUN

The last section of the Pacific Marine Circle Route crosses the Cowichan region, the warmest and only true Mediterranean climate zone in Canada. Its Coast Salish name, Quw'utsun, translates to "warm land." Oddly, perhaps, the most famous symbol of this balmy region is a bulky winter sweater, a traditional craft of the Cowichan peoples. Before knitting and sheep arrived in the nineteenth century, Cowichan weavers created pictorial textiles from fibers shorn from mountain goats and wool dogs (page 123). In the past seventy years

The map shows locations including: NANAIMO, PETROGLYPH P.P., COWICHAN LAKE, TS'UUBAA-ASATX FIRST NATION, LADYSMITH, LAKE COWICHAN, CHEMAINUS, PACHEEDAHT FIRST NATION, CROFTON, PACIFIC OCEAN, PACIFIC MARINE CIRCLE ROUTE, WESTHOLME TEA COMPANY, PORT RENFREW, DUNCAN, BLUE GROUSE ESTATE WINERY, COWICHAN BAY, COBBLE HILL, MILL BAY, SIDNEY, CANADA, USA, SOUTHERN GULF ISLANDS, VICTORIA, SAN JUAN ISLANDS

or so, non-Indigenous brands have co-opted the Cowichan sweater into a Canadian souvenir—but the real thing is a beauty to behold. To purchase knitted goods that actually support Indigenous craftspeople, look for the trademarked Genuine Cowichan label.

Agritourism has become another Cowichan hallmark, as the mild climate has nurtured several farm-to-table restaurants, wineries, and distilleries. Visit perennial favorites Blue Grouse Estate Winery and Merridale Cidery & Distillery. Or steep yourself in the unusual terroir of Westholme Tea Company, the only commercial tea farm in Canada.

COASTAL COWICHAN

Cowichan also includes part of the eastern shore, around Nanaimo. Vancouver Island's main highways and towns run up this coast (map on page 151), so even if your trip includes other parts of the island, you'll still end up here at intervals.

Don't miss the waterfront community of Cowichan Bay, with its buildings perched on wooden pilings and its collection of hand-built wooden boats. Nearby Duncan, nicknamed the City of Totems, has thirty-eight contemporary Indigenous totem poles arranged in a self-guided walking tour. Ladysmith also offers the self-guided Heritage Walk, featuring historic buildings from the town's origin as a coal-mining town named Oyster Harbour. Last is Nanaimo, Vancouver Island's second-largest city. History buffs should stroll through the Old City Quarter, then stop at the Bastion, an 1852 wooden blockhouse. And if Sooke whet your whistle for petroglyphs, you can find one of the island's highest concentrations of them at Petroglyph Provincial Park. Finish your tour with a Nanaimo bar—a sweet snack of a coconut-graham crust topped with layers of custard and chocolate.

Nanaimo is a major ferry hub. From here you can catch a BC Ferries boat to Horseshoe Bay (page 178), Tsawwassen, and Gabriola Island (page 166). Or hop the Snuneymuxw First Nation's foot ferry to Saysutshun (Newcastle Island), a popular summer destination (page 168).

▼ In the ultimate nod to Norway, Old Country Market comes complete with a herd of goats nibbling on the roof.

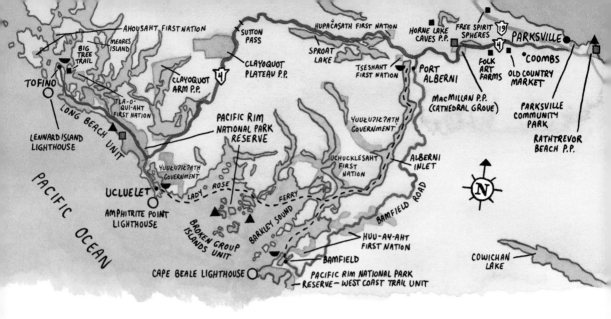

(Map labels, reading roughly west to east and north to south:)

AHOUSAHT FIRST NATION

MEARES ISLAND

BIG TREE TRAIL

TOFINO

LONG BEACH UNIT

PACIFIC OCEAN

LENNARD ISLAND LIGHTHOUSE

TLA-O-QUI-AHT FIRST NATION

CLAYOQUOT ARM P.P.

SUTTON PASS

CLAYOQUOT PLATEAU P.P.

HUPAČASATH FIRST NATION

SPROAT LAKE

TSESHAHT FIRST NATION

HORNE LAKE CAVES P.P.

FREE SPIRIT SPHERES

PARKSVILLE

COOMBS

FOLK ART FARMS

OLD COUNTRY MARKET

PORT ALBERNI

MacMILLAN P.P. (CATHEDRAL GROVE)

PARKSVILLE COMMUNITY PARK

RATHTREVOR BEACH P.P.

PACIFIC RIM NATIONAL PARK RESERVE

YUUŁUʔIŁʔATH GOVERNMENT

UCHUCKLESAHT FIRST NATION

ALBERNI INLET

UCLUELET

YUUŁUʔIŁʔATH GOVERNMENT

LADY ROSE

AMPHITRITE POINT LIGHTHOUSE

BROKEN GROUP ISLANDS UNIT

FERRY

BARKLEY SOUND

BAMFIELD ROAD

N

HUU-AY-AHT FIRST NATION

COWICHAN LAKE

CAPE BEALE LIGHTHOUSE

BAMFIELD

PACIFIC RIM NATIONAL PARK RESERVE—WEST COAST TRAIL UNIT

▼ If you're sad to leave the trees of Cathedral Grove, you can spend the night in an actual treehouse at Free Spirit Spheres, near Qualicum Beach.

INLAND AND UNDERGROUND

Beyond Nanaimo, Highway 19 hugs the east coast of the island all the way to Campbell River. To reach the west coast again, you'll need to turn inland at Parksville. On the way, make a pit stop at Coombs, home of Old Country Market, a slow-food "mall" built with a traditional sod roof by Norwegian immigrants. Nearby is MacMillan Provincial Park, which is still called Cathedral Grove by locals. The park protects the island's most human-accessible stand of giant old-growth evergreens. Just north of MacMillan is Horne Lake Caves Provincial Park. Vancouver Island is home to more than a thousand known caves, and this park is the easiest and most popular destination to explore them.

ISLAND CROSSROADS

Port Alberni is located both on the west coast *and* smack in the middle of the island. Long, narrow Alberni Inlet connects the city to the Pacific. The Nuu-chah-nulth people, who include fourteen sovereign nations along the west coast, have their tribal council headquarters here. Visit for the Port Alberni Salmon Festival held over Labor Day weekend. Salmon derbies like this one are held all over the Pacific Northwest, in a tradition dating back to just after World War II. In the autumn, Victoria Quay is a great (and safe!) spot to watch bears catching spawning salmon across the river. Port Alberni also offers a scenic ferry to Bamfield or (via the Broken Group Islands) Ucluelet.

WEST COAST, PART DEUX

If you're a music fan, you may have chosen Bamfield as your next destination. The fishing village is home to the annual Music by the Sea festival, featuring performances ranging from classical to, well, nautical. In 2017 the orchestra included a horn player in a rowboat and a chorus of boats honking out "O Canada."

Across Barkley Sound (but not ferry-served from Bamfield) is laid-back Ucluelet (called "Ukee" by locals), home to Canada's first catch-and-release aquarium. Nearby Tofino's wicked waves make it a major cold-water surfing destination. Winter storm-watchers can curl up at the sumptuous Wickaninnish Inn, named for an eighteenth-century chief of the Tla-o-qui-aht people. Local water taxis connect to Meares Island, home to the Big Tree Trail. Boaters or floatplane passengers can continue on to Maquinna Marine Provincial Park (map on page 140), prized for its natural hot springs—and natural surprises. A 2015 earthquake shook up the "plumbing," turning the waters cold for a few days!

EXPLORE THE PACIFIC RIM

Tofino and Ucluelet's main attraction is Pacific Rim National Park Reserve, which protects a long stretch of coastline, islands, and temperate rain forests. The park actually has three separate units—only the Long Beach unit, between the two towns, is accessible by car (motorists must purchase a parking pass or risk being fined). Bamfield is the western terminus of the West Coast Trail unit (page 148), and the Broken Group Islands unit lies between the other two.

The Long Beach unit offers a campground and many short trails to choose from. For cultural context, don't miss the Nuu-chah-nulth Interpretive Trail or the Kʷisitis Visitor Centre. The Broken Group Islands are a pristine archipelago of islets and reefs. Often, local park maps detail the many shipwrecks in this area. The entire west coast lies within what historians call the Graveyard of the Pacific, which stretches from Cape Scott (page 155) to the northern Oregon coast. Keep this in mind when paddling the islands—ocean conditions can be fierce here, and safety is paramount.

THE OCEANSIDE ROUTE

To continue up island by car, you'll need to backtrack to the east coast once more. At Parksville, Highway 19 splits, and slower, scenic 19A (locally called Old Island Highway or the Oceanside Route) hugs the shore all the way to Campbell River. This route takes you through the Comox Valley, a scenic swath of coastline below craggy peaks and the Comox Glacier. This is the traditional land of the K'ómoks (Coast Salish) peoples, who include the K'ómoks and Qualicum First Nations on Vancouver Island, and the Tla'amin and Klahoose First Nations across the Strait (page 176). The Oceanside Route

▲ The Comox Glacier is one of five remaining mountain glaciers on Vancouver Island (there were over 150 in the 1970s). Due to climate change, scientists worry that it will melt completely by 2040.

▼ The two car-accessible areas of Strathcona Provincial Park are not contiguous. The Forbidden Plateau is served only by rugged logging roads west of Courtenay.

offers a parade of lighthouses, lovely beaches, and small towns. If you visit in the spring, check out the Brant Wildlife Festival, which celebrates the return of geese and other species to this region, as they gorge themselves during the annual herring run. Don't miss the oyster havens of Fanny Bay (home of the famous Fanny Bay and Kusshi Oysters, as well as a massive sea lion haul-out spot) and Union Bay. You can harvest your own at the Baynes Sound Recreational Shellfish Reserve, near Buckley Bay. Bring your own oyster knife to practice your shucking skills, and make sure you heed any current warnings about paralytic shellfish poisoning (PSP, or red tide) before you set out.

FOSSILS AND FAIRWAYS

Greater Victoria has the legend of Caddy, the local Loch-Ness-like sea monster called the Cadborosaurus. The city of Courtenay has the real thing—an actual marine dinosaur called the elasmosaurus. In 1988 twelve-year-old Heather Trask discovered the first elasmosaur fossil recorded west of the Canadian Rockies. You can see the skeleton at the Courtenay and District Museum and Paleontology Centre.

The Comox Valley bills itself as the Recreational Capital of Canada and a haven for Canada's most popular sport: golf (did you guess it was hockey?). Ninety percent of Canada's courses are public, and Courtenay's Crown Isle Resort is a scenic choice. If you prefer winter sports, you can tackle the slopes at Mount Washington Alpine Resort or lace up your hockey skates at the Comox Valley Sports Centre.

CAST YOUR LINE

Campbell River traditionally marks the northwestern boundary of the Salish Sea. The town is Canada's capital of a specific type of salmon angling called tyee fishing. Derived from the Nuu-chah-nulth word for "chief" or "champion," a tyee salmon is a Chinook weighing thirty pounds or more.

Freshwater streams teem with steelhead (page 157), so Campbell River is also a major flyfishing locale. If this all sounds a bit intimidating, you can simply show up at the Discovery Fishing Pier in August, rent a rod, and try your luck. When you've fished your limit, visit the Maritime Heritage Center, or hike the jaw-dropping suspension bridge at Elk Falls Provincial Park, just outside town.

INTO THE WILD
Head inland once more to visit Strathcona, BC's oldest provincial park. There are only two areas in this sprawling park accessible by road: Buttle Lake and the Forbidden Plateau. Everything else in the park requires backcountry hiking by experienced outdoorspeople with the correct survival gear and wild animal know-how. Encountering dangerous animals—black bears, cougars, elk, and even wolves—is a possibility here. For everyone's sake, take this seriously.

BEYOND THE BOUNDARY
Northern Vancouver Island is rainy, rugged, and remote—and endlessly rewarding, for those willing to make the trek. Past Campbell River, Highway 19 turns westward, leaving the Salish Sea behind. The road runs inland for close to 200 kilometers (124 miles) before rejoining the shore again at Port McNeill. You can break up the long drive with a stop at Steam Locomotive 113, a restored historic logging train in Woss, or Little Huson Cave Park (see map on page 140), where a short trail leads to impressive limestone arches and pits.

BOARDWALK EMPIRE
Just before you reach Port McNeill, take the short detour to tiny Telegraph Cove. The village was built in 1912 as the terminus to the Campbell River telegraph line and became a small hub for the canning and logging industries. Today it's picture postcard for tourists and a departure point for kayakers and whale-watching boats looking to search Johnsons Strait for orcas and other wildlife.

▲ This piece of roadside advice near Holberg is good for a laugh—and also a reminder that the "North Island" is a truly wild and unpredictable place.

▼ Telegraph Cove is one of BC's famous (and disappearing) "boardwalk communities"—where the whole town is built on stilts over the water, and wooden boardwalks take the place of streets.

OF POTLATCHES AND PERSEVERANCE

Northern Vancouver Island is part of the traditional homeland of the Kwakwa̱ka'wakw peoples, one of the cultural groups associated with totem poles and potlatches—gift-giving feasts central to social and political life, from which the term *potluck* may be derived. In 1884 federal laws in both Canada and the United States ordered the assimilation of Indigenous people. Ceremonial goods were banned, along with potlatches in BC. Kwakwa̱ka'wakw, Nuu-chah-nulth, and Coast Salish peoples continued conducting potlatches in secret—authorities imprisoned those they caught and confiscated many cultural objects, until the law was finally repealed in 1951. Children were removed from their communities and sent to residential schools to replace their languages and customs with white culture and Christianity. These boarding schools, the last of which ran until 1996, had a high rate of child deaths, and abuse was rampant and systemic. Anti-Indigenous laws and systems wrought devastating cultural loss and tore communities apart—and the wounds and trauma are still fresh among survivors and their families.

In recent decades BC's Indigenous peoples have worked hard to reclaim their stolen objects and restore their cultural traditions and languages. Kwakwa̱ka'wakw peoples have created a thriving Indigenous-owned tourist industry. Sea Wolf Adventures in Port McNeill operates wildlife-viewing tours of the Broughton Archipelago. In Port Hardy, the Kwa'lilas Hotel runs k'awat'si Tours, offering outdoor ecotours and cultural experiences like cedar weaving and storytelling. And in Alert Bay on Cormorant Island, the U'mista Cultural Centre displays a collection of repatriated potlatch regalia (as does the Nuyumbalees Cultural Centre, page 172), and offers group tours and salmon tastings. In summer the T'sasala Cultural Group performs there regularly.

▲ Many of Alert Bay's totem poles are still in their original location at the 'Na̱mgis burial grounds. They are easily viewable from the road, but the grounds are closed to the public.

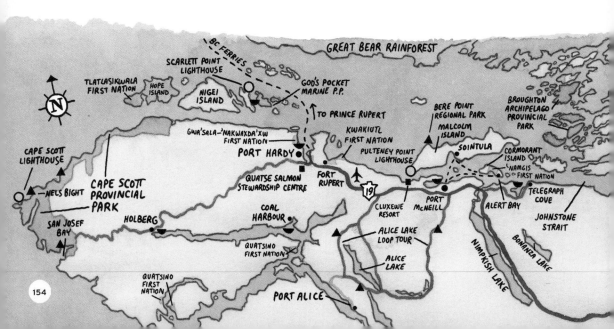

THE EDGE OF THE EARTH

From Port McNeill, BC Ferries runs a triangle route to Cormorant and Malcolm Islands. On the latter is the small town of Sointula, settled by Finnish immigrants in 1901 as a socialist utopia. At nearby Bere Point Regional Park, orcas are known to swim right up to shore and rub themselves on the beach. Port McNeill also links to the Alice Lakes Loop Tour, an inland series of limestone and karst rock formations along logging roads. Highway 19 ends in Port Hardy, but secondary roads lead to some west-coast communities and Cape Scott Provincial Park. The park is open to hikers and boaters only (the last restaurant is the Scarlet Ibis Pub in Holberg). Highlights include San Josef Bay and the muddy, full-day hike to Nels Bight. Along the way you'll see ghostly remnants of the area's settlement and logging history, including village ruins and corduroy (wooden-plank) roads. Shore camping is allowed, but dogs are banned from most of the park, as wolves are present. Serious kayakers can explore the shore for more than sixty nautical miles from Port Hardy to Coal Harbour, along the Cape Scott Marine Trail.

THE DOMAIN OF THE SPIRIT BEAR

The Great Bear Rainforest, a 25,000-square-mile labyrinth of fjords and islands, begins at Johnstone Strait and stretches to the Alaska border. The Broughton Archipelago is the southernmost extent of the rainforest—this area is easily accessible to boaters and various fishing and ecotour outfits. Indigenous peoples, particularly the Kitasoo/Xai'xais, have evolved their land stewardship to include sustainable wilderness tourism as an alternative to resource extraction and trophy hunts. This new ecotourism centers on remote lodges and wildlife watching, specifically grizzly bears and the Kermode bear—a rare white variant of the black bear that Indigenous peoples call the spirit bear.

THE CALL OF THE NORTH

Port Hardy is also the southern terminus of the Inside Passage—the waterway up to Alaska. Haida Gwaii (the Queen Charlotte Islands) is a major destination, reached via a long, two-boat BC Ferries route (many fly instead). At the southern tip of the archipelago is Gwaii Haanas National Park Reserve, home to the famous Haida Watchmen poles depicted by white BC artist Emily Carr. Because of the sensitive nature of Gwaii Haanas, a park permit, cultural orientation training, and a tour from a licensed operator (or your own boat or long-haul kayak) are required to visit.

▲ A canopy of buoys welcomes hikers to the entrance to Nels Bight, near the northwesternmost point on Vancouver Island.

▼ According to Kitasoo/Xai'xais oral traditions, Raven the Trickster made one in every ten black bears white to remind people of the ice age and the bounty of today's world.

Gone Fishing

A staple food of humans and animals alike, salmon are an icon of the Pacific Northwest. Though places like Campbell River do big business during the sport fishing seasons, salmon are also a threatened keystone species of the Salish Sea ecosystem.

▼ **COLOR CODED.** There are five true salmon species, and each undergoes a dramatic color change between its oceangoing and spawning phases.

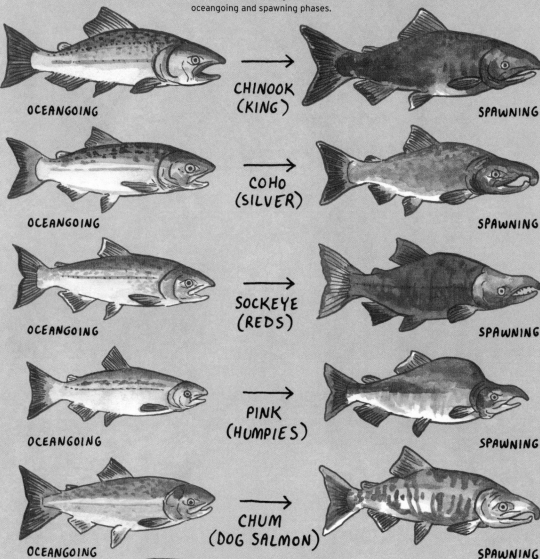

OCEANGOING — CHINOOK (KING) — SPAWNING

OCEANGOING — COHO (SILVER) — SPAWNING

OCEANGOING — SOCKEYE (REDS) — SPAWNING

OCEANGOING — PINK (HUMPIES) — SPAWNING

OCEANGOING — CHUM (DOG SALMON) — SPAWNING

◀ **REEL 'ER IN.** The sport of tyee fishing began in 1924 with strict rules. No motors allowed—anglers fish from a rowboat, using a single, barbless hook and a rod between six and nine feet long.

▲ **WATCH THE CALENDAR.** Each species has a different spawning and fishing season—so do your research before you book that fishing trip. In addition, pinks have a two-year life cycle, so you might find yourself fishing in an off year.

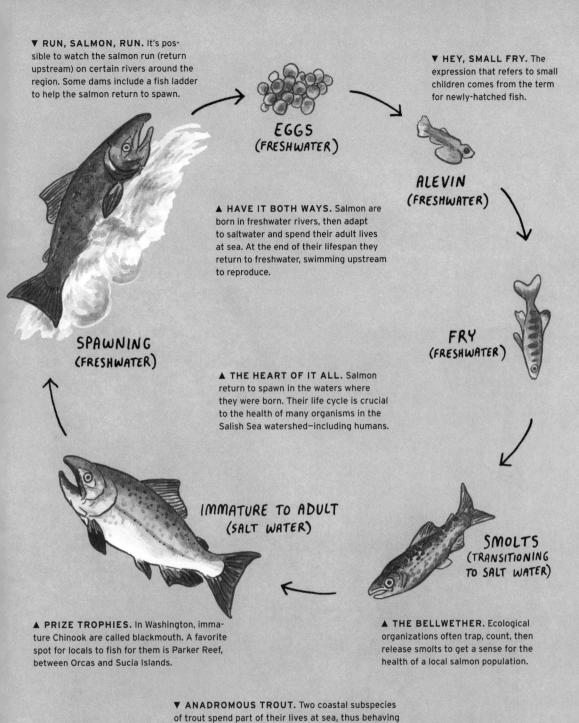

▼ **RUN, SALMON, RUN.** It's possible to watch the salmon run (return upstream) on certain rivers around the region. Some dams include a fish ladder to help the salmon return to spawn.

EGGS (FRESHWATER)

▼ **HEY, SMALL FRY.** The expression that refers to small children comes from the term for newly-hatched fish.

ALEVIN (FRESHWATER)

▲ **HAVE IT BOTH WAYS.** Salmon are born in freshwater rivers, then adapt to saltwater and spend their adult lives at sea. At the end of their lifespan they return to freshwater, swimming upstream to reproduce.

SPAWNING (FRESHWATER)

FRY (FRESHWATER)

▲ **THE HEART OF IT ALL.** Salmon return to spawn in the waters where they were born. Their life cycle is crucial to the health of many organisms in the Salish Sea watershed—including humans.

IMMATURE TO ADULT (SALT WATER)

SMOLTS (TRANSITIONING TO SALT WATER)

▲ **PRIZE TROPHIES.** In Washington, immature Chinook are called blackmouth. A favorite spot for locals to fish for them is Parker Reef, between Orcas and Sucia Islands.

▲ **THE BELLWETHER.** Ecological organizations often trap, count, then release smolts to get a sense for the health of a local salmon population.

▼ **ANADROMOUS TROUT.** Two coastal subspecies of trout spend part of their lives at sea, thus behaving (and tasting) like salmon. Coastal rainbow trout become steelhead when they go to sea, and some cutthroat also make the journey—and transformation.

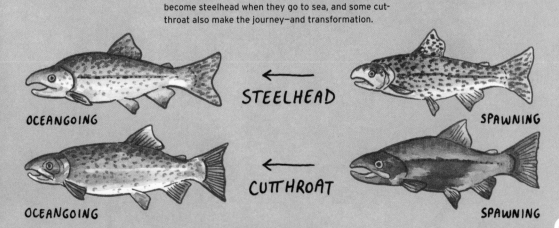

OCEANGOING

STEELHEAD

SPAWNING

OCEANGOING

CUTTHROAT

SPAWNING

THE GULF ISLANDS

▶ For the sake of scale, this map depicts the Southern Gulf Islands only. You'll find a northern islands map on page 171, and the Discovery Islands on page 173.

▼ Gulf Islands National Park Reserve maintains many historic orchards (see map, right), preserving heritage varieties of apples, pears, quince, and other fruit. Hand-harvesting by the public is permitted within the park.

The Gulf Islands occupy much of the northern Salish Sea and are some of the most popular (and sunny) vacation spots on the Canadian west coast. There are too many islands to fit into one trip, so think of this chapter as a tasting menu to help you sample the region.

When defining the archipelago, it depends on whom you ask. The term "Gulf Islands" is often used as shorthand to refer only to the Southern Gulf Islands (map on facing page), the Canadian half of the archipelago that includes the San Juan Islands (page 74). The more northerly islands are more loosely defined—some call them the Northern Gulf Islands, and others simply lump them in with other provincial districts. For simplicity's sake, this chapter deals with all the major islands occupying the Strait of Georgia (once called the Gulf of Georgia, hence the name). Listed first are the Southern Gulf Islands, and we'll move northward from there. Because of their proximity to other destinations, you'll find a few small outliers in the Vancouver Island (page 140) and Sunshine Coast (page 176) chapters.

For the most part, the major Gulf Islands are accessible by BC Ferries, either from Vancouver or Tsawwassen on the mainland, or from various points along the east coast of Vancouver Island. A few islands require an interisland ferry or a transfer on Vancouver Island, and currently, the ferry to Texada (page 169) departs only from the Sunshine Coast. Hopping around to multiple islands takes planning to navigate multiple ferries (pro tip: you can get discounted fares by paying with a preloaded BC Ferries Experience Card). Only Salt Spring (page 160) has public bus transit—for the most part, in the Gulf Islands, you are on your own for ground transportation.

VANCOUVER

ENTRANCE ISLAND LIGHTHOUSE

GABRIOLA ISLAND

NANAIMO

SNUNEYMUXW FIRST NATION

VALDES ISLAND

STUART CHANNEL

STZ'UMINUS FIRST NATION

SOUTHERN GULF ISLANDS

BC FERRIES

STRAIT OF GEORGIA

VANCOUVER INTERNATIONAL AIRPORT

SAND HEADS LIGHTHOUSE

RICHMOND

LADYSMITH

THETIS ISLAND

PORLIER PASS RANGE FRONT + REAR LIGHTHOUSES

BC FERRIES

PENELAKUT TRIBE

CHEMAINUS

PENELAKUT ISLAND

STZ'UMINUS FIRST NATION

BARE POINT LIGHTHOUSE

GALIANO ISLAND

GULF ISLANDS

TSAWWASSEN

POINT ROBERTS (WASHINGTON)

VESUVIUS

TRINCOMALI CHANNEL

TRANSCANADA HIGHWAY

VANCOUVER ISLAND

BC BC FERRIES

CROFTON

LONG HARBOUR

GANGES

SALT SPRING ISLAND

STURDIES BAY

PORTLOCK POINT LIGHTHOUSE

PREVOST ISLAND

VILLAGE BAY

ACTIVE PASS LIGHTHOUSE

MAYNE ISLAND

BC FERRIES

CANADA

UNITED STATES

GULF ISLANDS NATIONAL PARK RESERVE

QUW'UTSUN FIRST NATION

DUNCAN

COWICHAN BAY

FULFORD HARBOUR

RUSSELL ISLAND

OTTER BAY

PENDER ISLAND

LYALL HARBOUR

SATURNA ISLAND

PORTLAND ISLAND

HISTORIC ORCHARDS

PIERS ISLAND

MORESBY ISLAND

GOWLLAND POINT LIGHTHOUSE

EAST POINT LIGHTHOUSE

SWARTZ BAY

COAL ISLAND

VICTORIA INTERNATIONAL AIRPORT

SIDNEY

WASHINGTON STATE FERRIES

ISLE-DE-US (RUM ISLAND)

STUART ISLAND (WASHINGTON)

159

Salt Spring

Starting at the archipelago's largest, most touristy island, or using it as a base camp for island hopping, is a logical choice. You'll find diverse lodging options here—resorts, inns, vacation rentals, even yurts—as well as three ferry terminals: Fulford Harbour for the Swartz Bay crossing, Vesuvius for the Crofton ferry, and Long Harbour for Tsawwassen and Swartz Bay, as well as the interisland boat to Galiano, Mayne, Pender, and Saturna Islands.

DIVERSE FROM THE BEGINNING

Salt Spring is an ancestral land of several Coast Salish peoples, and thus has been known by different names—including Klaathem, the Cowichan word for "salt"—for millennia. You can find an ancient petroglyph of a harbor seal's face at Drummond Park, across from the ferry landing in Fulford.

In the 1850s the British government opened the island for pre-emption—in which settlers could occupy and improve land *before* purchasing it. Many of these early settlers were Kanakas—Native Hawaiians who had previously worked for Hudson's Bay Company. (In fact, the trade language called Chinook Jargon spoken by many of HBC's international workers was mainly comprised of Indigenous, French, and Hawaiian words.) The Hawaiian community built Saint Paul's Church in Fulford and established heritage fruit orchards on Salt Spring, Russell, and Portland Islands.

Black pioneers were also central to Salt Spring's history. In 1858 colonial Governor Sir James Douglas invited Black people in California—who were freed from slavery but could not legally vote or homestead—to take up land claims in BC. About six hundred settlers sailed north (you can find paving bricks commemorating many of them in Bastion Square in Victoria—map on page 143), and about a dozen pre-empted homesteads on Salt Spring. The island's first teacher, John Craven Jones, was one of them, and a few descendants of other early Black pioneers remain on Salt Spring today.

By the early 1900s there were also Japanese communities on Salt Spring and Mayne Islands. But like their American counterparts (page 28), Japanese Canadians were forced into internment camps during World War II, and their property was seized and sold off by the government. You can discover the triumph and tragedy of the island's immigrant history at the Salt Spring Museum, near Ganges.

▲ Saint Paul's Church is one of the oldest on the island, built of local fieldstone and finished in 1885. The door, windows, and bell were brought over by canoe from Cowichan Bay.

▼ Government docks, like this one at Vesuvius Bay, provide public water access to islanders and visitors alike. Easily identifiable by their bright red railings, they are spottable all around the islands.

▶ Salt Spring's roads are well paved but congested and narrow, with many blind curves. Consider biking early in the day or during the shoulder season (spring and fall) to avoid heavy car traffic.

STUART

THETIS ISLAND

REID ISLAND

SCHOOL

HALL ISLAND

CHEMAINUS

BC FERRIES

BARE POINT LIGHTHOUSE

SECRETARY ISLANDS

CHANNEL

PENELAKUT ISLAND

HOUSTOUN PASSAGE

GALIANO

STZ'UMINUS FIRST NATION

TENT ISLAND

PENELAKUT TRIBE

WALLACE ISLAND MARINE P.P.

MINERAL SPRINGS RESORT

SAINT MARY LAKE

TRINCOMALI CHANNEL

ISLAND

CROFTON

BC FERRIES

VESUVIUS

SALT SPRING WILD CIDER

SALT SPRING SEA SALT

LONG HARBOUR

N

VANCOUVER ISLAND

MOUNT ERSKINE PROVINCIAL PARK

GANGES

SALT SPRING MUSEUM

LAKE MAXWELL

SALT SPRING APPLE COMPANY

SANSUM NARROWS

QUW'UTSUN FIRST NATION

MOUNT MAXWELL PROVINCIAL PARK

CUSHEON LAKE

THIRD SISTER ISLAND

PORTLOCK POINT LIGHTHOUSE

PREVOST ISLAND

VILLAGE BAY

MAYNE ISLAND

COWICHAN BAY

BURGOYNE BAY PROVINCIAL PARK

SALT SPRING VINEYARDS

GARRY OAKS ESTATE WINERY

LAKE WESTON

BC FERRIES

OTTER BAY

HOPE BAY

(NORTH)

SATURNA ISLAND

MUSGRAVE POINT

SALT SPRING ISLAND

DRUMMOND PARK

FULFORD HARBOUR

RUCKLE P.P.

ROESLAND PARK

PENDER ISLAND (SOUTH)

SATELLITE CHANNEL

PAUQUACHIN FIRST NATION

RUSSELL ISLAND

PRINCESS MARGARET MARINE PARK

BC FERRIES

THIEVES BAY MARINA

WOODS ON PENDER

GOLF ISLAND DISC PARK

SWANSON CHANNEL

BEDWELL

POET'S COVE RESORT

BC FERRIES

SWARTZ BAY

PORTLAND ISLAND

MORESBY ISLAND

HARBOUR

MILL BAY

SAANICH INLET

SAANICH PENINSULA

SIDNEY

GOWLLAND POINT LIGHTHOUSE

BC FERRIES

BRENTWOOD BAY

▲ Mount Erskine's fairy doors are a great way to introduce kids to hiking. You'll find even more doors hidden around Ganges and at Mouat Park.

CURES, CUISINE, AND CULTURE

In the nineteenth century, health retreats became a hybrid of vacations and healthcare. Travelers flocked to resorts built over natural mineral or hot springs to "take the cure." Salt Spring's namesake mineral springs, long known by Indigenous peoples, are now owned by Mineral Springs Resort. The springs have inspired Salt Spring's island-wide emphasis on wellness—many tourists come for spa treatments, meditation retreats, or even paddleboard yoga classes.

The local food scene is also serious business here. Dining options abound in Ganges, including sandwiches at Buzzy's Luncheonette or Tree House Cafe, Sunday brunch at Salt Spring Inn, and prix fixe dinners at Hastings House's Manor Dining. Grab picnic fare at the Salt Spring Saturday Market, or try one of the island's many honor-system farm stands. Salt Spring Sea Salt produces fleur de sel, a culinary salt made from evaporated seawater. You'll find local cider at Salt Spring Apple Company and Salt Spring Wild Cider, as well as the Salt Spring Island Apple Festival, held every October. The event showcases more than four hundred heritage varieties from local orchards—fresh, baked, or pressed.

For a dash of Salt Spring culture, try the Studio Tour circuit (look for the blue and white sheep signs around the island), a year-round, self-guided circuit of working artist studios, gallery spaces, and artisan-made goods for sale. Salt Spring Pride Festival, held each September, is one of Canada's largest LGBTQ+ events. In October, you can take a writing class at the Paper Covers Rock literary festival. Or just browse the shelves at Salt Spring Books or Black Sheep Books, both in Ganges. Consider shopping with local Salt Spring Dollars, which are exchanged on par with Canadian currency. Look for the $$ symbol at businesses that accept them.

BIKE, BOAT, OR BIVOUAC

Though Salt Spring is as mountainous as Orcas Island (page 100), it's also a favorite of cyclists. Bike rentals (including e-bikes, which help with the steep hills!) are available at several locations in Ganges. Boaters will find full-service marinas and kayak rentals at Ganges and Fulford Harbours. Ruckle Provincial Park, which preserves the island's oldest working farm, is a favorite paddling spot. More seasoned

▼ Poets Cove Resort was built in 1959 as Bedwell Harbour Resort. It's run along the same "village" model as Rosario and Roche Harbor Resorts in the San Juan Islands.

kayakers might want to set out on the Gulf Islands Marine Trail (similar to the Cascadia Marine Trail). Or take a sea kayak tour from Ganges out to Third Sister Island, where you'll see a large Indigenous shell midden at Chocolate Beach. There's also a marine campsite at Musgrave Point for kayakers. Hikers will love Mount Maxwell Provincial Park (warning: feral sheep!) and Burgoyne Bay Provincial Park. And though the view at the summit is its own reward, the trails at Mount Erskine Provincial Park have a little extra enchantment. Look for a series of handmade fairy doors hidden in plain sight along the forest trail.

▲ Hope Bay (pictured) and Port Washington on North Pender are home to historic store buildings. Hope Bay's store has been restored and runs as part of a group of cooperative businesses.

Pender

The next island east of Salt Spring, thanks to a steamship canal cut through in 1903, is actually two islands—locals call it either the singular Pender or the Penders. BC Ferries offers service from Tsawwassen and Swartz Bay, as well as an interisland ferry that makes the rounds between Salt Spring, Galiano, Mayne, and Saturna Islands. Floatplane service operates out of Bedwell Harbour, and you can reach South Pender overland via a one-lane bridge built in 1955.

Kayakers love Pender, and with thirty-three well-marked public beach access points, you can take your pick of put-ins. North Pender is the more populous island, though it has no incorporated town center. A large suburban subdivision built here in the 1970s (inspiring the formation of the anti-development Islands Trust group) is now home to a well-known disc golf course, Golf Island Disc Park. Nearby Roesland—protected by Gulf Islands National Park Reserve (page 167)—is a former 1920s resort that now houses the Pender Islands Museum. The breakwater at Thieves Bay Marina is an excellent spot to watch Southern Resident orcas as they pass by close to the shore along the Whale Trail. WOODS on Pender offers a variety of hipster lodging accommodations, including vintage Airstream trailers.

South Pender curves around Bedwell Harbour, a sheltered anchorage from the winds coming off the Strait.

▼ Since Pender Island built its network of car stops in 2008, Mayne and Saturna Islands (page 164) have since followed suit.

Poets Cove Resort offers upscale lodging, meals, and spa treatments, plus a full-service marina for boaters (including a seasonal border checkpoint for people sailing in from the San Juan Islands). Look for the 1905 British surveyor's mark carved into a rock along the cove.

If you arrived without your own vehicle, you might have use for one of the island's most charming quirks: the car stop. Since there's no bus service here, and hitchhiking is a time-honored tradition in the Gulf Islands, locals created a volunteer "taxi" network. At each of the forty-odd stops is a place to wait for a willing driver (yes, stick your thumb out!), and a brief list of rules: neither party is obligated to accept a ride, and no money can change hands.

Saturna and Mayne

Wild and windswept Saturna Island is surrounded on three sides by the US border and is accessible via the interisland ferry to Lyall Harbour. The island is nearly empty and truly wild—close to half its land area is encompassed by Gulf Islands National Park Reserve. There are few services here, but you'll find a campground at Narvaez Bay. Geocaching is a popular activity around the island, with about sixty sites maintained by the Saturna Ecological Education Centre. Don't miss the views from Mount Warburton Pike (accessible by trail) and East Point Regional Park—the latter offers sweeping views of Boundary Pass, Mount Baker, and the San Juan Islands (page 74). The lighthouse there is a new replacement, but the the historic fog alarm building is still there. Just offshore are Tumbo and Cabbage Islands, the outermost in the archipelago. These are both also part of the national park (there's a campsite on Cabbage), and at low tide are connected to each other by an exposed reef.

Also served by the interisland ferry is Mayne Island, Saturna's more populous, gently rolling sister. Check out the Coast Salish welcome figure, carved by Indigenous artist Johnny Aitken, at Emma & Felix Jack Park. Then see the Mayne Island Museum, located in the historic 1896 jail in Miner's Bay. Visit the Japanese garden at Dinner Bay Park, built as a memorial and meditation spot on farmland confiscated from Japanese families during World War II. Bring a picnic lunch to Georgina Point Heritage Park (home of Active Pass Lighthouse), and do a bit of ferry watching. This is also an excellent bird-watching spot for black oystercatchers and harlequin ducks. Divers can explore the wreck of the *Zephyr*, a wooden barque that sunk just offshore in 1872. And if you can snag a reservation, stay at one of Canada's most popular vacation rentals, a quirky cottage made from cob, a material similar to adobe (page 172).

Galiano

The last stop on the interisland ferry is a long skinny strip of sedimentary rock flanking the eastern boundary of the archipelago. Check out Montague Harbour Marine Provincial Park, a favorite of boaters and campers, or Dionisio Point Provincial Park, with three-thousand-year-old shell middens and a pair of lighthouses just outside the park. The western shore is dotted with unusual sandstone formations and sea caves. You can access some of these by land at Retreat Cove and others by kayak (rentals available at the Montague Harbour Marina). For a moment of extra peace, climb the Stairway to Heaven at Tapovan Peace Park. The two-hundred-acre park, named for the Sanskrit word for a "spiritual wilderness," features a trail with a statue of Indian spiritual leader Sri Chinmoy (and stunning views) at the top.

Most of Galiano's businesses are located at the southern end. After you step off the ferry, pop into Sturdies Bay Bakery for a seasonal peach scone. Since 2009 Galiano Island Books has hosted the Galiano Literary Festival, featuring authors from near and far. Hummingbird Pub is a popular restaurant and watering hole with its own bus. "Tommy Transit" Tompkins makes free runs between the pub and the Montague Harbour Marina and campground each evening, and passes out musical instruments to entertain riders along the way. Finally, Pilgrimme Restaurant lives up to its name, as travelers come here from around the world for prix fixe locally sourced and foraged meals. You'll also find plenty of lodging on the island, from cottages and bed-and-breakfasts to the luxurious Galiano Oceanfront Inn & Spa.

▲ Don't miss the Briary—arguably the islands' most beautiful honor-system farm stand—where you can purchase artisanal jams, chutneys, and vinegars.

▼ East Point Park on Saturna Island is the southeasternmost point in the Gulf Islands. Its unprotected bluff is buffeted by excellent kite winds.

Thetis and Penelakut

Named for a mythic Greek sea nymph fathered by Zeus, Thetis Island is connected by BC Ferries to Vancouver Island. (Note that Thetis is not included on the interisland ferry that connects Salt Spring to Galiano, Mayne, Saturna, and Pender.) There are nine miles of public road and twelve of public shoreline on Thetis—everything else is privately owned. Still, tourists are welcome, and there are services (including a bistro and a pub), mostly clustered around two full-service marinas. You'll find a handful of overnight accommodations on Thetis, and also a one-room schoolhouse that's still in operation—one of the last in Canada.

Adjacent Penelakut Island, once called Kuper, was renamed in 2010 for the Penelakut people who have lived there and on Galiano for millennia. From 1890 to 1978, the Catholic Church ran a residential school (page 154) on the island, and its abuses have left scars on today's Penelakut community. Though the island is connected to Thetis and Vancouver Islands by BC Ferries, all of Penelakut is First Nation reserve property. Thus, it is generally not open to the public—visitors require the invitation of a tribal member.

▲ A hike at Galiano's Bodega Ridge Provincial Park leads you to a vista point more than one thousand feet above the Trincomali Channel.

Gabriola

The northernmost large island in the chain is reached by a short BC Ferries run from downtown Nanaimo. Both city and island lie within the traditional territory of the Snuneymuxw (Coast Salish) people. Gabriola is home to more than seventy known Indigenous petroglyphs, carved into stone all over the island. Some are ancient, some modern—some sit along the shore, and others are tucked away in hidden woods. There's an interpretive trail highlighting some in the Garry oak meadow next to Christ Church. Local Indigenous elders have asked visitors not to photograph the island's carvings—

but you can learn more about them and view replicas on the grounds of the Gabriola Museum.

Nature's carving tools are on display at the Malaspina Galleries, at the northwestern end of the island. This spectacular, tsunami-shaped sandstone formation was scooped out over centuries by wind and water. Make sure to visit at low tide to get the full effect, and see the honeycomb of tafoni weathering on the floor of the hollow.

With all this sculpting going on, it's not surprising that Gabriola is yet another creative haven. The ten-day Isle of the Arts Festival each spring includes a variety of workshops in visual arts, dance, writing, and music. There's also a studio tour on Gabriola around Thanksgiving (which, remember, is in October here), with some studios open year-round. After sampling the art, try the cioppino at Woodfire, a restaurant that also sells its own spice blends. Or head to the pub at Surf Lodge, at the northern tip of the island. And every August since 1955, the Gabriola Island Community Hall has hosted the world's largest salmon barbecue, serving over six hundred meals as a local fundraiser.

▲ A former resort cabin on Wallace Island is "shingled" with oars and other island flotsam inscribed with vessel names of boaters who have visited over the years.

Other Islands

The Southern Gulf Islands also include many small non-ferry islands. Most are privately owned or wildlife reserves, and thus offer no public access. However, several are public parks and worth a visit. Wallace Island Marine Provincial Park, just north of Salt Spring, is an especially lovely kayaking spot, with several sheltered coves, a picnic shelter, and eighteen campsites. There are hiking trails from one end of the skinny island (which until 1905 was called Narrow Island) to the other, offering great spots for wildlife viewing, including bald eagles, otters, and—if you're lucky—mink.

A FLOATING NATIONAL PARK
A patchwork of island parklands southeast of Salt Spring are collected into Gulf Islands National Park Reserve (see the green areas of the map on page 161). The park is almost entirely backcountry, with no visitor center and few services. Boaters should take care around ferry traffic and strong tidal

▼ The Malaspina Galleries have been impressing visitors for centuries— they were recorded in land survey logs by Spanish explorers in 1792.

▲ Separate private foot ferries connect Nanaimo to Protection Island and Saysutshun. Note that the Protection Island fare is cash only—and don't mix up the two!

▼ Jesse Island itself is private, but kayakers love to explore the rock formations along the shore, eroded into sea stacks, tunnels, and caves.

currents. And watch the tides—tidal ranges can be extreme, so anchor carefully to avoid being left high and dry.

Prevost Island is in the thick of the ferry traffic lanes—though no routes actually stop here. Similar to Sucia Island in the San Juans (page 132), there are many bays, sheltered coves, and long fingers of land. There are two park areas here, on opposite ends of the island, with a campground at James Bay and Portlock Point Lighthouse at the southern tip. Portland and Russell Islands both had farms established by Kanaka (Native Hawaiian) families. Between them five heritage orchards remain, plus historic Mahoi House on Russell. Both islands also have significant Indigenous cultural sites, including a thousand-year-old clam garden on Russell. Portland Island also doubles as Princess Margaret Marine Park—it was once owned by the princess herself, and she donated it back to the province in 1958. Tiny Isle-de-Lis, formerly named Rum Island, was a base for Prohibition-era rumrunners. Today there's a backcountry campsite and great views of Turn Point Lighthouse (page 129) on Stuart Island. D'Arcy and Sidney Islands are more easily accessed from Sidney (page 146).

THE TOP OF THE ARCHIPELAGO

There are also several non-ferry destinations at the other end of the Southern Gulf Islands. Much of Valdes Island is private, belonging to the Lyackson First Nation reserve—a community of about two hundred people, plus about sixty archaeological sites, some of which date back five thousand years. Valdes does provide a few tourist highlights, including Wakes Cove Provincial Park, a day-use recreation space for kayakers. There's a marine campsite at Blackberry Point, part of the Gulf Islands Marine Trail.

Protection Island is a bedroom community for adjacent Nanaimo, but it does have three public parks, several hiking trails, and a small museum at the lighthouse. The island is also home to the Dinghy Dock, Canada's only floating pub. Nearby Saysutshun (formerly Newcastle Island) is a marine provincial park operated (with a seasonal ferry) by the Snuneymuxw First Nation. You can even book a walking tour with a Coast Salish guide, a salmon barbecue with traditional singing and storytelling, or other cultural experiences, by contacting the Snuneymuxw event coordinator.

The string of islands between Valdes and Vancouver Islands is known as the De Courcy Group, including Mudge, De Courcy, Pylades, and others. There's no ferry service, though Gulf Island Seaplanes offers service to De Courcy.

You'll find two marine provincial parks here: Pirates Cove on De Courcy Island (camping available), and Whaleboat Island Marine Provincial Park (day use only).

Lasqueti and Texada

For tourists, the Northern Gulf Islands seem to begin a bit reluctantly. A privately run "foot ferry" (no cars, no BC Ferries passes!) serves Lasqueti from French Creek Harbour on Vancouver Island. Until recently this off-grid island's electricity came from diesel generators that switched off each night, leaving locals to rely on candlelight and lanterns. Today much of the island has converted to solar power—as well as other green infrastructure like composting toilets— making Lasqueti a local pioneer in renewable energy and sustainable living. The tourist activities here are equally quiet and off-grid. Many come for the kayaking—especially at Squitty Bay Provincial Park and, just offshore, Sabine Channel and Jedediah Island Marine Provincial Parks. No camping is allowed on Lasqueti, but there are a few guest cottages and bed-and-breakfasts.

Texada Island, on the other hand, is technically considered part of the Sunshine Coast. BC Ferries offers service from Powell River (page 182)—though at times it has also expanded service to Comox on Vancouver Island in a triangle run. Texada's tourist draws are definitely in the "roughing it" category. The island's lakes, trails, and provincial parks are remote, often requiring a high-clearance, four-wheel-drive vehicle to reach by land. Shingle Beach is popular with paddlers—waterfront camping is available here, as well as at Shelter Point Regional Park. For pilots and airplane enthusiasts, there's also the Texada Annual Fly-In (which has its own dance party, the Fly-In Fling) each August at the Gillies Bay airfield. Bring picnic supplies with you, as there are only a handful of dining options on the island. Remote as the island is, however, you won't need to worry about *becoming* lunch yourself. Texada advertises itself as one of the few BC islands with no large carnivorous wildlife.

Denman and Hornby

BC Ferries runs the world's longest cable ferry—a boat crossing back and forth on a tether—to Denman Island from Buckley Bay. Here, too, be artists: check out the potters' studio tour in May. Definitely stop at the Free Store, a donation-based sharing and reuse "shop" that is a community tradition

▲ Fossil Beach Farm's orchard was planted in 1921. You'll have to visit the farm in person to taste the small-batch cider made from its apples.

▼ The Hornby Island Community Hall is the pinnacle of creative reuse and eco-artistry. The structure is built from a fallen old-growth stump, log-round cladding, and a sod roof.

▲ Kayakers can paddle right up to Discovery Islands Lodge on Quadra Island. The inn also offers paddling instruction and sea kayaking tours of the islands.

▼ There are several scuba diving sites along the western shore of Quadra Island, including an artificial reef created by intentionally sinking the HMCS *Columbia* off adjacent Maude Island.

on several Gulf Islands. Fillongley Provincial Park was an early-twentieth-century private estate, whose former bowling green is now a wildflower meadow ringed by imported deciduous trees. Ten campsites flank the beach (reservations highly recommended). At the southern tip of the island is Boyle Point Provincial Park, with views of Chrome Island Lighthouse, just offshore.

Continue on from Denman with another ferry to Hornby Island (note that Hornby's ferry does not connect directly to Vancouver Island, but you can purchase your "thru fare" to Hornby when you buy your Denman ticket). You'll find a few camping options here, including "glamping" tents at the Fossil Beach Farm cidery. Helliwell Provincial Park, at the island's eastern tip, protects an old-growth forest of Douglas fir and Garry oak trees. And Tribune Bay Provincial Park is home to what might be the best swimming beach on the Salish Sea. The bay's southern exposure keeps its shallow waters warm. The white sand, balmy microclimate, and vivid aquamarine waters have led locals to call the beach "Little Hawaii."

The Discovery Islands

Occupying the area between Desolation Sound and Johnstone Strait (see the Vancouver Island overview map on page 138), the Discovery Islands mark the northern boundary of the Salish Sea. These are considered Northern Gulf Islands by some, though not all. BC Ferries serves Quadra and Cortes, flights and water taxis reach the outer islands, and Desolation Sound is best accessed from the Sunshine Coast (page 176). Protected coves and 360-degree scenic views make this a boating paradise. (Paddlers beware: there are so many islands and waterways here that navigation can be tricky.) Johnstone Strait, especially, is a favorite of whalewatchers and marine scientists. In the summer a population of about 150 orcas—including both transients and the Northern Residents (page 99)—feed along the passage.

PRESERVING THE POTLATCH

A short ferry from Campbell River runs to Quadra Island, landing at Quathiaski Cove, home of the island's few services. The north end includes Main Lake Provincial Park (a wilderness camping spot), Octopus Islands Marine Provincial Park

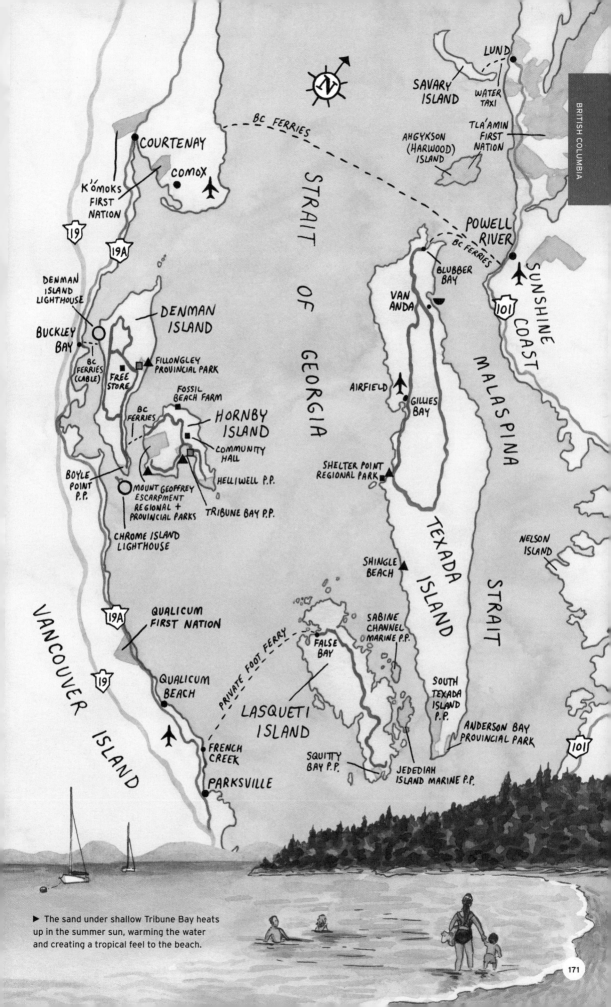

N

LUND

SAVARY ISLAND

WATER TAXI

TLA'AMIN FIRST NATION

AHGYKSON (HARWOOD) ISLAND

BC FERRIES

COURTENAY

COMOX

K̓ÓMOKS FIRST NATION

19

19A

STRAIT OF GEORGIA

POWELL RIVER

BC FERRIES

BLUBBER BAY

VAN ANDA

SUNSHINE COAST

101

DENMAN ISLAND LIGHTHOUSE

BUCKLEY BAY

DENMAN ISLAND

BC FERRIES (CABLE)

FREE STORE

FILLONGLEY PROVINCIAL PARK

FOSSIL BEACH FARM

BC FERRIES

HORNBY ISLAND

COMMUNITY HALL

HELLIWELL P.P.

AIRFIELD

GILLIES BAY

SHELTER POINT REGIONAL PARK

MALASPINA

BOYLE POINT P.P.

MOUNT GEOFFREY ESCARPMENT REGIONAL + PROVINCIAL PARKS

TRIBUNE BAY P.P.

TEXADA ISLAND

NELSON ISLAND

CHROME ISLAND LIGHTHOUSE

SHINGLE BEACH

STRAIT

QUALICUM FIRST NATION

19A

SABINE CHANNEL MARINE P.P.

QUALICUM BEACH

PRIVATE FOOT FERRY

FALSE BAY

SOUTH TEXADA ISLAND P.P.

ANDERSON BAY PROVINCIAL PARK

VANCOUVER ISLAND

19

LASQUETI ISLAND

101

FRENCH CREEK

SQUITTY BAY P.P.

JEDEDIAH ISLAND MARINE P.P.

PARKSVILLE

▶ The sand under shallow Tribune Bay heats up in the summer sun, warming the water and creating a tropical feel to the beach.

▲ Cob buildings like the Sanctuary at Hollyhock are fairly common in the Gulf Islands. This traditional building material comprised of earth, straw, water, and lime is durable, fireproof, and heat-efficient.

▼ Though it serves an official government function, Cortes Island's post office looks more like a local fishing shack or garden shed.

(popular with boaters), and Small Inlet Marine Provincial Park (home to tidal rapids). Halfway down Quadra's eastern shore is Rebecca Spit Marine Provincial Park—great for a long beach walk or a windsurfing adventure. At the southern tip of the island is Cape Mudge Lighthouse (illustration on page 184), built in 1916. Cape Mudge Village is the seat of the We Wai Kai First Nation, a band of Kwakwaka'wakw people. Make sure to visit the Nuyumbalees Cultural Centre, home of seven of the island's many ancient petroglyphs—as well as the Kikasuw (Sacred Potlatch Collection), a group of Kwakwaka'wakw ceremonial objects repatriated back from white-owned museums decades after federal authorities confiscated them under anti-potlatch laws (page 154).

A PLACE TO UNPLUG

The ferry to Cortes Island leaves from Heriot Bay on Quadra—as with Hornby Island, you can buy your thru fare to Cortes when you purchase your Quadra ticket. The main attraction on the island is the Hollyhock Lifelong Learning Center, a day and overnight facility founded by Greenpeace veterans in 1982. Hollyhock offers workshops, conferences, and retreats in yoga and wellness, sustainability, writing, performing arts, and leadership. Nearby are the sandy beaches of Smelt Bay Provincial Park, named for the small fish that spawn here by the tens of thousands every fall. Bike the island in June for the Creative Spaces Tour of artist studios. And Whaletown, the setting for Ruth Ozeki's novel *A Tale for the Time Being*, offers a handful of restaurants.

BEYOND THE FERRY

The Discovery Islands also have many large and small outer islands. There are no cities and few permanent residents out here, but plenty of outdoor recreation spots. Fish the waters of Rendezvous Island South Provincial Park, view wildflower blooms on Mitlenatch, kayak around East Thurlow, or watch the Shark Spit Regatta sail around Marina Island. Mail your travel postcards from the Surge Narrows floating post office on Read Island. Stay at the swanky wilderness resort on Sonora, or try the "glamping" accommodations on Maurelle. If you can't decide, take a guided "island-tasting" tour—Misty Isle Adventures runs sailing day trips, and Coast Mountain Expeditions offers multiday kayak camping trips.

▶ Refuge Cove, the upper islands' easternmost year-round community, is the last supply stop for boaters heading up the remote fjords of Toba and Bute Inlets.

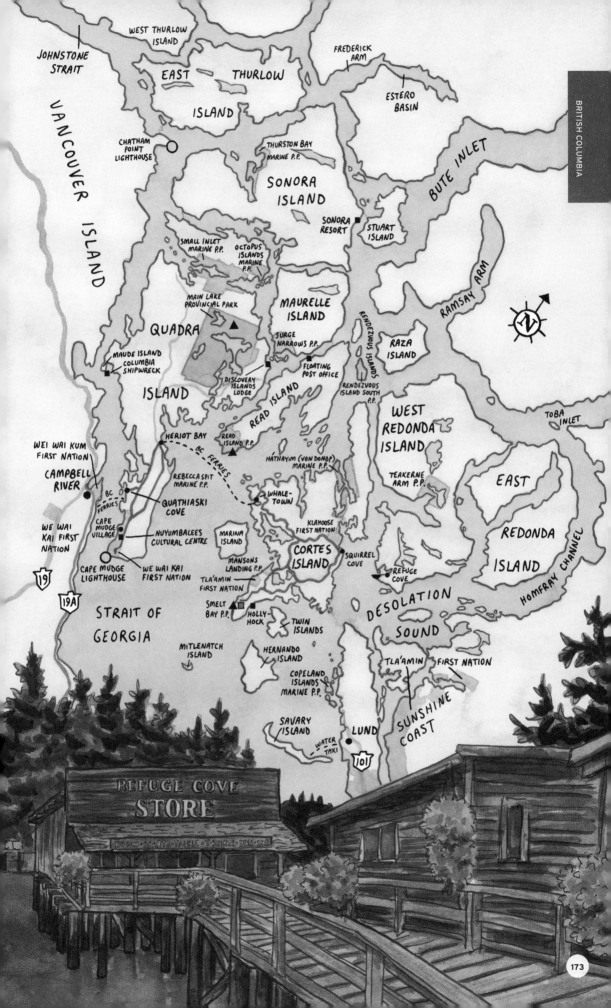

JOHNSTONE
STRAIT

WEST THURLOW
ISLAND

FREDERICK
ARM

EAST THURLOW

ISLAND

ESTERO
BASIN

VANCOUVER ISLAND

CHATHAM
POINT
LIGHTHOUSE

THURSTON BAY
MARINE P.P.

BUTE INLET

SONORA
ISLAND

SONORA
RESORT

STUART
ISLAND

SMALL INLET
MARINE P.P.

OCTOPUS
ISLANDS
MARINE
P.P.

RAMSAY ARM

MAIN LAKE
PROVINCIAL PARK

MAURELLE
ISLAND

RENDEZVOUS ISLANDS

RAZA
ISLAND

QUADRA

SURGE
NARROWS P.P.

FLOATING
POST OFFICE

MAUDE ISLAND
COLUMBIA
SHIPWRECK

DISCOVERY
ISLANDS
LODGE

RENDEZVOUS
ISLAND SOUTH
P.P.

TOBA
INLET

ISLAND

READ ISLAND

WEST
REDONDA
ISLAND

HERIOT BAY

READ
ISLAND P.P.

WEI WAI KUM
FIRST NATION

BC FERRIES

HÁTHAYIM (VON DONOP)
MARINE P.P.

TEAKERNE
ARM P.P.

EAST

CAMPBELL
RIVER

REBECCA SPIT
MARINE P.P.

WHALE-
TOWN

BC
FERRIES

QUATHIASKI
COVE

REDONDA

WE WAI
KAI FIRST
NATION

CAPE MUDGE
VILLAGE

NUYUMBALEES
CULTURAL CENTRE

MARINA
ISLAND

KLAHOOSE
FIRST NATION

CORTES
ISLAND

SQUIRREL
COVE

ISLAND

19

CAPE MUDGE
LIGHTHOUSE

WE WAI KAI
FIRST NATION

MANSONS
LANDING P.P.

REFUGE
COVE

HOMFRAY CHANNEL

19A

TLA'AMIN
FIRST NATION

SMELT
BAY P.P.

HOLLY-
HOCK

DESOLATION

STRAIT OF

TWIN
ISLANDS

SOUND

GEORGIA

MITLENATCH
ISLAND

HERNANDO
ISLAND

TLA'AMIN FIRST NATION

COPELAND
ISLANDS
MARINE P.P.

SUNSHINE

SAVARY
ISLAND

LUND

COAST

WATER
TAXI

101

REFUGE COVE
STORE

Wild Bouquet

Spring and summer bring a burst of color to the islands. Whether you sail to Yellow Island (page 129), hike up the Forbidden Plateau (page 153), or simply stop along the roadside, you'll find many different wildflower species along your way. Here are just a few to watch out for:

▼ **WOODLAND EPHEMERA.** These short-lived, shade-loving blossoms can be found on the forest floor. Many are fragile or rare. Be a good island steward and refrain from picking these or any other wildflowers.

PACIFIC
BLEEDING HEART

SKUNK CABBAGE
(SWAMP LANTERN)

FAIRY SLIPPER
(CALYPSO ORCHID)

COAST
FAWN LILY

WHITE TRILLIUM
(WESTERN WAKE-ROBIN)

▶ **BEACH AND BOG.** These flowers need a lot of moisture, so you'll find them adding extra beauty (or in the case of the chocolate lily, a mighty stink) to marshy areas or along creeksides.

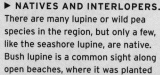

CHOCOLATE LILY

COMMON YELLOW
MONKEYFLOWER

▶ **NATIVES AND INTERLOPERS.**
There are many lupine or wild pea species in the region, but only a few, like the seashore lupine, are native. Bush lupine is a common sight along open beaches, where it was planted to help control erosion.

BUSH LUPINE

SEASHORE LUPINE

WESTERN
BOG LAUREL

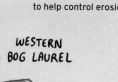

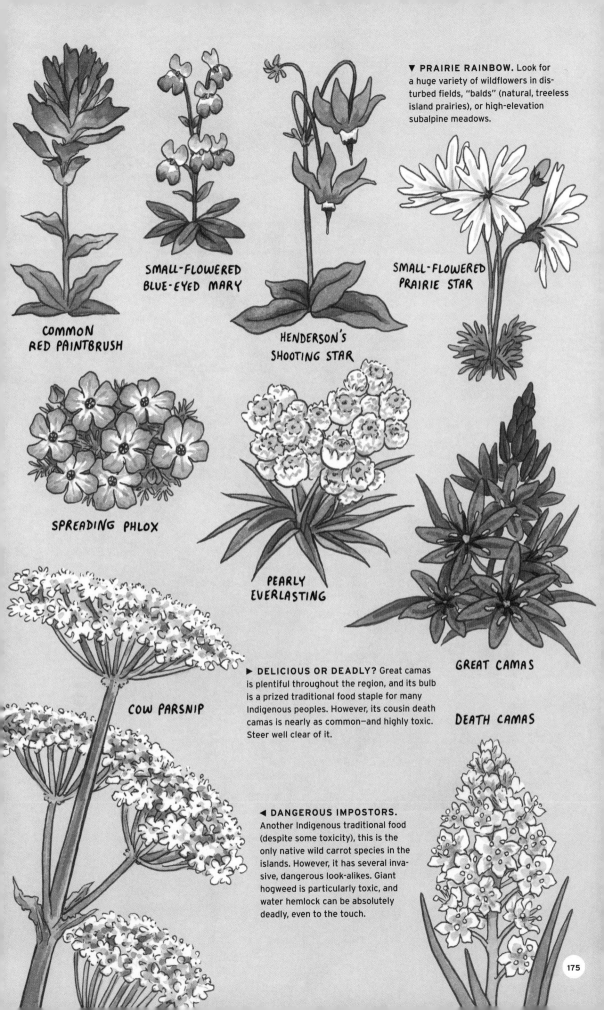

COMMON
RED PAINTBRUSH

SMALL-FLOWERED
BLUE-EYED MARY

HENDERSON'S
SHOOTING STAR

▼ PRAIRIE RAINBOW. Look for a huge variety of wildflowers in disturbed fields, "balds" (natural, treeless island prairies), or high-elevation subalpine meadows.

SMALL-FLOWERED
PRAIRIE STAR

SPREADING PHLOX

PEARLY
EVERLASTING

GREAT CAMAS

DEATH CAMAS

COW PARSNIP

▶ DELICIOUS OR DEADLY? Great camas is plentiful throughout the region, and its bulb is a prized traditional food staple for many Indigenous peoples. However, its cousin death camas is nearly as common—and highly toxic. Steer well clear of it.

◀ DANGEROUS IMPOSTORS. Another Indigenous traditional food (despite some toxicity), this is the only native wild carrot species in the islands. However, it has several invasive, dangerous look-alikes. Giant hogweed is particularly toxic, and water hemlock can be absolutely deadly, even to the touch.

THE SUNSHINE COAST

THE

▲ Logging threatens the elusive marbled murrelet, a small seabird that nests high in old-growth forests. Scientists didn't document this behavior until the 1970s, and only a few nests have ever been found.

▼ Princess Louisa Inlet is known by the shíshálh people as Suivoolot, a name that means "sunny and warm." There are no roads here—the fjord is accessible only by boat or floatplane.

This wild, fjordy pocket of the BC mainland is a great place to end your Salish Sea adventure. With quaint seaside communities, many small islands, and rugged mountains, you'll find beauty to explore in every direction. The area includes the ancestral homelands of the Squamish, shíshálh, Tla'amin, and Klahoose peoples. White settlement began in the 1880s with the fishing, logging, and paper mill industries, and tourism followed in the twentieth century.

The sunny name can be a bit misleading—this region has the same annual rainfall as Seattle and the same wet-winter-dry-summer climate. The moniker originated in 1914, when a local businessman painted "The Sunshine Belt" onto a wharf building to promote tourism. When Black Ball Ferries began the first car ferry service to the area in 1951, it used the term "Sunshine Coast" for promotion—and the name stuck. If you're truly committed to maximizing sunshine on your trip, the Cowichan region (page 148) is warmer and Victoria (page 142) is drier.

This chapter assumes you're starting your Sunshine Coast journey from Vancouver (the city), so we'll journey northward from there. (Highway 101 technically runs southeast-northwest, so some travelers may consider it an east-west journey. But the highway is officially designated as a south-north route, so this chapter follows that logic.) You could, however, do the trip in reverse and begin in Powell River, arriving on the Comox ferry from Vancouver Island. And of course, if you are traveling in your own boat, you can pick up the thread wherever you make landfall.

BUTE INLET

TOBA

INLET

KLAHOOSE WILDERNESS RESORT

MOUNT DENMAN

ELDRED VALLEY

CHATTERBOX FALLS

PRINCESS LOUISA INLET

N

WEST REDONDA ISLAND

EAST REDONDA ISLAND

PAGE 182

REFUGE COVE

DESOLATION SOUND

DESOLATION SOUND MARINE P.P.

POWELL LAKE

KLAHOOSE FIRST NATION

GOAT LAKE

CORTES ISLAND

MALASPINA P.P.

TLA'AMIN FIRST NATION

GOAT ISLAND

THE KNUCKLEHEADS SKI AREA

LUND

DODD LAKE

INLAND LAKE P.P.

HASLAM LAKE

HORSESHOE LAKE

SAVARY ISLAND

LOIS LAKE

JERVIS INLET

AHGYKSON ISLAND

POWELL RIVER

101

NARROWS INLET

SECHELT INLET

SQUAMISH

BC FERRIES

BC FERRIES

NELSON ISLAND

SALMON INLET

STRAIT

TEXADA ISLAND

PAGE 180

SPIPIYUS PROVINCIAL PARK

HOWE SOUND

COURTENAY

COMOX

OF

TETRAHEDRON PROVINCIAL PARK

GAMBIER ISLAND

19

HORNBY ISLAND

DENMAN ISLAND

101

SHÍSHÁLH FIRST NATION

SISTERS ISLETS LIGHTHOUSE

LASQUETI ISLAND

GEORGIA

MERRY ISLAND LIGHTHOUSE

SECHELT

LANGDALE

BOWEN ISLAND

VANCOUVER

QUALICUM BEACH

SANGSTER ISLAND LIGHTHOUSE

GIBSONS

PAGE 178

HORSESHOE BAY

PARKSVILLE

ISLAND

WEST VANCOUVER

VANCOUVER

BC FERRIES

NANAIMO

GABRIOLA ISLAND

ONE IF BY LAND, TWO IF BY SEA

The Sunshine Coast region is bound between Howe and Desolation Sounds, and the Strait of Georgia. And many consider some of the Northern Gulf Islands, like Cortes and Texada, to be included as well. The 156-kilometer (96-mile) Sunshine Coast Highway (BC Highway 101) runs most of the length of the region, but the route is not contiguous with any other mainland highway. There's a ferry on either end—and since the coast is bisected by Jervis Inlet, there's one in the middle too. The 17.6-kilometer (9.5-nautical-mile) ferry run between Earls Cove and Saltery Bay is officially part of the highway route. Thanks to road, weather, and tidal conditions, this region is notorious for missed, delayed, or canceled ferries. Save yourself a major headache by building in plenty of extra time, and try not to schedule more than one ferry crossing per day.

NAVIGATING BY PURPLE FLAG

The Sunshine Coast has more artists per capita than any other region in Canada, so get ready for some serious inspiration. The year-round Purple Banner Tour of open studios, galleries, and events stretches the entire length of the region. Wherever you see a purple banner, you'll know artists work there. A flying banner is often an invitation for the public to enter a studio or venue—but not always. Some locations require calling ahead, and others are only open on certain days. There's also an Art Crawl each October, where many studios and galleries are all open at once. Do your research ahead of time to get the most out of your tour.

MAINLAND, INTERRUPTED

Your Sunshine Coast journey begins with BC Ferries at Horseshoe Bay, a West Vancouver enclave perched on the eastern shore of Howe Sound. (If you're biking, you can even skip the car and take a Vancouver city bus to Horseshoe Bay!) Horseshoe Bay is a BC Ferries hub, offering service

▲ To see individual studios of working artists on the Purple Banner Tour, be sure to call ahead for an appointment. Unlike galleries or performance venues, many of these locations are not open for walk-ins.

to Langdale, Nanaimo (page 149), and adjacent Bowen Island—home to the historic Union Steamship cottages resort. Howe Sound is a favorite of both paddlers and scuba divers, and a number of adventure tour outfits in Horseshoe Bay and on Bowen Island offer snorkeling, scuba diving, and sea kayaking trips. Within reach of boaters and paddlers are Halkett Bay Marine Provincial Park on Gambier Island, the Pasley Island Group archipelago, Anvil Island, and Keats Island—Gambier and Keats are also accessible by BC Ferries (passenger only) from Langdale, but Bowen Island is not.

WELCOME TO THE OTHER SIDE

The ferry lands at the tiny village of Langdale. There's a wildlife viewing platform at the ferry terminal, where you can watch coho and chum salmon return to spawn in the autumn. From Langdale you'll begin your journey up Highway 101—or you can first take a short detour up Port Mellon Highway and back, for more views of Howe Sound. From Port Mellon, rugged Rainy Road leads you to the "back door" of Tetrahedron Provincial Park (page 181).

THE TV TOWN

Originally incorporated in 1929 as Gibson's Landing, the town now officially called Gibsons became a star thanks to the television show *The Beachcombers*—which ran on the CBC from 1972 to 1990. With fans around the world, the show's main filming location is still widely recognizable, even decades later. Gibsons is small, but its scenic location makes it a great stop to stretch your legs or have a meal (note that the town is located away from the main highway, on the water). Explore the region's history at the Sunshine Coast Museum and Archives. Tour the waterfront on the wheelchair-accessible Seawalk, grab a cuppa at Beachcomber Coffee, then buy local produce or artisan-made goodies at the Gibsons Public Market. Visit the hop and barley fields at the Beer Farm, owned by local favorite Persephone Brewing

▲ Howe Sound is one of British Columbia's many fjords—narrow inlets carved by glaciers. The water here reaches a maximum depth of 1,000 feet, below mountains topping out at over 5,000 feet in height.

▼ Gibsons began hosting a fall lantern festival in 2019, inspired by the ancient Chinese tradition of displaying painted paper lanterns to celebrate the lunar new year.

Molly's Reach began as a fictional setpiece for *The Beachcombers*, but after the show ended it became a real restaurant, which remains a Gibsons icon to this day.

TO POWELL RIVER
SALTERY BAY
SUNSHINE COAST TRAILHEAD
SALTERY BAY P.P.
JERVIS INLET
BC FERRIES
EARLS COVE
NELSON ISLAND (PRIVATE)
RUBY LAKE
EGMONT
SAKINAW LAKE
SKOOKUMCHUCK NARROWS P.P.
PENDER HARBOUR
SPIPIYUS PROVINCIAL PARK
INLET
NARROWS INLET
101
SMUGGLER COVE MARINE P.P.
SECRET COVE
SALMON INLET
SECHELT
HALFMOON BAY
MOUNT RICHARDSON P.P.
COOPER'S GREEN PARK
MERRY ISLAND LIGHTHOUSE
PORPOISE BAY P.P.
STRAIT OF GEORGIA
SECHELT
SHÍSHÁLH FIRST NATION
DAVIS BAY
TO GIBSONS
N
ROBERTS CREEK

Company. And if you visit in late July, don't miss the annual Sea Cavalcade, a weekend-long nautical festival.

A SPLASH OF COLOR

Just down the road is Roberts Creek, a quiet village nicknamed the Gumboot (galoshes) Capital of the World. Rain or shine, its long, sandy beaches are perfect for a contemplative walk. You can finish your meditative meandering at the community mandala—an ongoing pavement mural begun in 1997, with the help of hundreds of local and tourist painters. Afterward, stop for a meal at the Gumboot Restaurant. Or if your timing is right, catch the Slow Sundays in the Creek, a summer music and outdoor market event.

Next up is Davis Bay, home to a pebbled beach that is a favorite among locals and visitors alike. Walk the length of Davis Bay Pier to catch the sunset—or if you're lucky, a whale sighting. On clear days you'll have an expansive view of Vancouver Island, just across the Salish Sea.

THE SMORGASBORD

The largest town in the southern Sunshine Coast is Sechelt, named for the shíshálh people who have lived here for thousands of years. The name translates to "land between two waters," referring to the narrow isthmus between the Strait of Georgia and Sechelt Inlet. You can discover local Indigenous history by visiting the tems swiya Museum, which houses artifacts that include a 3,500-year-old mortuary stone. At nearby Porpoise Bay there's a paddle center run by Talaysay Tours, a Coast Salish–owned ecotour company in Vancouver, which also offers themed day trips to Sunshine Coast sites.

Sechelt has carved out a niche as a haven for foodies. Try a meal at the Wobbly Canoe, Shift Kitchen & Bar, or the Lighthouse Pub—or coffee and a pastry at Lone Wolf Bakery. Sechelt is also a capital of the other BC:

the Brewer's Coast, also called the BC Ale Trail. You can enjoy a pint at Batch 44 Brewery & Kitch or Brickers Cider Company—or take to the air for a "Flights to Flights" float-plane tour, including lunch and several tasting rooms.

A PECK OF PARKS

This section of the Sunshine Coast has many parks to choose from—some right off the road, others tucked away in the backcountry or offshore. Family-friendly Porpoise Bay Provincial Park offers camping, mountain bike trails, and a swimming beach. Winter adventurers love Dakota Ridge's cross-country trails and Tetrahedron Provincial Park's cozy backcountry cabins. Be warned that avalanches are a major risk in Tetrahedron's mountains. Halfmoon Bay is the gateway to Spipiyus Provincial Park, which protects pockets of some of the world's oldest specimens of yellow cedar and western hemlock trees. The park's name is the shíshálh term for the marbled murrelet, which nests in the trees there. Near Secret Cove is Smuggler Cove Marine Provincial Park, whose calm waters are beloved by paddle boarders (you can access this park by land or sea). Afterward, if money is no object, you can stay at Rockwater Secret Cove Resort, which features a quartet of luxury "tenthouse suites" perched on the cliffside. You can easily access all these parks, especially if you're a boater, from the unincorporated community of Pender Harbour, a haven for sailing, kayaking, scuba diving, and recreational salmon fishing. Soak in a bit of culture at the Pender Harbour Blues Festival in June or the Pender Harbour Chamber Music Festival in August.

THE TURN OF THE TIDE

Before you catch your ferry at Earls Cove, take the short side road east to Egmont. Nearby Skookumchuck Narrows Provincial Park is worth the detour. Its Chinook name ("strong water") refers to the Sechelt Rapids, which form when tidewater is forced through the Narrows. You'll see whirlpools at ebb tide (page 21) and dramatic waves at flood tide—the size and timing of these depend upon the tides themselves. Keep your tide chart handy, and stop in at the Sechelt Visitor Centre for information on when to arrive at the viewing platform. A fairly easy, hour-long (each way), 4-kilometer (2.5-mile) hike is required to reach the rapids.

For even more coastal drama, try a tour of Jervis Inlet—boat, kayak, and floatplane tours leave from Egmont, if you don't have your own vessel. Near the end of the waterway lies

▲ Visit Roberts Creek in July, and you can help "refresh" the mandala with a brand new, annual design under the direction of a lead artist.

▼ Experienced kayakers and surfers like to ride the waves at Skookumchuck Narrows, but this is not a feat for beginning paddlers.

Princess Louisa Inlet (map on page 177)—a small but spectacular fjord, at the head of which Chatterbox Falls plunges 40 meters (120 feet) to the water below.

THE WOODS BECKON

The northern half of the Sunshine Coast is even more rural than the southern half, with just one major town and a handful of small communities. Most of the attractions up here revolve around backcountry woods and water. This is where outdoor lovers come for the ideal "forest bathing" experience, a Japanese concept that has become popular in the West of late. Called shinrin-yoku in Japan, the idea refers not to a literal bath but to soaking in the atmosphere of the woods—an act that restores the mind, body, and soul.

The Powell Forest Canoe Route combines the best of the forest and the water. This trail runs for fifty-seven kilometers (thirty-five miles) and includes five portages to cover eight lakes near Powell River. It takes at least five full days to do the whole thing, but beginners can get their feet wet (so to speak) at Inland Lake Provincial Park.

For the ultimate forest hike, look no further than the Sunshine Coast Trail, which extends to Sarah Point and begins right at the ferry landing in Saltery Bay. This 180-kilometer (110-mile) trek is Canada's longest "hut-to-hut" trail—punctuated by fourteen rustic sleeping huts, plus some tent pads for overflow campers. Like the West Coast Trail (page 148), it's designed for experienced hikers with wilderness experience—but this trail is free of charge. Meeting dangerous wildlife is a possibility here, and you'll need to purify any water you collect for drinking.

PAPER AND PRESERVATION

The Sunshine Coast's largest town, Powell River, sits on the homelands of the Tla'amin people. Once home to the world's largest paper mill, it's now a hub for BC Ferries, with service to Texada and Vancouver Islands.

History buffs will like the original Historic Townsite, a 1910 planned community with more than 400 original buildings still intact. This led the area to be designated one of Canada's National Historic Districts in 1995—one of only seven at the time, and still the only one in western Canada. Don't miss the Patricia Theatre, the oldest continuously operating movie house in Canada.

There's plenty to do outdoors here too. Snow hounds love the Knuckleheads, a group of backcountry ski and snowshoe trails northeast of Powell River (same hazards as

▼ The huts along the Sunshine Coast Trail are available on a "first-come, first-sleep" basis. Three are winterized for four-season camping, but most have just three walls.

at Tetrahedron apply here). Experienced rock climbers tackle the sheer granite walls of the Eldred Valley, a wilderness area that parallels Powell Lake. And with many dive sites to choose from, the Powell River area is also a major destination for scuba divers. (Of note is the Emerald Princess, a large underwater mermaid statue at the Mermaid Cove dive site, at Saltery Bay Provincial Park.)

COASTAL POSTSCRIPT

The Sunshine Coast Highway continues past Powell River to Lund, and then a rough logging road ends at the Sunshine Coast Trailhead, near Bliss Landing and Sarah Point. Lund offers a water taxi (definitely call ahead for a reservation) to Savary Island, home to white-sand beaches and, according to locals, the warmest swimming water north of Mexico. Just offshore from Bliss Landing are the Copeland Islands, protected as a marine provincial park. The park features a handful of backcountry campsites for kayakers.

DESOLATION AND INSPIRATION

The Sunshine Coast ends at Desolation Sound, where the waters are surprisingly warm, thanks to a convergence of tidal currents. Beyond are the fjords of Toba and Bute Inlets, and distinctive Mount Denman is visible from many points in the area. Visitors without their own boat can explore the area and its remote provincial parks via adventure tours operating out of Lund and Powell River. With the exception of Refuge Cove (page 172), most services in and around Desolation Sound are seasonal. The only major lodging in the area is the new Klahoose Wilderness Resort (formerly Homfray Lodge), an Indigenous-owned eco-resort run by the Klahoose First Nation. A stay here is pricey but all-inclusive, with guided cultural and wildlife-viewing boat tours, Indigenous storytelling, foraging and cedar weaving lessons, and sustainable, traditional cuisine.

END OF THE LINE, OR A NEW BEGINNING

Instead of returning to Vancouver, you can hop the Comox ferry to Vancouver Island, then complete the loop back to Horseshoe Bay on a ferry out of Nanaimo (page 149). If you're not ready to say farewell to the fjords yet, from Horseshoe Bay you can drive the Sea-to-Sky Highway, which runs up the eastern shore of Howe Sound, then up to Whistler Ski Resort. From there it's possible to continue on to points north, including the ALCAN (Alaska-Canada) Highway.

▲ Many Coast Salish peoples traditionally prepare chum salmon by slow-roasting butterfly-cut filets on cedar skewers and split stakes over an alderwood fire.

▼ Inland Lake Provincial Park features a boardwalk bike trail, part of which is built right on the lakeshore. Watch out for crowds on this popular trail.

Beacons in the Night

Lighthouses represent one of humanity's best qualities: the desire to protect others. There are more than forty lighthouses in the Salish Sea region, and many of them are open to the public. On this spread are a few outstanding historical specimens; though some are only reachable by boat.

◄ **TEMPLATES.** Several lighthouse styles follow a stock architectural form, such as the tower, Cape Cod, and pepper-pot (or salt shaker) style. Cape Mudge's tapered silhouette is copied all over Canada, and a number of Puget Sound (page 22) lighthouse were built using standardized shapes and paint colors.

POINT ROBINSON LIGHTHOUSE (1914)
MAURY ISLAND, WA

CAPE MUDGE
LIGHTHOUSE (1916)
QUADRA ISLAND, BC

▶ **LONELY OUTPOSTS.** Vancouver Island has a number of extremely remote lighthouses that are accessible only by boat, or else by overland hiking trail that stretches for many miles.

RACE ROCKS LIGHTHOUSE (1859)
OFF THE SOUTHERN TIP OF VANCOUVER ISLAND, BC

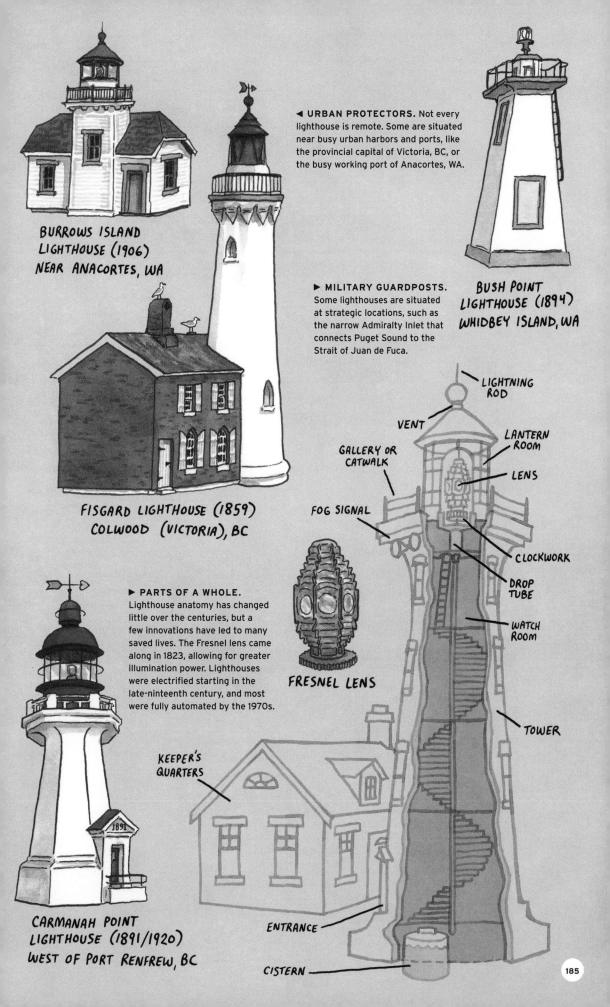

BURROWS ISLAND
LIGHTHOUSE (1906)
NEAR ANACORTES, WA

◀ **URBAN PROTECTORS.** Not every lighthouse is remote. Some are situated near busy urban harbors and ports, like the provincial capital of Victoria, BC, or the busy working port of Anacortes, WA.

BUSH POINT
LIGHTHOUSE (1894)
WHIDBEY ISLAND, WA

▶ **MILITARY GUARDPOSTS.** Some lighthouses are situated at strategic locations, such as the narrow Admiralty Inlet that connects Puget Sound to the Strait of Juan de Fuca.

FISGARD LIGHTHOUSE (1859)
COLWOOD (VICTORIA), BC

LIGHTNING ROD

VENT

GALLERY OR CATWALK

LANTERN ROOM

LENS

FOG SIGNAL

CLOCKWORK

DROP TUBE

WATCH ROOM

▶ **PARTS OF A WHOLE.** Lighthouse anatomy has changed little over the centuries, but a few innovations have led to many saved lives. The Fresnel lens came along in 1823, allowing for greater illumination power. Lighthouses were electrified starting in the late-nineteenth century, and most were fully automated by the 1970s.

FRESNEL LENS

TOWER

KEEPER'S QUARTERS

CARMANAH POINT
LIGHTHOUSE (1891/1920)
WEST OF PORT RENFREW, BC

ENTRANCE

CISTERN

AFTERWORD

Even with a couple hundred pages at my disposal, it's impossible to convey the sheer breadth and depth of the Salish Sea region—inevitably there is something here I've left out, some island given short shrift, some road (or ferry) not taken. This is why I like to be a perennial tourist, even in my own backyard—there is always something new to see, even on the hundredth visit. Not only does that help me plan future island adventures, but it also keeps my excitement evergreen (and ensures that I'll never want to skip the view and stay in my car for a ferry crossing). My hope is that this book has whet your appetite for the Northwest's islands—and that it will inspire you to help take care of them, so they will continue to thrive for all who love and depend upon them.

TAKE IT IN PIECES
If you find yourself overwhelmed by all the options before you, it can help to plan your trip in terms of a single geographic area at a time. The distinct subregions (Puget Sound, the San Juans, the Gulf Islands, etc.) make for an easy place to start. If even that feels daunting, narrow your scope a bit more. Perhaps your itinerary includes just what you can reach along the Anacortes ferry route, or a series of day trips radiating outward from your hotel in Seattle. Or start with

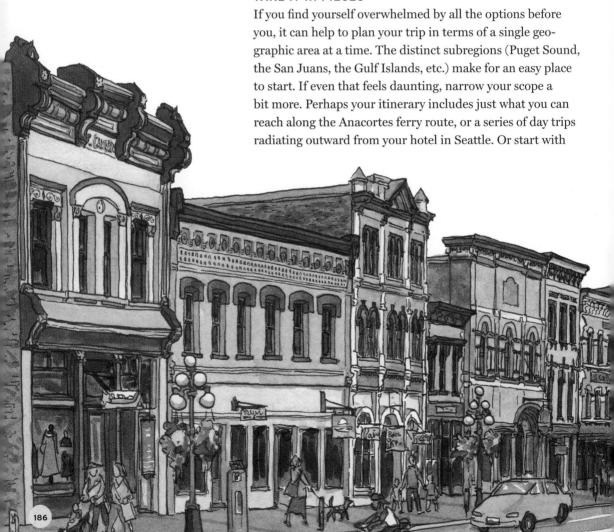

just one island, get to know it thoroughly, then move onto someplace else. This last one is a great approach for Northwesterners, for whom at least some of the islands are local destinations. Breaking your trip down into pieces is also a great strategy for traveling with children. Though ferries are entertaining for most kids, waiting for a ferry is . . . not so much. Cramming too much into your trip can lead to cranky kids and stressed-out parents. Creating a more manageable itinerary will make your island memories that much sweeter.

LEAVE 'EM WANTING MORE

As someone who tends to ignore her own advice and shoehorn absolutely *everything* into her travel plans, I can tell you how I try to approach a healthier balance. I tell myself that this is only the first trip—that *next time*, I'll get to the things I missed. Many times, I keep my word to myself: I do get to make those return trips, and each time I cross a few more items off my wish list. And for other places, I'm still waiting for that return trip one day. I am okay with this. It keeps my travel memories fresh and ensures that every time I step onto another ferry (even just for an errand!), I feel that wave of excitement.

Among all this careful planning, it's important to leave room for serendipity—you never know what surprises you might find along the way. Indeed, those surprises might well come in the form of missed ferries or closed roads—or they might include unexpected delights that have you happily canceling reservations and adding extra days to your trip. In the end, all these things—good and bad, easy and difficult— become part of your journey, part of your story. If you can approach the islands with an open mind and heart, the story you create on your adventure might become one of your most cherished memories.

▼ Lower Johnson Street in Victoria is lined with tiny shops and indie fashion boutiques housed in candy-hued, nineteenth-century storefronts.

PRONUNCIATION GUIDE

PRONUNCIATION KEY

Accented syllables appear in capital letters.

AY	(bay, sail)
A	(cat, tab)
AH	(cod)
AL	(pal)
ALL	(all, ball)
AW	(ought, saw)
AIR	(fair, rare)
EAR	(pierce)
EE	(bee, see)
E	(bet, said)
ER	(birch, fir)
EYE	(island, sight)
EEUH	(gloria)
I	(bit, hit)
OH	(go, sew)
OW	(out, sound)
OO	(food, suit)
O̲O̲	(bush, foot)
OR	(door, roar)
OY	(point)
YOO	(hue, menu)
UH	(cup, rough)
G	(gull)
J	(jewelry)
S	(cement, sailboat)
SS	(fuss, miss)
K	(cup, kayak)
TS	(cats)
Z	(zero, rosy)

MOST-HEARD PLACES

Anacortes (anna-COR-tiss)
Mount Rainier (ray-NEER)
Orcas Island (OR-cuss)
Puget Sound (PYOO-jit)
Rosario Strait (roh-ZAHR-ee-oh)
Salish Sea (SAY-lish)
Seattle (see-AT-ull)
Strait of Juan de Fuca (WAHN duh FYOO-cuh)
Vancouver Island[1] (vang-COO-ver)
Whidbey Island (WID-bee)

ON THE MENU

Chanterelle mushrooms
  (shan-tuh-REL)
Chinook salmon (shi-NO̲O̲K)
Coho salmon (COH-hoh)
Dungeness crab (DUN-jen-ess)
Geoduck (GOO-ey-duck)
Morel mushrooms (muh-REL)
Poutine (poo-TEEN)
Sashimi (sah-SHEE-mee)
Siegerrebe (zee-ger-EBB-ay)
Terroir (tair-WAHR)

NATURE TERMS

Alevin (AL-uh-vin)
Anadromous trout
  (uh-NA-druh-muhss)
Anemone (ah-NEM-uh-nee)
Archipelago (AHR-kuh-PEL-uh-goh)
Camas (CAM-us)
Isthmus (ISS-muhss)
Marbled murrelet (MER-luht)
Minke whale (MEENK-uh)
Nudibranch (NOO-di-brank)
Salal (suh-LALL)
Shinrin-yoku (SHIN-rin YOH-koo)
Tombolo (TAHM-buh-loh)

MISCELLANEOUS TERMS

Bowline knot (BOH-lin)
Fresnel lens (fruh-NEL)
Issei (EE-say)
Kanakas (kuh-NAH-kahs)
Lopezians (lo-PEEZ-shuns)
Mainsail (MAYN-suhl)
Nisei (NEE-say)
Sansei (SAHN-say)
Tyee fishing (TEYE-EE)
Windlass (WIND-luhss)

▼ Dragon boat racing began in southern China more than two thousand years ago and is now the world's fastest-growing team water sport.

INDIGENOUS NAMES AND TERMS

Ahgykson (AH-geyek-suhn)
Ahousaht (ah-HOWZ-aht)
Duwamish (doo-WAH-mish)
Gilakas'la (GEE-lah-kas-lah)
Gwa'Sala-'Nakwaxda'xw[2] (GWAH-sah-lah-NAHK-kwah-dahk-w)
Haida (HEYE-duh)
Haida Gwaii (HEYE-duh GWEYE)
Haleets/Xalilc (hah-LEETS)
Hibulb (HEYE-bulb)
Hupačasath (hoo-puh-CHESS-et)
Huu-ay-aht (hoo-WAY-aht)
Kamilche (kuh-MIL-chee)
k'awat'si (ka-WAHT-see)
Kikasuw (kee-kah-SOO)
Kitasoo/Xai'xais (KIT-ah-soo/KAY-kayz)
Klahoose (kluh-HOOSS)
Ko-Kwal-Alwoot (koh-KWAHL-uhl-woot)
K'ómoks (COH-mahks)
Kwakiutl (KWAH-gul)
Kwakwaka'wakw[2] (kwah-KWAH-kay-wahk-w)
Kwaḱwala (KWAH-kwah-lah)
Kwa'lilas (KWAH-lee-lahss)
Lekwungen (Luh-KWUNG-en)
Lhaq'temish (LAHK-tuh-mish)
Lushootseed (luh-SHOOT-seed)
Makah (muh-KAW)
Malahat (MAL-ah-hat)
Musqueam (MUHSS-kwee-uhm)
'Namgis (NAHM-geess)
Nisqually (ni-SKWAH-lee)
Nooksack (NOOK-sak)
Nootka (NOOT-kuh)
Nuu-chah-nulth (noo-CHAW-nulth)
Nuyumbalees (neye-YUHM-bah-lees)
Pacheedaht (pah-CHEE-daht)
Pauquachin (PAH-kwuh-chin)
Pe'pi'ow'elh[3] (puh-pee-OW-ech)
Potlatch (PAHT-lach)
Puyallup (pew-ALL-up)

Q'emásən (KEM-ah-suhn)
Quatsino (kwaht-SEE-noh)
Quileute (KWILL-ee-yoot)
Quw'utsun (koo-WOOT-suhn)
Qwe 'lhol mechen (kwuh-HALL-much-sten)
Saanich (SA-nich)
Samish (SAM-ish)
Sc'ianew (CHEE-nuh)
Semiahmoo (SEM-ee-AH-moo)
Shíshálh (SHEE-sha)
Si'ahl[4] (SEE-ah-lsch)
Sk'aliCh'elh[3] (SKAL-ee-CHUH)
Skéxe (SKIK-shuh)
S'Klallam[5] (skuh-LAH-lum)
Snohomish (snuh-HO-mish)
Snuneymuxw[6] (snoo-NAY-muh)
Songhees (SAHN-geez)
Spipiyus (SPI-pee-yuhss)
Sq'emenen (SKUH-muh-nen)
Squamish (SKWAH-mish)
Squaxin (SKWAHX-in)
Stillaguamish (still-uh-GWAH-mish)
Stz'uminus (shuh-MAY-nuhss)
Suivoolot (swee-VOO-luht)
Suquamish (suh-KWAH-mish)
Swədəbš/Swadabs (swuh-DAHBS)
Swinomish (SWIN-uh-mish)
Sxʷáləʔ (SHWAH-lah)
tems swiya (temz SWEE-yah)
Tla'amin (sleye-AM-uhn)
Tlatlasikwala (KLAHT-la-seek-KWAH-la)
Tla-o-qui-aht (klah-OH-kwee-aht)
Tlingit (KLING-it)
Tlo:kwa:na (klo-KWAH-nah)
Tsartlip (SART-lip)
T'sasala (TSAH-sah-lah)
Tsawout (TSAY-owt)
Tsawwassen[7] (tsa-WAH-sen)
Tsaxis (TSAYK-sis)
Tseshaht (TSAY-shaht)
Ts'el-xwi-sen/Chulxwesing (SHUL-hwuh-suhn)
Tseycum (TSAY-coom)
T'Sou-ke (TSAW-awk)

Ts'uubaa-asatx (TSOO-bah-set)
Tulalip (too-LAY-lip)
Txiwuc (SHEE-wook)
U'mista (oo-MEE-stuh)
Uchucklesaht (yoo-CHUCK-le-sat)
We Wai Kai (WEE-wah-KAY)
Wei Wai Kum (WEE-wah-kuhm)
Wh'lehl-kluh (whuh-LAYL-kluh)
Xwemelch'stn (hwuh-MULCH-stuhn)
Yalis (YAH-lis)

NOTES

1. Vancouverites pronounce a "hidden G" inside of the name Vancouver—if you want to sound like a local, don't forget that letter!

2. The "w" that ends some Indigenous words (as well as the "wh" consonant within some others) is difficult for many non-native speakers to pronounce. It sounds a bit like a soft blowing of air, similar to a whispered "whoo."

3. The "elh" sound that ends some Indigenous words is a guttural "h" sound, similar to the "ch" sound in Hebrew.

4. A common Indigenous pronunciation of Chief Si'ahl is "SEE-ah-lsch," but Camp Sealth and the ferry MV *Sealth*, both derived from a misspelling of Si'ahl, are pronounced in the Americanized way, which rhymes with "wealth."

5. The "S'K" syllable in "S'Klallam" is spoken very quickly in a short "skuh" sound, as if the "LAH" syllable interrupts it.

6. Snuneymuxw ends in the same guttural "h" sound as "Sk'aliCh'elh."

7. The Indigenous pronunciation of Tsawwassen is similar to "tsa-WAH-sen." However, people who live in and near Tsawwassen, BC, pronounce it "tuh-WAH-sen." Many Canadians who live in other parts of BC pronounce it "suh-WAH-sen."

WSF VESSELS

MV *Cathlamet* (cuth-LAM-it)
MV *Chelan* (shuh-LAN)
MV *Chetzemoka* (CHET-zuh-MOKE-uh)
MV *Chilkat* (CHILL-kat)
MV *Chimacum* (CHIM-uh-kuhm)
MV *Elwha* (ELL-wah)
MV *Issaquah* (ISS-uh-kwah)
MV *Kalakala* (Kuh-LAH-kuh-lah)
MV *Kaleetan* (kuh-LEE-tuhn)
MV *Kitsap* (KIT-sap)
MV *Kittitas* (KIT-uh-toss)
MV *Puyallup* (pew-ALL-up)
MV *Spokane* (spo-KAN)
MV *Tillikum* (TILL-uh-kuhm)
MV *Tokitae* (TOKE-ah-tay)
MV *Wenatchee* (wuh-NAT-chee)
MV *Yakima* (YACK-uh-muh)

BC FERRIES VESSELS

MV *Kahloke* (kuh-LOH-kee)
MV *Klitsa* (KLIT-suh; KLEET-suh)
MV *Kuper* (KYOO-per; KOO-per)
MV *Kwuna* (KOO-nuh)
MV *Queen of Coquitlam*
  (Coh-KWIT-luhm)
MV *Quinitsa* (kwin-IT-suh)
MV *Quinsam* (KWIN-sum)
MV *Tachek* (TAY-check; TAH-check)

WASHINGTON PLACE NAMES

Alki Point (AL-keye)
Bellingham (BELL-ing-ham)
Ben Ure Island (BEN-yuhr)
Bloedel Reserve (bloh-DEL)
Cama Beach (CAM-uh)
Camano Island (ca-MAY-no)
Camp Sealth[4] (SELTH)
Cap Sante Park (CAP-SANT)
Colvos Passage (COHL-vohss)
Coupeville (COOP-ville)
Decatur Island (de-CAY-ter)
Dugualla State Park (doo-GWALL-uh)
Ebey's Landing (EE-beez)
Elger Bay (ELL-jer)
Fidalgo Island (fi-DAL-goh)
Guemes Island (GWEE-miss)
Haro Strait (HAHR-oh)
Harstine Island (HAR-steen)
Hoypus Point Forest (HOY-puhss)
Ika Island (EE-kuh; EYE-kuh)
Jarrell Cove (JAIR-uhl)
Ketron Island (KE-tron)
Kiket Island (KICK-it)
Kitsap Peninsula (KIT-sap)
Klahanie (klah-HAH-nee)
Kukutali Preserve (kook-uh-TAH-lee)
Legoe Bay (LEE-goh)
Leque Island (luh-KWAY)
Lisabeula Park (LEYE-zah-BYOO-lah)
Lummi Island (LUHM-ee)
Mackaye Harbor (muh-KAY)
Marrowstone Island (MAIR-oh-stuhn)
Matia Island[8] (MAY-shuh)
Mercer Island (MER-ser)

Moran State Park (muh-RAN)
Mukilteo (muckle-TEE-oh)
Neah Bay (NEE-uh)
Odlin County Park (AHD-lin)
Padilla Bay (puh-DILL-ah)
Palouse Winery (puh-LOOSS)
Patos Island[9] (PA-toess)
Pelindaba Lavender (pel-in-DAH-buh)
Poulsbo[10] (PALLZ-bo)
Roche Harbor (ROHsh)
SeaTac International Airport
  (SEE-tak)
Skagit Valley (SKAJ-it)
Snee-oosh Beach (SNEE-oosh)
Spieden Island (SPEYE-dun)
Squaxin Island (SKWAK-sin)
Steilacoom (STILL-a-coom)
Sucia Island[8] (SOO-shuh)
Suyematsu Farm (soo-ye-MAHT-soo)
Swadabs Park (swuh-DAHBS)
Tahlequah (TAL-uh-kwah)
Tillicum Village (TIL-uh-cuhm)
Utsalady (uht-suh-LAD-dee)
Vashon Island (VASH-on)
Vendovi Island (ven-DOH-vee)
Waldron Island (WALL-druhn)
Watmough Bay (WAHT-moo)
Yeomalt (YOH-mult)

BRITISH COLUMBIA PLACE NAMES

Abkhazi Garden (AB-KAH-zee)
Bowen Island (BOH-uhn)
Butchart Gardens (BOOTCH-art)
Bute Inlet (BYOOT)
Buttle Lake (BUH-tuhl)

▼ Straitsview Farm on San Juan Island boasts a beautifully restored historic barn, built in the gable-on-hip style in 1863.

Carmanah Point Lighthouse
  (car-MA-nuh)
Chemainus (shuh-MAY-nuhss)
Clayoquot Plateau (KLA-kwaht)
Comox (COH-mahks)
Coombs (COOMS)
Cortes Island (COR-TEZ)
Courtenay (CORT-nee)
Cowichan (COW-i-chuhn)
Craigdarroch Castle (CRAIG-DAIR-uhk)
De Courcy Island (De-COR-see)
Dionisio Point Provincial Park
  (deye-oh-NEE-see-oh)
Esquimalt (es-SKWEYE-malt)
Fillongley Provincial Park
  (fi-LAHN-glee)
Gabriola Island (GAY-bree-OH-lah)
Galiano Island (GAL-ee-AN-oh)
Ganges (GAN-jeez)
Gillies Bay (GILL-eez)
Gwaii Haanas National Park Reserve
  (gweye HAH-nuhss)
Háthayim Marine Provincial Park
  (HAH-thah-yim)
Hesquiat Peninsula Provincial Park
  (HESS-kwee-uht)
Kuper Island (KOO-per)
Lasqueti Island (luh-SKEE-tee)
Little Huson Cave Park (HOO-sahn)
Lyackson First Nation (lee-AK-suhn)
Lyall Harbour (LEYE-uhl)
Mahoi House (muh-HOY)
Malahat Summit (MAL-ah-hat)
Malaspina Galleries (mal-uh-SPEE-nuh)
Maquinna Marine Provincial Park
  (mah-KWIN-nah)
Mayne Island (MAYN)

Meares Island (MEERS)
Mitlenatch Island (MIT-uhl-natch)
Nanaimo (nuh-NEYE-moh)
Narvaez Bay (NAR-vez)
Penelakut Island (puh-NEL-uh-ket)
Port Alberni (al-BER-nee)
Port Renfrew (REN-froo)
Pylades Island (pi-LAH-deez)
Quadra Island (KWAH-drah)
Qualicum Beach (KWALL-i-c<u>oo</u>m)
Quathiaski Cove (KWAH-thee-ask-ee)
Quatse Salmon Stewardship Center
  (KWAHT-see)
Redonda Islands, West and East
  (ruh-DAHN-dah)
Saanich (SA-nich)
Saturna Island (suh-TER-nah)
Savary Island (SAY-vree)
Saysutshun (Newcastle Island)
  (SAY-suht-shuhn)
Sechelt (SEE-shelt)
Sointula (soyn-TOO-lah)
Sooke (SOOK)
Strathcona Provincial Park
  (strath-COHN-ah)
Swartz Bay (SHWORTZ)
Texada Island (tek-SAY-duh)
Thetis Island (THEE-tiss)
Tofino (tuh-FEE-noh)
Trincomali Channel (TRIN-coh-
  MAH-lee)
Tsawwassen[7] (tuh-WAH-sen)
Ucluelet (yoo-CLOO-let)
Van Anda (van-AN-duh)
Wickaninnish Inn (WICK-uh-NIN-ish)

NOTES (CONTINUED)

8. The pronunciations of Matia and
    Sucia Islands depend on which
    locals you ask. Most still seem
    to adhere to the Americanized
    pronunciations of "MAY-shuh"
    and "SOO-shuh," but some use
    "mah-TEE-uh" and "soo-SEE-uh,"
    which are based on their colonial
    Spanish names.

9. Some locals pronounce Patos
    Island as "PAH-toess," or even
    "PAY-toess."

10. Some locals pronounce Poulsbo
    as "POHLZ-bo." However, the
    name was originally derived from
    the Norwegian name for Paul's
    place, and is correctly pronounced
    like a man's first name.

INDEX OF PLACES

Note: Page numbers in *italic* refer to maps.

CITIES AND TOWNS
Anacortes, 78-80, 82-83
Bamfield, *141*, 150
Bellingham, 124, *125*
Brentwood Bay, *145*, 146
Campbell River, *141*, *151*, 152-153
Chemainus, *141*, *151*, *159*
Clinton, *43*, 44
Comox, *151*, 169, 176
Coupeville, *43*, 47-50
Courtenay, *141*, *151*, 152, *171*, *177*
Cowichan Bay, 148-149, *151*, *159*
Duncan, 149, *151*, *159*
Esquimalt, 142, *143*
Everett, *43*, 71
Friday Harbor, 76, 77, 86-91, *87*, *89*
Ganges, *161*, 162
Gibsons, *177*, *178*, 179-180
Horseshoe Bay, *177*, 178-179
La Conner, *43*, 66-67, 77, 79
Ladysmith, 149, *151*
Langley, *43*, 44, 45-47
Mukilteo, *43*, 44. 71
Nanaimo, *141*, 149, *151*, 166, 168, *177*
Oak Bay, *143*, 144, *145*
Oak Harbor, *43*, 50
Olympia, 54, *55*, 58-59
Parksville, 150-151, *177*
Port Alberni, *141*, 150
Port Angeles, *v*, 9, 11, *24*
Port Hardy, *140*, 154-155
Port Renfrew, *141*, 147-148
Powell River, 169, 176, *177*, 182-183
Qualicum Beach, 150, *151*, *177*
Seattle, viii-ix, 4-5, 9, 22-23, *24*,
  25-26, *27*, 28, 31, 62, 68-69
Sechelt, *177*, *178*, 180-181
Sidney, *141*, *145*, 146-147
Sooke, *141*, *146*, 147
Stanwood, *43*, *63*, 64
Steilacoom, *55*, 56-57
Swartz Bay, *141*, *145*, 146
Tacoma, vi-vii, 34, 39, 54, *55*, 56, 57
Telegraph Cove, *140*, 153, *154*
Tofino, 139, *141*, *150*, 151
Ucluelet, *141*, *150*, 151
Vancouver, 4-5, 176, *177*, *178*, 180, 183
Victoria, *141*, 142-146

West Vancouver, *177*, 178
Winslow, 26-29

WASHINGTON ISLANDS
Anderson, *55*, 56, *57*
Bainbridge, 26-31
Blakely, *113*, *127*, 128
Camano, 62-65
Cypress, *125*, 126
Decatur, 126-128
Fidalgo, 78-83
Fir, *63*, 66-67
Fox, 57
Guemes, 123, *125*
Harstine, *55*, 58-59
Jetty, *43*, 71
Ketron, *55*, 56, *57*
Lopez, 112-117
Lummi, 123-124, *125*
Marrowstone, *43*, 70
Maury, 34, *35*, 37, 39
McNeil, *55*, 57
Mercer, 68-69
Orcas, 100-109
Samish, 124, *125*
San Juan, 86-97
San Juans (archipelago), 74-133
Shaw, 120-122
Spieden, 130
Squaxin, *55*, 58, 59
Steamboat, *55*, 58, 59
Vashon, 34-39
Vendovi, 124, *125*
Waldron, 130
Whidbey, 42-51
Yellow, *121*, 128-129

BRITISH COLUMBIA ISLANDS
Bowen, *177*, *178*, 179
Broughton (archipelago), *140*, 154-155
Cormorant, xi, 154
Cortes, 172, *173*
Denman, *151*, 169-170, *171*
Discovery (archipelago), 170-173
East Redonda, *170*
Gabriola, *151*, *159*, 166-167
Galiano, *151*, *159*, *161*, 164, 165-166
Gulf (archipelago), *138*, *141*, *149*,
  158-173
Haida Gwaii (archipelago), *138*, 144, 155
Hornby, *151*, 169-170, *171*
Lasqueti, *151*, 169, *171*

Malcolm, *154*, 155
Mayne, *159*, *161*, 164-165
Pender, *159*, *161*, 163-164
Penelakut, *159*, *161*, 166
Prevost, *159*, *161*, 164, 168
Quadra, 170, 172
Salt Spring, 159-163
Saturna, 159, 164
Savary, 171, 183
Sidney, 145, 147
Texada, *151*, 169, *171*
Thetis, *151*, *159*, *161*, 166
Valdes, *159*, 166, 168
Vancouver, 4, 140-155
West Redonda, *173*

LIGHTHOUSES
Active Pass, *159*, 164
Admiralty Head, *43*, 48-49, *50*
Alki Point, 69
Amphitrite Point, *150*
Ballenas Islands, *151*
Bare Point, *151*, *159*, *161*
Berens Island, *143*
Bickford Tower, *143*
Burrows Island, 82, 185
Bush Point, *43*, 44, 185
Cape Beale, *150*
Cape Mudge, *151*, 172-173, 185
Cape Scott, *154*
Carmanah Point, *141*, 185
Cattle Point, *87*, 92, 94
Chatham Point, *173*
Chrome Island, *151*, 170, *171*
Denman Island, *151*, *171*
Discovery Island, *145*
East Point, *159*, 164
Entrance Island, *151*, *159*, 166
Fisgard, *143*, 147, 185
Gallows Point, *151*, 166, 168
Gowlland Point, *159*, *161*
Lennard Island, *150*
Lime Kiln Point, *87*, 96, 97
Marrowstone Point, *43*, 70
Merry Island, *177*, *178*, *180*
Mukilteo, *43*, 71
Ogden Point Breakwater, *143*
Patos Island, 131-132
Point Atkinson, *178*
Point Robinson, *35*, 39, 184
Point Wilson, *43*, 49, 70

Porlier Pass (front and rear), *151*, *159*, *164*, 165
Portlock Point, *159*, *161*, *164*, 168
Pulteney Point, *154*
Race Rocks, *147*, 184
Sand Heads, *159*
Sangster Island, *151*, 177
Scarlett Point, *154*
Sheringham Point, *147*
Sisters Islets, *151*, 177
Trial Islands, *143*
Triangle Island, *146*, 147
Turn Point, 129, *145*, 168
West Point, *27*
Whiffin Spit, *146*

WASHINGTON STATE PARKS
Bay View, *79*
Cama Beach, *62-63*, 65
Camano Island, *63*, 65
Deception Pass, *43*, *50-51*, 77, *79*, 80-81
Dugualla, *43*, *50*, *51*
Fort Casey, *43*, 48, *50*
Fort Ebey, *43*, 48, *50*
Fort Flagler, *43*, 70
Fort Worden, *43*, 70
Harstine Island, *58*, *59*
Jarrell Cove, 54-55, *58-59*
Joseph Whidbey, *43*
Larrabee, *125*
Lime Kiln Point, *87*, 88, *96*, *97*
Moran, *101*, 104-107
Obstruction Pass, *101*, 108, *109*
Possession Point, 44
South Whidbey, *43*, *44*, *45*
Spencer Spit, *113*, 114-115
Stretch Point, *58*, *59*

WASHINGTON MARINE STATE PARKS
Blake Island, 69-70
Blind Island, *121*, 122
Burrows Island, *79*, 82
Clark Island, *76*, *101*, *125*, *131*, 133
Doe Island, 109
Eagle Island, *56*, *57*
Hope Island (north), *43*, 51, *79*
Hope Island (south), *55*, *58*, 59
James Island, *113*, *127*, 128
Jones Island, *87*, *121*, 129, *130*
Matia Island, *101*, *131*, 133
McMicken Island, *55*, 58-59
Mystery Bay, 70
Patos Island, 131-132
Posey Island, *87*, 95
Saddlebag Island, *79*, 124, *125*
Skagit Island, *79*, 81
Stuart Island, 129, *130*
Sucia Island, *101*, *131*, 132-133
Turn Island, *87*, 90, *121*

BRITISH COLUMBIA PROVINCIAL PARKS
Anderson Bay, *171*
Bamberton, *145*, 146
Bodega Ridge, *164*, 166
Boyle Point, 170, *171*
Burgoyne Bay, *161*, 163
Broughton Archipelago, *154*
Cape Scott, *140*, 151, *154*, *155*
Clayoquot Arm, *150*
Clayoquot Plateau, *150*
Dionisio Point, *164*, 165
Drumbeg, *166*
Elk Falls, *151*, 153
Fillongley, 170, *171*
Gabriola Sands, *166*
Goldstream, *145*, 146
Gowlland Tod, *145*, 146
Helliwell, 170, *171*
Hesquiat Peninsula, *140*
Inland Lake, *177*, 182
Kitty Coleman Beach, *151*
MacMillan, 150
Main Lake, 172, *173*
Malaspina, *177*, *182*
Mount Erskine, *161*, 162-163
Mount Geoffrey Escarpment, *171*
Mount Maxwell, *161*, 163
Mount Richardson, *178*, *180*
Mquqʷin/Brooks Peninsula, *140*
Porpoise Bay, *178*, 180
Rathtrevor Beach, *150*, *151*
Read Island, *173*
Rendezvous Island South, 172, *173*
Ruckle, *161*, 162
Saltery Bay, *182*
Sandwell, *166*
Skookumchuck Narrows, *180*, 181
Sooke Potholes, *146*, 147
South Texada Island, *171*
Spipiyus, *177*, *180*, 181
Squitty Bay, 169, *171*
Strathcona, *141*, 152-153
Surge Narrows, *173*
Teakerne Arm, *173*
Tetrahedron, *177*, *178*, *179*, 181
Tribune Bay, 170, *171*
Wakes Cove, *166*, 168

BRITISH COLUMBIA MARINE PROVINCIAL PARKS
Copeland Islands, *182*, 183
Desolation Sound, *177*, *182*
Discovery Island, *145*, 147
God's Pocket, *154*
Halkett Bay, *178*, 179
Háthayim (Von Donop), *173*
Jedediah Island, 169, *171*
Maquinna, *140*, 151
Montague Harbour, *164*, 165

Octopus Islands, 172, *173*
Pirates Cove, *166*, 169
Princess Margaret Marine Park, *161*, 168
Rebecca Spit, 172, *173*
Sabine Channel, 169, *171*
Saysutshun (Newcastle Island), *166*, 168
Small Inlet, 172, *173*
Smuggler Cove, *180*, 181
Thurston Bay, *173*
Wallace Island, *161*, *164*, 167
Whaleboat Island, *166*, 169

MUSEUMS
Anderson Island Historical Society, 56, *57*
Bainbridge Island Historical Museum, 28
Bainbridge Island Museum of Art, *28*, 29
Civilian Conservation Corps (CCC) Interpretive Center at Deception Pass State Park, 51, 80
Courtenay and District Museum and Paleontology Centre, 152
Crow Valley School Museum, 103
Fort Casey Historical State Park, *43*, 48, *50*
Gabriola Museum, 167
Hibulb Cultural Center, *43*
Island County Historical Museum, 49
Maritime Heritage Center (BC), 153
Maritime Heritage Center (WA), 83
Maritime Museum of British Columbia, *143*, 146
Mayne Island Museum, 164
Moran Mansion museum, *106*, 107
Nuyumbalees Cultural Centre, 154, 172, *173*
Orcas Island Historical Museums, 102, *103*
Orcas W.I.L.D., 104
PBY Naval Air Museum, 50
Pender Islands Museum, 163
Royal BC Museum, *143*, 144
Salt Spring Museum, 160, *161*
San Juan Historical Museum, 89
San Juan Islands Museum of Art, 89
Shaw Island Library & Historical Society, *121*, 122, 124
Squaxin Island Museum Library and Research Center, 59
Sunshine Coast Museum and Archives, 179
Suquamish Museum, 30, 31
Teacherage Museum, 129
tems swiya Museum, 180
U'mista Cultural Centre, 154
The Whale Museum, 88, *89*

THANK YOU

First and foremost, to my adopted home of Washington State and the people with whom I share it: thank you for all your support and for welcoming me as one of your own. I also owe a debt of gratitude to the Puyallup people, on whose unceded traditional homelands I live and work.

I am forever thankful for Hannah Elnan, my editor at Sasquatch Books for many years now, who trusted my instincts and let me soar. She also guided me through the uncertain time of the COVID-19 pandemic, lighting the way whenever I got lost (which was often, I'm sorry to say). I'm deeply grateful to Rena Priest and Jenn Ashton for their knowledge, insight, and perspective, as well as their thoughtful suggestions for how I might make this book more inclusive of and sensitive to the experiences of Indigenous peoples. Thanks also to Jen Worick, Bridget Sweet, Rachelle Longé McGhee, Anna Goldstein, and the team at Sasquatch Books for their help in bringing this book to life.

To my favorite travel companion on the road and in life, Donald Sidman: thank you for your love, your encouragement, and your patience. And to my sweet son, Gale, who so far loves everything life has to offer—especially, to my endless delight, ferries, sailboats, and lighthouses. I hope you'll grow to love the islands as much as I do.

I owe infinite thanks and love to the dear friends who have become part of my family. Mary-Alice Pomputius and Walter Smith have given me so much—including company on many of my sojourns, spot-on recommendations, and a perennial space to write and draw at their home on San Juan Island. Dianne and Fred Matthaei have lent knowledgeable and sympathetic ears, and helped introduce my son to the Salish Sea. Ann and Peter Darling nurtured my fledgling ideas for this book—their years spent sailing the outer San Juans have given them a wealth of experience, and they were a weather vane whenever I needed direction. Carol Serdar Tepper lived on Hope Island before it was a state park and once commuted by kayak with a toddler aboard. She is a fount of knowledge about every nook and cranny of the Puget Sound region. Jessica Spring has helped me put down roots and form connections in the Pacific Northwest and the

▼ Gulls are ubiquitous and easy to take for granted, but they are iconic symbols of the islands—and their calls are some of my favorite sounds in the world.

ADIEU

FARE THEE WELL AND IF FOREVER
STILL FOREVER FARE THEE WELL

YOUR COMING GAVE US PLEASURE
YOUR GOING GIVES US PAIN
FOND MEMORIES OUR ONLY TREASURE
UNTIL YOU COME AGAIN

wider world—she also happens to be a human divining rod for good restaurants on the road. And I would be lost without the local knowledge, professional eye, endless kindness, and moral support of Mary Holste.

A cadre of Vashon Island colleagues provided warm hospitality and let me pick their brains about local quirks. Many thanks to Don Glaister, Suzanne Moore, and Gerry and Michael Feinstein. Thanks also to Bainbridge Island supporters Cynthia Sears, Amy Goldthwaite, and the staff of the Bainbridge Island Museum of Art. I am grateful for the McMillen Foundation, whose MAC Fellowship supported me while I drafted this book. And many more friends, colleagues, and fellow travelers led me to buried island treasure or other Salish Sea gems—especially Erik Hanberg, Debbie and Terry Parks, Ellie Mathews and Carl Youngmann, Ric Matthies, Jill Frey, Trevor McInnis and Trish Harkess, Candace Rardon, the late Vera Campbell, Gabriel Campanario, Yoshiko Yamamoto and Bruce Smith, Mary Mikel Stump, Rozarii Lynch, and Laura Bentley.

To the tireless, dedicated crew members of the Washington State Ferries: you have kept aging vessels shipshape and gotten us all to and fro safely, despite budget shortfalls, complaining taxpayers, and a global pandemic. You chocked my tires a thousand times, kept me in jigsaw puzzles, pointed out the best views when you saw my sketchbook, and patiently taught me how to do that terrifying backward ramp-loading thing onto the Lopez ferry. Thank you.

Finally, librarians and booksellers have supported my work from the beginning. Sending special thanks to Jane Carlin, Jamie Spaine, Lisa Bitney, Mariesa Bus, Kelsey Smith, Eli Gandour-Rood (and his spouse, Ro), Sandra Kroupa, Kate Leonard, Jeff Hudson, Amy King-Schoppert, and sweet pea Flaherty. You have all helped me find my place in our community, and I hope I can repay you in kind.

▲ On my trips to San Juan Island, I like to take a walk under the Roche Harbor rose trellis on my last day, to say goodbye until next time.

▼ Whenever I return to Victoria, my first stop is always the pair of botanical orca topiaries in front of the Empress Hotel. These cheerful living sculptures are the perfect welcome to Vancouver Island.

195

Images and Text

The illustrations in this book are inspired by my island travel sketchbooks, but I've redrawn each one anew in my studio in order to tell a seamless story and fit the format of these pages. Each scene was drawn by hand and painted with watercolor. All the chapter headings are hand lettered and the maps are hand drawn as well.

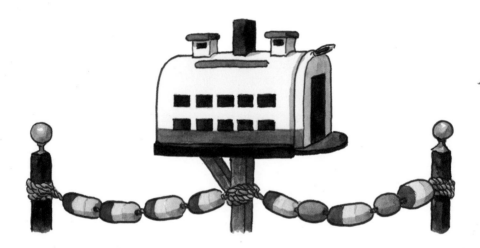

About the Endpapers

The images on the inside covers of this book depict the quirky artistic touches you'll find all over the Salish Sea islands. Islanders have hidden unique markers in plain sight for anyone observant enough to spot them: wayfinding signs, house numbers, hand-hewn schoolbus shelters, roadside farmstands, wooden water towers, little free libraries, and more. Keep your eyes peeled on your adventure—how many can you spot?